A Critical History of Police Reform

A Critical History of Police Reform

The Emergence of Professionalism

Samuel Walker
University of Nebraska at Omaha

Lexington Books
D. C. Heath and Company
Lexington, Massachusetts
Toronto

Library of Congress Cataloging in Publication Data

Walker, Samuel, 1942-
   A critical history of police reform.

   Includes index.
   1. Police—United States—History. 2. Police professionalization—
United States—History. I. Title.
HV8138.W34   363.2'2'0973   76-53866
ISBN 0-669-01292-0

Research for this book was supported in part by grants No. 72–CD–99–
0002 and No. 73–CD–99–0002 from the Law Enforcement Assistance
Administration.

Second printing, July 1978

Published simultaneously in Canada

Printed in the United States of America

International Standard Book Number: 0–669–01292–0

Library of Congress Catalog Card Number: 76–53866

Contents

	Acknowledgments	vii
	Introduction	ix
Part I	*The Police in the Nineteenth Century, 1830–1900*	1
Chapter 1	**The Police Unreformed**	3
	The Creation of the New Police	3
	The Patrolman on the Beat	8
	The Police and the Public	14
	The Police and the Criminals	19
	The Politics of Police Administration	25
	Social Control in an Urban–Industrial Society	28
Chapter 2	**The Emergence of Professionalism**	33
	The Beginnings of a Police Literature	33
	New Ideas in Police Service	37
	The Reform of the Cincinnati Police	40
	The Frustration of Reform: Theodore Roosevelt as Police Commissioner	43
	The Emergence of Professional Associations	47
Part II	*Professionalism Arrives, 1900–1918*	51
Chapter 3	**Cleaning House: Professionalization as Administrative Reform**	53
	An Age of Organization	56
	Efficiency Applied: Reform in Philadelphia	61
	The Frustration of Reform	66
	Uplifting the Patrolman	70
	New Approaches to Law and Order	75
Chapter 4	**Reforming Society: Cops as Social Workers**	79
	Cops as Social Workers: August Vollmer Reconsidered	80

The Introduction of Policewomen   84
Rehabilitating Adults: The Golden Rule Policy
   and the Sunrise Court   94
Suppressing the Social Evil   98
Cops as Social Workers: Critique from the
   Old Guard   103

Part III   *The Police and the Nation, 1919–1940*   107

Chapter 5   **The Age of the Crime Commission, 1919–1931**   109

The Rise and Sudden Fall of Police Unionism   110
The Cops in the Ghetto: Racism and Riots   120
The Police and the Crime Commissions   125
The Police in the Twenties: Progress with Problems   134

Chapter 6   **The Law-and-Order Decade, 1932–1940**   139

The Police Occupation in Hard Times   139
The Police and the Labor Movement   146
The New Deal, the FBI, and the "War on Crime"   151
The FBI and the New Professionalism   159

Epilogue: The Legacy of Professionalism   167

Notes   175

Index   201

About the Author   209

Acknowledgments

As a contribution to scholarship in the field of criminal justice, this book is dedicated to Vince Webb, chairperson of the Department of Criminal Justice at the University of Nebraska at Omaha. Without his initial and continued support this book would not have been possible. In addition to that direct support, I should like to express my appreciation for a warm friendship, a stimulating intellectual relationship, and my respect for his capable leadership of the department. It is through such leadership that the field of criminal justice will transcend its past history and take its place as a legitimate and respected academic discipline. In this regard it is also appropriate to mention Hubert Locke, former dean of the College of Public Affairs and Community Service at the university. The first steps toward academic respectability were possible only because Dean Locke, at considerable personal cost, assumed leadership and fought the battles that needed to be fought.

Much of the research for this book was conducted at four libraries: the University of Chicago and University of California at Berkeley libraries, the New York Public Library, and the Library of Congress. I should like to extend my appreciation to the staffs of those institutions for their cooperation and excellent service.

Finally, my thanks to Linda Stoner who typed the entire manuscript, and to Meg Oleson who wrestled with the last-minute corrections and revisions.

Introduction

The myth of the unchanging police dominates much of our thinking about the American police. In both popular discourse and academic scholarship one continually encounters references to the "tradition-bound" police who are resistant to change. Nothing could be further from the truth. The history of the American police over the past one hundred years is the story of drastic, if not radical change. Neither the citizen nor the police officer of one hundred years ago would recognize contemporary police service. The most obvious changes are technological: the adoption of the patrol car and the other paraphernalia of crime fighting. Even more important are the less obvious changes in the idea of police service. Not only are public expectations of the police vastly different, but the attitudes of police officers themselves about their work have undergone dramatic change.[1]

This book is a study of the changes that have overtaken police service in America during the past century. It is an examination of police reform from the middle of the nineteenth century through the end of the 1930s. At the turn of the century, reform ideas coalesced around the idea of professionalization. The goal of achieving professional status for the police became the dominant rationale for a wide variety of reform strategies. This book examines the origins, development, and fruition of the idea of police professionalization.

By the end of the 1930s the dominant features of modern American police administration has taken shape. Police organizations conformed to a single model: large bureaucratic structures organized along hierarchical, semimilitary lines. For the rank and file, police work was a life-long career and the officers themselves were increasingly drawn into a tight-knit subculture. Almost no new ideas or techniques were introduced in police administration from the 1940s through the mid-1960s. The national crisis over the role of the police that erupted in the 1960s, then, was a direct consequence of several decades of police reform. The history of the police professionalization movement sheds new light on the origins of our contemporary police problems.

The concept of professionalism provides a framework for the various reform ideas that were proposed for the police as well as the actual changes that were effected. This history of the police, then, draws upon the theoretical literature of the sociology of the professions. According to the dominant school of thought, professional status consists of three basic dimensions: professional knowledge, professional autonomy, and the service ideal. A profession is characterized by a complex and esoteric body of knowledge, capable of being codified and applied to social problems. Professionals are the experts who have mastered that body of knowledge through intensive training. Professionals also hold a monopoly on the right to use their expertise and to exclude others from dealing with their area of interest. Professional autonomy comes with monopoly status:

they assume the responsibility for recruiting, training, and supervising new practitioners. They are responsible not only for maintaining standards of performance, but also for generating new knowledge in the field. In return for their monopoly power, professionals commit themselves to a service ideal. Their activities are directed not toward self-gain but toward the interests of their clients and the general public.

No single occupation, of course, fully achieves the professional ideal. These attributes of professionalism form a continuum which makes it possible to compare different occupations and changes within particular occupations. The history of the police, for example, becomes intelligible when we think of it in terms of its halting progress along the scale of professionalism. The idea that policing was a calling, a life-long career, did not begin to emerge until very late in the nineteenth century. By the same token, the idea of a police science, an abstract body of knowledge related to police work, was also extremely slow in developing. The outward forms of professional autonomy—professional associations, journals, etc.—did not fully appear until the twentieth century. Finally, the notion that the police should be committed to an abstract ideal of public service, rather than narrow parochial or political service, has also been slow in developing. Change with respect to all of the various attributes of professionalism help to illuminate the evolution of the police in the United States.[2]

A rigorous definition of professionalism serves to clarify how far short of the goal of full professional status the police now stand. It also helps to expose the emptiness of much of the rhetoric concerning police professionalism. For much of the public the term professionalism is a vague and ill-defined synonym for something better than what presently exists. Frequently, the demand for professionalism translates into little more than calls for improved training and more education for police officers. The writings of liberal critics of the police are filled with simplistic ideas of this sort. At the same time, police officials frequently define professionalism in terms of technology. Sophisticated equipment is often taken as evidence of professional status. Police officials have also used the rhetoric of professionalism quite selectively to deflect criticism. The idea of professional autonomy is used to argue that outsiders (that is, liberal critics, the courts, militant blacks) are incapable of understanding the realities of police work and, thus, should have no voice in police affairs.[3]

Equally important, a rigorous definition of professionalism helps to clarify the distinction between professionalism and bureaucracy. The distinction is crucial to understanding the nature of the contemporary police. Despite the rhetoric of professionalism, the American police have not developed along lines similar to the acknowledged professions of law, medicine, and education. Rather, police service has evolved along bureaucratic lines. The most "professional" departments have been those in which the rank-and-file officer is subject to the tightest internal supervision. The trend has been to limit rather than enhance the autonomy of the front-line practitioner. Moreover, police careers are largely restricted to closed bureaucratic structures, with little or no opportunity for advancement by way of moving laterally from one agency to another. The closed structure of police organizations has become one of the prime points of attack for police reformers in the 1970s.[4]

The emergence of nearly autonomous police bureaucracies is one of the main themes of modern police history. A major part of that theme is the growing self-consciousness and assertiveness of the rank and file. That self-consciousness finally found an institutional framework with the dramatic upsurge in police unionism in the late 1960s. Today, the rank and file, through their unions, are major actors in determining the future of policing in America. Although the reformers around the turn of the century failed to recognize it, the eventual autonomy of the rank and file was an inevitable consequence of the reforms they sought.[5]

Police unions serve as the focal point of much of the contemporary concern about the police. To some, the possibility of police strikes represents the spectre of lawlessness and anarchy. The record suggests that these fears are grossly exaggerated. More seriously, however, the power of police unions on a day-to-day basis raises fundamental questions about the responsiveness of the police to the public. Without indulging in fantasies of incipient fascism, it is appropriate to ask whether independent and aggressive police unions pose a threat to the idea of a democratic police, one that is responsive to the public at large.[6]

These concerns connect with issues that are the proper subject of any history of the police. The most fundamental issue is simply the question of what role the police have played in American society. A brief review of the slim body of literature on police history reveals three distinct schools of thought. The first school of thought might be called the "heroic" view of the police. As the agents of law and authority, the argument runs, the police contribute to the progress of civilization. This view is most popular among historians of the English police. Charles Reith introduced his account with a chapter on "The Overlooked Dependence of Authority, in History, on Means of Securing Observance of Laws." In short, the police have made a notable contribution to the growing civility of English society. This view has not received a forceful statement with respect to the American police, however.[7]

An alternative to the heroic view, and the dominant school of thought on the police, is the urbanization–social control thesis. The police as a formal social agency, this argument holds, emerged in response to the growing urbanization and resulting social disorder of Anglo-American society in the early nineteenth century. Roger Lane and James Richardson, in their histories of the Boston and New York City police departments, emphasize the impact of urban growth, immigration, and a wave of riots in stimulating the establishment of the first police departments. Perhaps the most sophisticated version of this argument is to be found in Allan Silver's seminal essay on "The Demand for Order in Civil

Society: A Review of Some Themes in the History of Urban Crime, Police and Riot." Like the schools and numerous other social agencies, the modern police penetrated the daily lives of citizens as never before and were designed to create, maintain, and extend order in an increasingly complex urban-industrial society.[8]

Although it remains the dominant view of the police, the urbanization-social control thesis is not without problems. First, it tends to overestimate the degree of social order prior to the modern police era. Abundant evidence, however, suggests that violence and lawlessness did not necessarily increase in the early nineteenth century. Second, and perhaps more important, the social control view assumes a neutral role for the police. It is based on the assumption, implicit or explicit, that there is a shared definition of "public order," and that all groups in society share the benefits of the order that the police maintain. Such a view, however, ignores some of the most obvious conflicts in American history. The fierce struggle over the control of the police developed precisely because the police could be and were in fact used to benefit different groups in different ways.

The major alternative to the urbanization-social control view is a Marxist interpretation of American police history. There is as yet no fully developed Marxist history of the American police. Nonetheless, one finds the outlines of such an interpretation in the writings of an emerging school of radical criminology. The Marxist interpretation is rather straightforward: American society is based on a capitalist economy; the institutions of society reflect the interests of the dominant economic groups; the police play their assigned role by repressing those groups and individuals who threaten the elite.[9]

The Marxist view offers a challenging argument. It is difficult to deny, for example, that the police have actively harrassed dissident political movements and played a major role in preserving white supremacy both north and south. Furthermore, the history of American labor relations is punctuated with numerous incidents of police attacks on labor unions and their leaders. Finally, much police reform has been motivated by a desire to enhance the legitimacy of the police by eliminating the more blatant abuses. This certainly explains the periodic campaigns against the third degree and other forms of police misconduct.

In the end, however, the Marxist interpretation fails to account for some of the more important aspects of police history. The main failure lies in the confusion of intent with result. There can be no doubt that members of an American elite sought to control the police for their own ends. Yet it is equally clear that they failed to achieve this goal. Throughout the nineteenth century and into the twentieth, the police remained firmly in the grip of political machines that were not controlled by any elite. The police were hardly the passive tools of industrialists. Indeed, most police reform efforts sprang from an attempt to break the control of immigrant and working class-based political machines. The heart of much of the controversy around the police was that the police openly subverted the intent of the laws, particularly those concerned with drinking.

The history of police reform that follows opts for a view that falls somewhere in between the urbanization–social control and the Marxist views. It attempts to take into account the complexities and ambiguities of the American social structure. American society has been divided not just along economic lines, but along racial, ethnic, and religious lines as well. The result has been that both middle and lower classes have been deeply divided internally. In many respects, divisions of race and ethnicity have overshadowed those of economic class. Unable or unwilling to challenge the economic elite working class groups have often directed much of their hostility toward rival working class groups. Often, these divisions have been consciously manipulated by the economic elite.[10]

The social structure of American society is further complicated by its relative political openness. It has been possible for groups with little economic power to gain a modicum of political power and social status through electoral politics. The urban political machine became one of the principal means by which various groups could gain some control over their lives. The police were perhaps the most important part of the political machines, because of the patronage jobs they offered, the status of being the official agents of the established order and because of the very real power to enforce or subvert the law.

Finally, this history of the police attempts to take into account another aspect of modern society: the steadily growing autonomy of organized interest groups. The most powerful of these groups represent some common economic or occupational interest. The history of the police in the twentieth century is the story of the growing occupational identity and search for autonomy by local police bureaucracies. This development was one of the unintended consequences of the professionalization movement. The occupational identity of the police further complicates the class and ethnic divisions of society. Consider the predicament of the white police officer, perhaps a second generation American of eastern European stock. Is he a "worker" in the traditional blue collar sense of the word, or is he a "new professional"? Consider, for that matter, the even more complex situation of the black police officer. Does he identify primarily as a black person, with deep-seated grievances against the established order? Or does he identify as a police officer, the agent of that established order? Or do both white and black police officers identify primarily as policemen and think of themselves as a completely distinct and isolated group in society? There are no easy answers to these questions. They are raised primarily to suggest the hazards of making facile generalizations about the American police.

It is appropriate at this point to indicate the scope and methodology of this history of police reform. It seeks to trace the development of reform, of the professionalization movement, on the national level, indicating the general periods of change. Any national history of the American police confronts certain inescapable problems. The historic localism of American policing, the existence of an estimated 25,000 different law enforcement agencies, makes generalization difficult. The police in various cities are subject to unique factors. Moreover, the process of reform has been extremely uneven. Some departments reformed long before others; some reformed only to quickly slide back into older patterns; some police departments, it has been suggested, have never reformed at all.

Despite these problems, it is possible to ascertain general patterns of development common to the police as a whole. One of the central arguments of this book is that around the turn of the century the *idea* of professionalization gained hegemony in police circles. Moreover, there developed a rough consensus about the specific items on the reform agenda. The techniques of managerial efficiency became the dominant motif of police professionalism. A subtheme, and often a conflicting one, was the definition of professionalism in terms of social reform: the idea that the police should be an instrument in the general betterment of society. One can trace these different ideas throughout the history of police reform.

To identify general patterns of development, this study of police reform is an exercise in historical sociology. That is to say, the insights of contemporary sociologists (and social scientists in other disciplines) are used to illuminate the history of the police, to bring order out of a chaotic mass of detail. The concept of professionalization, as an analytical framework, is drawn from the work of the sociology of the professions. Also, the literature on the sociology of the police is used to identify the central elements of policing in America. In a recent review of the literature, Lawrence W. Sherman identifies ten principal findings about the police. These, in turn, can be usefully arranged into three general categories: the nature of police work, the character of police officers, and the structure of police organizations.[11]

Police work in America is characterized by three distinct phenomena. First, the police officer exercises an enormous degree of discretion and, as a consequence, has an enormous impact on the overall operations of the criminal justice system. Second, Sherman points out that there is some evidence to suggest that police actions "amplify" deviant or criminal behavior. While this view remains arguable, the basic phenomenon remains: that police actions have an enormous impact on the behavior of the citizenry. Finally, social scientists have persuasively documented the fact that the bulk of police work is devoted to noncriminal "service" duties, and that most actions are *re*active—a response to a citizen request for service. These insights offer suggestive leads for historical investigation. Clearly, technological developments in the area of communications have wrought a revolution in the nature of police work and the pattern of police-community relations.

The characteristics of police officers is a second major area of investigation. Sherman identifies three major findings. First, "The police occupation is isolated from the general community, with great internal solidarity and secrecy." Second, it is generally argued that the attitudes of police officers are shaped less by their background characteristics and more by a process of occupational socialization. Finally, this socialization process has resulted in the emergence of a distinct police subculture that often contains "general values and practices which deviate widely from legal and organizational rules." The police subculture is an historical phenomenon. This history of the police argues that its development has been one of the profound indirect and unanticipated consequences of professionalization.

The nature of police organizations forms the third major area of concern. Sherman points out that "Policemen work within a nondemocratic organizational context which is antithetical to the democratic values they are supposed to protect in society." This fact has had profound implications for police behavior which is subject to a wide variety of influences. Sherman points out that the "Varieties of police behavior depend upon specific stituational, organizational and community factors." His final conclusion is that organizational change offers perhaps the best prospect for changing police behavior. He notes the wide interest in administrative decentralization and debureaucratization as reform strategies. The centralized and authoritarian nature of contemporary police organizations is also an historical phenomenon. This history of the police argues that militarization was a consequence of professionalization, often seized upon as a reform strategy. The story of the shift from decentralized, nonmilitaristic police organizations to centralized and militaristic ones can hopefully provide insight into both the promise and the pitfalls of contemporary decentralization strategies.

As a history of police reform on the national level an effort has been made to present as representative a picture as possible. The existing literature on the history of the police concentrates heavily on New York City, Boston, Chicago, and Los Angeles. This account attempts to balance that material by exploring the police experience in such midwestern industrial cities as Cleveland, Cincinnati, Detroit, Milwaukee, Kansas City, and St. Louis. The research is based on an extensive survey of annual reports, other municipal documents, and investigations of the police by public and private agencies. National developments have been traced through the work and publications of professional associations in the fields of law enforcement, social work, and public administration. The International Association of Chiefs of Police, the National Conference of Charities and Corrections, National Institute of Public Administration, and the International City Management Association have provided valuable insights into developments in policing.

Finally, this account could not have been written without the previous work done by a number of historians. The published work of Roger Lane, Mark Haller, Wilbur Miller and James Richardson yield invaluable insights. At the same time, much has been learned from the work of social scientists in other disciplines. The work of Jerome Skolnick, James Q. Wilson, William A. Westley, and David Bayley deserves particular mention. The author hopes this account will contribute to the ongoing study of the American police begun by these scholars.

Part I:
The Police in the Nineteenth Century, 1830–1900

1 The Police Unreformed

Professionalization was an attack upon the pervasive influence of partisan politics on American policing in the nineteenth century. From the moment of their creation, the police were the creatures of partisan politics. The officer on the beat was less a public servant than an agent for a given political faction. Police work was a form of casual labor, not a lifelong career. Officers received virtually no formal training and there were no pretenses toward a police science. Public attitudes reflected this nonprofessional approach. Policemen on the beat were subject to a remarkable degree of disrespect and outright abuse. To gain even a nominal amount of respect for their authority, policemen frequently resorted to violence—to gain by means of the nightstick the respect that was not freely granted. Thus began a cycle of disrespect and brutality on both sides. Finally, the police had only a minimal commitment to the enforcement of the laws. As political operatives they were more interested in furthering the interests of their sponsors. From the beginning the police became the central figures in an intricate system of racketeering and municipal corruption. In short, the American police represented the antithesis of professionalism.[1]

By the end of the nineteenth century the state of American policing was increasingly intolerable to a growing number of reformers. The critique of the police was an integral part of a general dissatisfaction with American local government. In 1887 the English commentator James Bryce declared in his classic study *The American Commonwealth* that municipal government was the most conspicuous failure in all of American society. Some years later Raymond B. Fosdick, one of the leading police reformers, argued that the police were "perhaps the most pronounced failure in all our unhappy municipal history." Moreover, "it cannot be denied," Fosdick added, "that politics lies at the root of much of it."[2] To understand the nature of police reform it is necessary to first examine the state of the unreformed police in the nineteenth century.

The Creation of the New Police

The precise dates of the origins of the modern-style police are difficult to determine. By modern policing we mean a system of law enforcement involving a permanent agency employing full-time officers who engage in continuous patrol of fixed beats to prevent crime. The modern police were not created out of whole cloth; they evolved out of the older system of the night watch. In

3

many cases the "new" police represented little more than a consolidation of a patchwork of existing systems. Although historians have never given the matter adequate attention, it would seem that the first modern-style police systems appeared in southern cities as a part of a general approach to the control of slaves. Regular patrol was a common feature of both rural and urban areas. Washington, D.C., apparently had an organized police patrol system before 1820. Other major cities, such as Charleston, also had rather elaborately organized police patrol systems.[3]

We know far more about the creation of the new police systems in northern cities. The first of these police departments, Boston (1838) and New York City (1844), are the subjects of detailed book-length studies. The new police were born of conflict and violence, as a direct consequence of an unprecedented wave of civil disorders that swept the nation between the 1830s and the 1870s. The extent of these disorders was truly remarkable, even by the standards of 1960s. Few cities escaped serious rioting and most of the major cities experienced repeated mob violence. There was no single cause of civil disorder. Conflict between different ethnic groups, a result of the advent of massive immigration from Ireland and Germany, was perhaps the major cause. But racial conflict was also widespread, as mobs of whites attacked both nonslave blacks and white abolitionists. Economic disorders also generated violence: ruined investors sacked banks that failed, while workingmen destroyed the property of their employers. Mob violence was a frequently used technique for settling questions of public morality. Medical schools were attacked by mobs of moralists who objected to such practices as experiments on cadavers, while brothels were mobbed by those who sought to clean up a city in a quick and efficient manner.[4]

So pervasive was violence and disorder by the mid-1830s that many thoughtful Americans feared that the young republic might not survive. There was good reason for doubting the survival of democratic institutions. Election day was a frequent occasion for mob violence in New York, Philadelphia, Baltimore, and other major cities. President Andrew Jackson, who on three occasions ordered federal troops to suppress labor riots, warned that "this spirit of mob-law is becoming too common and it must be checked or, ere long, it will become as great an evil as service war, and the innocent will be much exposed." Abraham Lincoln warned in 1837 that "there is even now something of ill omen amongst us. I mean the increasing disregard for law which pervades the country—the growing disposition to substitute the wild and furious passions in lieu of the sober judgment of courts, and the worse than savage mobs for the executive ministers of justice."[5]

The prevailing machinery of justice, inherited from colonial America and from England before that, was a weak reed at best in the face of mob violence. The chief law enforcement officers were the sheriff and usually a number of elected constables. But they were essentially a reactive force: upon complaint they would seek to apprehend an offender in the expectation of receiving a fee for their services. The riot act, the primary mechanism for the suppression of mob violence, was a cumbersome procedure that relied primarily on the calling out of the militia. In short, there was no continuous presence of a police power, except for the night watch during the night hours. And even the members of the night watch were ill-prepared to deal with major violence.

In city after city, a sequence of major riots ultimately led to the creation of what has been called the *new police*. The experience of St. Louis was typical of other major cities. On election day, 1844, groups of Catholic Irish-Americans battled Protestant native-born Americans in the streets. That same year an angry mob attacked the St. Louis University medical school to protest the use of cadavers in medical education. Five years later, volunteer fire companies representing the Irish and native-born communities fought each other in the streets. The next year, 1850, a mob ransacked the brothels in the city in another attempt to enforce standards of public decency through group violence. Election day in 1852 featured a riot between German-Americans and the native-born, while in both 1853 and 1854 there were more riots involving Irish-Americans.[6]

The succession of riots finally led to the reorganization of the St. Louis Police. Businessmen, concerned about the safety of their property, took the initiative. During the 1854 election day riot they mobilized a volunteer vigilante force to guard the city. The next year, after a decade of rioting, the St. Louis City Council created a modern-style police force. By consolidating the old day and night watches into a single administrative unit, the city was given a continuous police presence for the first time.

A similar sequence of events occurred in other major cities. Baltimore experienced a total of nine riots between 1834 and the creation of its new police in 1857. There was an election day riot in 1834, a bank riot the next year, fire company riots in 1847 and 1855, further election day riots in 1848 and 1856, and a labor riot in 1857. The ethnic group passions that afflicted other cities were further complicated by conflict over the slavery question in this southern-oriented city. Baltimore earned the title of "mob town" but other cities were equally deserving. Philadelphia had at least eleven major riots between 1834 and 1849, while New York, Boston, and Cincinnati also experienced frequent disorders.[7]

It would be a mistake to overemphasize the cause and effect relationship between mob violence and the creation of the new police. Most cities took a remarkably long time to reorganize their law enforcement systems, in some cases as long as two decades. Furthermore, the police did little to end mob violence. Violence continued to be a prominent feature of American life. Racial violence, industrial strife, and other forms of disorder continued with little interference from the police. A profound irony lies at the heart of American police history: the police had little effect on the very social problem that ostensibly brought them into being. The contradiction between official mandate and actual functions remains a central feature of the American police. As contemporary sociologists have adequately documented, the police maintain a law enforcement image but in reality spend little of their time actually fighting crime. Most of their time is devoted to miscellaneous social services. Although in a somewhat different form, a similar contradiction characterized the nineteenth-century American police.[8]

The reluctance of American civic leaders to create the new-style police was the product of several different factors. On the one hand, a permanent police presence was an unprecedented institution. The London Metropolitan Police, established in 1829 after decades of debate in England, was still a new and untested institution. Moreover, the paramilitary aspect of the London police conjured up images of the British army and the American War of Independence, an event that was still not too far distant in the American past. The most important obstacle, however, was simply the fact that the different political factions in American cities could not agree on what kind of a police to establish. They were much less afraid of the idea of a police in the abstract than they were afraid of what their political opponents would do with such a force.

The political maneuvering that led to the creation of new police forces was particularly evident in both Philadelphia and New York. It took Philadelphia two full decades to finally establish a modern police force. In 1833 a bequest from the wealthy merchant and philanthropist Stephen Girard allowed the city to hire twenty-four day policemen and add another 120 men to the night watch. But two years later, even after several major riots, the ordinance that had consolidated these men into a single administrative unit was rescinded. Philadelphia was not yet ready for the new police. Thirteen years later, in 1848, day policemen were again established, but this thirty-four-man force remained administratively distinct from the night watch. The major obstacle to consolidation was the prevailing system of neighborhood localism. Democrats, who were largely Irish-Catholic and proslavery, dominated the outlying districts of the city, while Whigs (and later Native Americans), who were largely Protestant and antislavery, dominated the inner city. Police consolidation depended upon the unification of government agencies for the entire metropolitan area. Political leaders, whose power resided at the neighborhood level, resisted consolidation. A major race riot in 1849 in which a mob of whites invaded the black neighborhoods finally spurred action toward metropolitan reorganization. But even then it took almost six years to overcome the entrenched political opposition. Not until the summer of 1854 did Philadelphia get a consolidated, metropolitan police force. If the people of Philadelphia were concerned about civil disorder, they were more concerned about maintaining an existing political structure.[9]

The creation of the New York City police was also delayed by political maneuvering. Although rioting struck New York in 1834, it was the highly publicized murder of Mary Cecilia Rogers in 1841 that stimulated the movement for a new police. Mayor Robert Morris proposed, but the state legislature and the city council were long in disposing. The legislature passed enabling legislation in 1844, but the city council, under the control of the Native American Party, refused to act upon its provisions. Not until the next year, when the Democrats recaptured control of city government, did New York City create its first modern police force.[10]

The newness of the new police was both administrative and strategic. Administratively, the new police represented the consolidation of the night watch and day police, where they existed, into a single agency. Moreover, police work was now a full-time job (although not yet a career). Traditionally, members of the night watch had been elected and service was considered one of the duties of citizenship. This introduced the idea that law enforcement duties should be vested in a permanent bureaucratic agency.

At the same time, the new police were to perform a radically new function. Unlike the old constable night watch system, the new police were expected to prevent crime. To use modern terminology, they were to be *pro*active rather than merely *re*active. The crime prevention strategy, implemented by continuous and regular patrol over assigned beats, has remained the basic assignment of the police. This innovation, however, introduced a set of problems that have remained the essence of the police administration problem ever since. Once patrolmen were assigned to patrol, the problem of supervision became paramount. How to make sure that they were in fact working? And, if they were working, how to guarantee that their actions were consistent with official public policy? Control over individual patrolmen soon became not simply an internal administrative problem, but also one of the most important political questions in the urban community.

Ostensibly, the first American police departments were modelled after the London Metropolitan Police. In reality, the Americans borrowed selectively. The American police were drastically different not only in terms of their formal administrative structure, but, as a consequence, also in terms of their role in the community. Historian Wilbur Miller, in an insightful comparative study of the London and New York police during their first decades, illuminates some of the more important features of the American police.[11]

The London Metropolitan Police was an elitist and highly centralized agency. A creation of the Home Office, it was essentially an extension of the national government. The people of London, the policed, had no effective means of directly controlling or influencing police practices. This is not to say that the London police were not sensitive to the interests of Londoners. The commissioners of the London police, however, were able to make fine adjustments in policy while remaining aloof from the currents of popular feeling.[12] The commissioners themselves were recruited from the ranks of the upper class and were usually individuals trained for careers in the professional civil service. Generations of American reformers would look wistfully upon the "professional" administration of the London police, making invidious comparisons with the American police.

American police departments reflected the general style of local government. They were created in an era of increasing democratic participation. The mayor of New York City was first popularly elected in 1834; many municipal judgeships became elective in the following decade. City governments were also highly decentralized. Mayors were largely figureheads with little administrative power. The real power lay in the neighborhoods and in the wards. City councilmen, or aldermen, controlled the operations of city government, often combining both legislative and executive functions. The first police departments shared this style of participation and decentralization. The police were hardly even an extension of city government (much less the national government as in London), but rather an extension of different political factions. Neighborhood particularism meant that police officers were recruited by the political leaders in a given ward or precinct. In some cases, officers in different wards wore distinctive uniforms. Needless to say, police practices were hardly governed by universalistic criteria.

The administrative structure of American police departments, and the political style that determined that structure, was the major influence over police behavior. Historian Mark Haller, in an important exploration of police behavior in the nineteenth century suggests that we can understand the police in terms of four basic orientations. Police departments were not only decentralized and subject to direct partisan political influence but were also part of a relatively well organized system of rackets. Corruption was endemic in the entire criminal justice system and served important social and political purposes. Finally, police practices were characterized by a set of informal processes that bore little relationship to the official mandate of the police. Each of these aspects of the police became focal points for the professionalization movement.[13]

The Patrolman on the Beat

Thomas Byrnes, one of the most famous (or notorious) policemen in the history of New York City, if not the entire country, achieved immortality for his observation that there is more law in the end of a policeman's nightstick than in all the decisions of the courts. What Byrnes expressed in crude terms experts on criminal justice now accept as one of the fundamental issues in police administration: the question of police discretion. In 1919, Arthur Woods, commissioner of the New York City police wrote that "In this duty of law enforcement, the policeman is in a very real sense a judge."[14]

The history of that pivotal figure in American life, the patrolman, is shrouded in myths and stereotypes. The commonest myth is that of the "Irish cop." Like all myths, it contains an element of truth: that ethnicity has been an important ingredient in police recruitment. But it also obscures the more fundamental issue of the complex relationship between the police and the public. The nineteenth-century patrolman was essentially a political operative rather than a modern-style professional committed to public service. The political nature of the job began with the process of appointment. In New York City in 1845, "the Alderman, Assistant Alderman, and Assessors of each Ward, with the concurrence of the Mayor, were empowered to appoint a Captain, one first Assistant Captain, one second Assistant Captain, and as many Policemen as the Ward was entitled to, . . ."[15] Men (there were no women police officers until early in the twentieth century) received their appointments as rewards for political service. The structure of power within the department, meanwhile, paralleled that of city government. Police chiefs were as much figureheads as were mayors. The real power lay with the captains in the precincts. Technology conspired against centralized administration. Apart from a morning meeting with all the captains, there was no way a police chief could effectively supervise those under his command.

As political appointees, police officers enjoyed little job security. A dramatic turn of events on election day often led to a complete housecleaning of the police department. The Cincinnati police department prior to 1886 had a particularly unstable history. In 1880, 219 of the 295 members of the force were summarily dismissed, while another twenty resigned. Six years later, another political upheaval resulted in the removal of 238 of the 289 patrolmen and eight of the sixteen lieutenants. The Cincinnati experience was extreme, but not untypical; as late as the 1920s high rates of turnover could be found in unreformed departments.[16] Police work was essentially casual labor, a job that one took for only a short period at best. Perhaps the first rudimentary step in the development of policing as a profession was the idea of police work as a career. John Maniha's study of the St. Louis police department indicates one dimension of the professionalization process. In the 1870s and 1880s no members of the force left because of retirement; over 37 percent resigned voluntarily while the remainder were dismissed for cause. By the 1940s, however, nearly 78 percent were leaving either because of death or retirement.[17]

Although job security in the long run was low, police work in the nineteenth century had its attractions. Policemen were extremely well paid compared to alternative occupations. Because salaries were determined by local political factors rather than national market forces there were considerable variations from city to city. In 1880, for example, New Orleans paid its policemen only $600 a year while San Francisco paid a high of $1200. Most other major cities paid salaries in the neighborhood of $900 a year. A skilled tradesman in the building industry that year could expect to earn $774 a year, while those in manufacturing could expect about $450 a year. Mayor Fernando Wood told the members of the New York City police in 1855 that "your duties are light, the pay not illiberal; your social standing good and the term for which appointed renders you independent of the contingencies to which the operative and other laboring classes are subjected."[18] Although policemen were relatively insulated from the uncertainties of the business cycle, there were occasional problems. In 1880, for example, salaries in the New York police department were abruptly lowered from $1200 a year to a starting salary of $800 and a maximum of $1000. The reduction was undoubtedly a response to the financial strain on city government resulting from the depression of the late 1870s. Chicago responded to economic hard times not by reducing salaries but by cutting the size of the force 25 percent, from 565 to 409 officers.[19]

Another important attraction of police work was the fact that a patrolman was essentially unsupervised. There were ample opportunities to avoid official responsibilities, especially the unpleasantness of patrolling in inclement weather. And it is clear that police officers availed themselves of these opportunities liberally. What police administrators saw as laziness and what reformers saw as corruption—the fact that a patrolman spent a good deal of time in neighborhood saloons—was nothing more than an effort to lighten an otherwise boring and tiring patrol assignment. If one were to believe a 1915 investigation of the Chicago police, patrolmen spent *most* of their time in saloons.[20]

Because of its attractions, police departments recruited a large number of skilled tradesmen. Of the more than 200 men on the 1879 Cincinnati police force, there were sixty-five former common laborers but their numbers were more than outweighed by the seventeen butchers, thirteen iron moulders, eleven blacksmiths, seven machinists, seven painters, five engineers, and numerous other skilled tradesmen. In addition there were thirteen former clerks and five former merchants. Subsequent studies in the twentieth century indicated that the police continue to draw heavily from the ranks of blue collar workers. Eugene Watts' systematic study of recruitment in St. Louis indicates only relatively minor shifts in recruitment patterns.[21]

The political system of appointments opened the door for a significant number of black policemen in some northern cities. Chicago and Philadelphia were particularly receptive to the idea, while New York remained resistant. A Republican mayor in Chicago appointed the first black policeman there in 1872, a man who may well have been the first black policeman anywhere. Three years later a mayor elected by the People's Party replaced him with another black officer. The return of the GOP to power in 1880 resulted in the appointment of four black policemen. These men worked in plain clothes—in part not to offend the sensibilities of racist whites—and were assigned to the black neighborhoods. By 1894 there were twenty-three black policemen in Chicago. The introduction of civil service in 1895 significantly restricted the number of blacks. By 1905 the number had dropped to only sixteen. Only the spectacular growth of the Chicago ghetto in the next few years offset the impact of higher recruitment standards. By 1914 there were fifty black policemen and by 1922 Chicago led the nation with a total of 116.[22]

Black policemen were introduced in Philadelphia in 1884 by Republican Mayor Rufus King. Appointing thirty-five in one stroke, he declared grandly that "It was not done without mature consideration ... I determined to recognize the right of citizenship of all men, and proceeded, when I had an opportunity, to indulge my convictions, for with me it is a principle." These appointments at first generated considerable opposition and some of the first black officers were accosted on the streets by racist whites. Eventually, however, they were accepted as simply another part of the normal patronage system. Despite Mayor King's declaration of principle, politics ruled. In his classic study of *The Philadelphia Negro*, W. E. B. DuBois commented that "their jobs are in 'politics' and their holders must and do support the 'machine.'"[23]

New York City did not appoint its first black policeman until 1905. Samuel J. Battle endured the "silent treatment" from other members of the force who sought to preserve the police as an all-white institution. Battle endured, however. Assigned to patrol Central Park West, he expressed an eager willingness to patrol the Negro district if assigned to it.[24]

The long-standing myth of the "Irish cop" had a certain degree of factual basis. Because of the patronage system of appointments, lower-class immigrant groups managed to secure a substantial representation on police forces. In Boston, the appointment of Barney McGinniskin to the force in 1851 precipitated a major political crisis. The idea of an Irish-born police officer was abhorrent to many native-born Americans. In other cities, however, the Irish gained control of the police rather quickly. The first police chief in St. Louis, for example, was James McDonough, the son of Irish-born parents. In Scranton, Pennsylvania, Irish-Catholics dominated the police force under Mayor Mathew Loftus, himself Irish-born, between 1872 and 1875. The New York City Council in 1855 demanded an investigation of the police department to determine the exact number of Irish-born on the force. The department claimed that 305 of the 1149 officers were born in Ireland, a percentage (27 percent) that nearly matched the proportion of Irish-born in the city as a whole (28.2 percent). The city council's own investigation, however, suggested that the number of Irish-born police officers was closer to 600.[25]

The ethnic composition of the police continued to be a major political issue throughout the nineteenth century and much of the twentieth century as well. Although most of the attention focused on the Irish, the Germans achieved sizeable representation in such cities as Cleveland, Cincinnati, and St. Louis. There were thirty-five German-born police officers in Cleveland in 1872, compared with thirty-one Irish-born and forty-six American-born. Through most of the twentieth century the Cleveland police department remained a Protestant enclave from which Catholics of all ethnic background were largely excluded. German representation on the Cincinnati and St. Louis police forces was also a subject of frequent political controversy.[26]

Ethnicity was not an artificial issue. Since the police were primarily a political tool rather than a professional law enforcement agency, the composition of the force was all-important. In the absence of any conception of police work as a skilled occupation that demanded special training, political loyalty was the only real qualification for appointment. Policing was a job for amateurs, requiring little more than common sense. James Robinson, the reform-minded superintendent of the Philadelphia police observed in 1916 that "it was formerly the custom in Philadelphia, and I believe, in all other large cities, to equip newly appointed patrolmen with uniform, badge, police manual, revolver, blackjack, baton and keys for fire alarm boxes and police patrol boxes, and then assign the man to cover a beat."[27]

Formal training for recruits was virtually nonexistent. The "Advice to a Young Policeman" offered by Boston Police Chief Edward H. Savage consisted of little more than empty platitudes. "At the commencement," he advised, "do not forget that in this business your character is your capital. Deal honorably with all persons, and hold your word sacred, no matter when, where, or to whom given." Savage had little to say concerning the specifics of police work: "I might say more, but should I, you would still have to go out and *learn* your duty." Police officers received their real orientation—one hesitates to say training—on the street from experienced officers. There were a few notable exceptions to this rule prior to the turn of the century. Cincinnati in 1886 established a formal school of instruction that consisted of a remarkable seventy-five hours of class-room instruction over a three-month period. Even more important, the Cincinnati program appears to have remained a permanent feature. In other cities, formal training programs were established only to be quickly forgotten. Buffalo, for example, had a formal school of instruction as early as 1871, but its history was apparently rather brief.[28]

When the first police officers stepped out onto the streets of Boston, New York, Philadelphia, and other cities, they were hardly distinguishable from other civilians. Mayor Conrad in Philadelphia tried to put his men in uniform, but the officers successfully resisted the idea. They wore only a badge and an identifiable round patent leather hat. The New York City police initially wore blue frock coats, but this met with opposition from both the public and the police officers themselves. "The men did not take kindly to the uniform," Augustine Costello wrote, "because chiefly, the idea was borrowed from England. So adverse was the public to this innovation in police dress, that at the burning of the Old Bowery Theater a riot almost occurred, the populace threatening to mob the police whom they designated liveried lackeys." The uniform was dropped and the police wore only a copper badge on their coats. It is likely that opposition to police uniforms was an expression of ethnic group conflict as much as anything else. Members of the Irish-American community attacked a police force that represented a different political faction. The fact that the idea of police uniforms had been borrowed from the English served as a convenient point of attack.[29]

The uniform had important practical and symbolic uses. On the one hand it signified that police work was a distinct occupation, perhaps even a profession. In the 1830s, 1840s, and much of the 1850s, however, policemen refused to think of themselves in those terms. The uniform was a sign of a lower status caste, not of a higher status profession. The uniform also had practical implications in terms of supervision. It was relatively easier for a nonuniformed officer to simply remove his badge and melt into the crowd if he wished to avoid an unpleasant responsibility. The uniform, then, was partly an attempt by supervisors to establish control over their men. The New York City police were finally uniformed in 1857 and most other cities soon followed their lead. The Civil War also served to elevate the image of the blue uniform in the minds of both police and public. By 1880, the blue frock coat "made after the New York style" was fairly standard among police departments in major cities.[30]

Patrol duty was nominally an arduous task. Not only were officers expected to patrol on foot through all types of inclement weather, but they were required to put in extremely long hours. Through most of the nineteenth century, the two-platoon system prevailed. The force was divided into twelve-hour shifts. While an individual officer might be required to patrol only for two to six hours at one stretch, he was then expected to put in long hours at the station house "on reserve." The absence of any other means of rapid communication meant that officers had to be at the station itself in order to be on call for emergency duty. The two-platoon system left the men with very little time off. When Philadelphia finally adopted the three-platoon system in 1912, the number of hours policemen were required to serve dropped from 108 to 77 hours per week. Under the old system, men were required to do sixty-five hours a week on "street duty" and forty-two hours a week on "house detail," or reserve. A 1913 New York City Council investigation found that "the amount of extra duty required of policemen is so excessive that the policemen see very little of their homes and families." The three-platoon system became one of the major reforms of the professionalization movement.[31]

Actual patrol duty, of course, was a lot less onerous than it appeared. Since officers were beyond the reach of effective supervision while on patrol, they were able to avail themselves of the ample opportunities for taking it easy. The warmth and conviviality of a neighborhood saloon or barbershop was infinitely more attractive than the dull routine of patrolling the streets. The problem of supervision immediately became one of the paramount issues in police administration. Much of police history could be told in terms of a cat and mouse game between patrolmen and their supervisors. From the earliest call boxes to the modern two-way radio, administrators have sought some means of monitoring the activities of their men. Patrolmen, for their part, have been equally ingenious in their efforts to nullify and subvert the latest technological innovations.[32]

As we shall see, the primitive communications technology of the nineteenth century had enormous political ramifications. On one level, police chiefs were unable to supervise effectively their captains at the precinct level. Thus, policy was greatly influenced by the prevailing political and social mores of the various neighborhoods. But even the captains had limited ability to control either their sergeants or their patrolmen. As a consequence, police behavior was very much influenced by the interaction between individual officers and individual citizens. The nature of that interaction, what is now referred to as the problem of police-community relations, was perhaps even more complex and ambiguous in the nineteenth century than it is today.

The Police and the Public

The heart of the law enforcement function, as experts are fond of pointing out, is one of legitimacy. To carry out effectively any of their various assignments, the authority of the police must be generally accepted by the public as legiti-mate. The crux of the American police problem has long been the fact that the legitimacy of the police is so often challenged rather than accepted. From this issue alone stems some of the most serious and long-standing problems in American policing.

Precisely because they were essentially a political institution, and perceived as such by the public, the American police did not enjoy widespread acceptance by the public. Police officers, in fact, were subjected to an enormous amount of ridicule and outright hostility. The Cincinnati chief of police complained in 1887 that "a policeman's life is one of continual danger . . . He is considered fair sport for every gang of roughs and hoodlums who choose to assail him . . ." Leonard Fuld pointed out that "when patrol service was first introduced, the criminal class had little respect for the policeman and openly defied and at-tacked him; hence the patrol had to be by squads rather than by individual officers." In his colorful history of *The Gangs of New York*, Herbert Asbury vividly describes how youthful gangs made attacking the police a regular form of entertainment. Gang attacks, furthermore, were not meaningless events. The gangs were part of the institutional life of different ethnic group communities and soon became integrated into the political system. They were extremely useful during election day brawls with rival political factions and attacked not all policemen but only those identified with their political opponents.[33]

Much of the police problem was institutional. Wilbur Miller's comparative study of the New York and London police demonstrates how relations between the police and the public in the two communities were determined by the dif-ferent institutional structures of the two police departments. The London "bobby" appeared on the streets as the impersonal agent of national authority: "As a national institution the police could draw upon a reservoir of symbolic as well as physical power." The London police officer acted with the full weight of the state and a long legal tradition behind him. The New York City policeman worked in a very different social context. Miller writes, "His authority was *personal*, resting on a closeness to the citizens and their informal expectations of his power instead of formal bureaucratic or legal standards." The citizenry, then, were far less awed by police power and were much more willing to demand that the police conform to their standards. When the police represented a different political faction or ethnic group, relations could become openly hostile.[34]

The difference between the London and New York police in this regard represented a profound irony. The "professionalism" of the London police—their aloofness and commitment to impersonal legalistic norms—was based on an elitist institutional structure which, in turn, reflected an elitist and stratified society. Londoners had no more expectations of direct influence over the police in the mid-nineteenth century than into any of the other agencies of the national government. Thus, the commissioners could determine policy without being subjected to direct political influence. American reformers in the twentieth century admired this system of police administration without appreciating the social structure on which it was based. The participatory tradition of American local government demanded direct political influence. In a very real sense, this approach also guaranteed a certain degree of what might be called community control. If anything, the decentralized structure of police departments was community control run amok, with real power residing at the ward and precinct level. The advocates of professionalization in the twentieth century failed to see that by introducing impersonal and abstract norms of conduct they were also creating a new problem of police–community relations.

The American patrolman encountered resistance to his authority even in the process of making a simple arrest. Here again, technology conspired against the police. Once a suspect was arrested the officer faced the problem of physically transporting him to the station house. The bulk of arrests, moreover, were for drunkenness and disorderly conduct (anywhere from 60 to 80 percent of the total). Frequently, the arrestee resisted and the police officer had to physically subdue him. At times, other members of the community sympathized with the suspect and either harrassed the patrolman or attempted to "liberate" the prisoner. William J. McKelvey, Superintendent of the Brooklyn police in 1896 recalled that "when I first became a policeman, and thirty years is not so long ago, the work was vastly different . . . an officer was forced to lug his tipsy prisoner on a wheelbarrow for miles sometimes to the station." Some relief appeared in the 1880s with the development of the callbox and the horse-drawn patrol wagon. Because it relieved patrolmen of such an onerous and degrading duty, the patrol wagon was hailed as a revolutionary innovation in policing.[35]

The most tragic consequence of the problematic nature of police authority was the tradition of police brutality. There can be little doubt that brutality was widespread. As Wilbur Miller argues, the policeman's authority was uniquely personal and he had to establish it in any given situation in a personal way, which usually meant by force. One of the most famous of all New York City policemen was Captain Alexander S. ("Clubber") Williams, and it requires little imagination to guess the origins of his nickname. Lincoln Steffens in his *Autobiography* recalled, "Many a morning when I had nothing else to do I stood and saw the police bring in and kick out their bandaged, bloody prisoners, not only strikers and foreigners, but thieves, too, and others of the miserable, friendless, troublesome poor."[36]

Without training and virtually unsupervised, the nineteenth-century police dispensed "curbside justice." Mark Haller argues that they had virtually no orientation to the universalistic norms of a society based on the rule of law. Rather, their actions were highly personalized and generally arbitrary. One of the major goals of reformers in the twentieth century would be the introduction of universalistic norms. To achieve this, however, they had to not only redefine the role of the police, but also to introduce new mechanisms of command and control.[37]

Despite the prevalence of brutality, the nineteenth-century police did not make a fetish of guns—that would be a distinctly twentieth-century phenomenon. The first policemen in America did not carry weapons at all. The New York City police, for example, were not officially armed until 1853. Even as late as 1880 there was no consistent pattern across the country regarding weapons. In Boston, officers were permitted to carry revolvers "with the permission of their captains." Policemen in Brooklyn, then a separate municipality of over 500,000 people, did not carry weapons at all, but were issued "clubs only." In Albany, New York, the police carried "locust clubs by day and revolvers by night." The New Orleans police, meanwhile, were equipped only with a club and a whistle. Moreover, the Census Bureau survey reported "the law against carrying concealed weapons applies in full force to policemen."[38]

If the experience of New York City is typical, the police adopted weapons in response to the growing violence around them. The decade of the 1860s and the social dislocations wrought by the Civil War raised the level of violence in northern cities. Boston and New York experienced major draft riots. It was only then that weapons became standard equipment for the New York police. James Richardson reports that police violence then acquired a momentum of its own and complaints against the police in New York steadily mounted in the late 1860s and 1870s.[39]

While there can be no question about the prevalence of police brutality, the larger issue of police-community relations is extremely ambiguous. It is difficult to discern any systematic pattern of behavior toward particular groups, with the possible exceptions of blacks. Police violence, as Miller and Haller suggest, was both arbitrary and personalized. It was directed against individuals who in some way challenged the authority or offended the sensibility of a police officer. Police–community relations, as sociologists have demonstrated, is an interaction process. Much of it depends upon the expectations of each side. Since police brutality was so pervasive large segments of the public accepted it; they had no standard of fair and impartial public service against which to measure it. Much of the controversy about police brutality in the 1960s, for example, was the result not of a deterioration of police behavior (racism was a well established tradition) but of dramatically rising expectations on the part of blacks.[40]

While lower class immigrants received the bulk of police abuse, it is impossible to argue that there was a systematic pattern of repression. Police departments, after all, were often controlled by political machines that were themselves responsive to lower class immigrant communities. And, as we have already indicated, immigrant groups, especially the Irish, represented a significant proportion of police officers in most large cities. Contemporary research indicates that black police officers are just as likely to brutalize black suspects as are white officers (and white officers to brutalize white suspects). Thus, it seems reasonable to suggest that Irish-American police officers in the nineteenth century were not adverse to cracking the heads of fellow Irish-Americans when they became belligerent.[41]

The attitude of police officers is a complex phenomenon, involving the interplay of class, ethnic, and occupational sources of identity. Even though there was an extremely low level of professional consciousness through the nineteenth century, police officers did identify to a certain extent with their jobs. In times of crisis they were capable of thinking of themselves as the representatives of the law and of public order. A curious episode occurred during the so-called Orange Riots in New York in 1870 and 1871. When Protestant Northern Irishmen (the Orangemen) attempted to celebrate their national holiday with a parade and picnic, they were attacked by Catholic Irish-Americans. A minor incident was followed by a major riot in 1871. Curiously, the heavily Irish-American police force defended the right of the Orangemen to parade. In his contemporary account of the affair, Joel T. Headley commented that "to defend Protestant Irishmen against Roman Catholic friends and perhaps relatives, is a severe test of fidelity; but the Irish police have stood it nobly, and won the regard of all good citizens."[42]

The role of the police in labor disputes is equally ambiguous. The Marxist view that the police were the tools of industrialists cannot be supported in the face of the evidence. Most policemen, after all, were themselves former blue-collar workers who probably expected to return to their previous trade. Employers, moreover, complained bitterly over the fact that they could not always rely on the police during strikes. In Scranton, Pennsylvania, the Scranton family-controlled *Republican* opposed the enlargement of the police force out of a realistic fear that the opposition party, dominated by the Irish, would control it. Historian Samuel Hays argues that elite reformers in the Progressive Era sought reform as a device to break working class influence and ensure a more tractable police.[43]

Police history is indeed filled with incidents of police brutality against workingmen and strikers. One of the most famous episodes was the 1874 Tompkins Square Riot in New York City. The police viciously attacked workingmen who had gathered to demand relief for the unemployed during the depression. Police activities during the 1877 railroad riots were inconsistent, however. In Chicago, they were extremely brutal and, with "a taste for the sport of crowd busting," initiated much of the violence. But in Pittsburgh, they abandoned any pretense toward law enforcement and allowed the mob to do its will. A few spectacular episodes of police violence against the labor movement is not sufficent to support the view that the police were consistently repressive. The police, after all, were capable of making fine distinctions. A police force dominated by Irish and German-Americans, for example, was far less likely to attack kindred skilled tradesmen than a strike by unskilled Eastern European immigrant laborers.[44]

As we have already suggested, police attitudes and behavior were determined less by abstract norms and more by an informal socialization process. Leonard Fuld captured something of the complex social relations surrounding the police when, quoting another observer, he wrote that "the poorer classes fraternize with the policeman, the middle classes keep aloof, and the upper classes despise them." More recently Historian Eugene Watts formulated the same idea in another way, observing that the upper classes made the laws but the lower classes policed the city. The police were not completely the tools of any one group and their activities cannot be reduced to any simple formula.[45]

To fully appreciate the role of the police in the community, one must recognize that the police were one of the most important social welfare institutions in the nineteenth-century cities. The police provided overnight lodging in the station houses for indigents. This now forgotten function was practically universal in the nineteenth century. The number of lodgers was enormous. An estimated 127,000 were lodged annually in Philadelphia during the 1880s. During economic hard times the numbers rose dramatically. Providence, Rhode Island, lodged 11,002 people in the depression year of 1877, but only 1,873 two years later when prosperity had returned. Lodgers generally received some form of sustenance, usually tea and crackers, and this expense was listed in annual reports as a major item in police department budgets. Not everyone was entitled to lodgings, however, nor was it always free. The Philadelphia police believed that many men simply gravitated from one station house to another. The police dispensed social welfare in the same arbitrary manner that they meted out "curb-side justice": the "undeserving poor" were simply turned away and often threatened with arrest if they did not promise to leave town. Some cities, such as Lowell, Massachusetts, required lodgers to saw firewood in return for their keep.[46]

The practice of lodging had a dreadful impact on the station houses themselves. In addition to the hordes of lodgers, the station houses contained barracks where policemen on reserve duty slept. The superintendent of the District of Columbia police complained of "the close proximity of the cells, lodging rooms, and water closets to the rooms occupied as sleeping rooms by the officers and privates, and although the greatest attention is paid to the cleanliness of the cells and water-closets, it is found nearly impossible to keep them so clean, especially at night, when occupied by prisoners and lodgers, as to prevent them from being extremely offensive to the sense of smell." William G. McAdoo, commissioner of the New York City police, described conditions in the station house as "a positive disgrace"; they were "unsanitary, poorly ventilated, and without modern improvements . . . heated by stoves in winter which give out a poisonous coal-gas. They are damp, gloomy, forbidding."[47]

Around the turn of the century, the police began to unburden themselves of the responsibility for providing lodgings. In part, this was the result of a campaign for housing reform. Jacob Riis and other housing reformers were largely responsible for the creation of separate municipal lodging houses in New York City in 1896. Riis' photographs of New York City police station houses, in fact, are vivid evidence of the disgraceful conditions that prevailed. Elimination of the practice of offering lodging was also part of the effort to improve the image of the police, if only by providing a clean and modern-looking station house.[48]

The Police and the Criminals

The relationship of the police to the problem of crime and criminals was at least as ambiguous as their relationship to the public generally. Although the official mandate of the "new police" was the crime prevention strategy of continuous patrol, it is doubtful that it had much effect on the incidence of crime. Indeed, Mark Haller has suggested that the police served to regulate rather than prevent crime. In recent years a number of studies have indicated that traditional police patrol does little to prevent crime and that detective work is usually successful only when the name of a suspect is immediately known. The nineteenth-century policeman, working without the benefit of the patrol car, two-way radio communications, and the trappings of the scientific crime lab, was probably even less effective as a crime fighter.[49]

There is in fact considerable evidence about the ineffectiveness of police work. In a number of cities police protection was withdrawn completely, usually as a result of a political dispute over control of the force. Yet, the record does not indicate either that these cities were engulfed in unchecked lawlessness or that there was a great deal of public concern about the absence of the police. These incidents provide an illuminating glimpse into the actual role of the police in the community and the expectations of the public.

In 1862 the Denver City Council suspended the $45-a-month salaries for police officers and decided that they should be paid by fees for specific services. The officers refused to accept this arrangement and, for all practical purposes, went out on strike. For a few days Denver was policed by the marshal and the chief of police alone. Finally, the city council capitulated and approved a new salary scale of $30-a-month plus expenses. The men returned to work, but in the interim there had been no breakdown in law and order. In Scranton,

Pennsylvania, an industrial town of 35,000 in 1875 with a history of industrial and ethnic strife, the city was left without police protection for several months. Two men claimed the office of mayor and both lined up support from within the city's small fourteen-man police department. After three months of struggle the courts resolved the issue in favor of Mayor McKune. But for those three months the city had been without meaningful police protection or, for that matter, much city government at all. The local press, however, gave no evidence of public fears of lawlessness. Indeed, one might legitimately ask what a fourteen-man police force would do in a city of 35,000 people anyway.[50]

In Omaha, Nebraska, police service was virtually suspended in 1887 when a dispute arose between the city council and a new board of police commissioners. The state legislature had just assumed control of the Omaha police, with the creation of a gubernatorial-appointed board. The Omaha City Council, resentful of this usurpation of power, refused to appropriate funds for the new police chief or the new patrolmen. The issue went into the courts, but for most of the summer of 1887 Omaha had only minimal police protection. Voluntary contributions to the Police Relief Association provided some income for some of the police officers who remained on duty for the duration. The public, however, betrayed no great fears of a breakdown in law and order.[51]

Even in the most famous suspension of police service in all of police history, the 1919 Boston police strike, the extent of lawlessness was greatly exaggerated. There was no dramatic upsurge in normal crimes against persons or property and even the looting and vandalism was relatively minor. The public reaction to the strike and the fears of "anarchy," were primarily an expression of antilabor, antiradical, and antiforeign hysteria in the troubled year of 1919—the year not only of the famous Red Scare, but also of major strikes in the coal and steel industries. During a similar police strike in Cincinnati the year before there had been neither lawlessness nor a public backlash.[52]

Even the most readily available statistics of police departments suggest that patrol was a perfunctory and rather empty gesture. The number of police per population remained extremely low. In fact, the creation of the so-called new police with their crime prevention mandate did not significantly increase the number of men actually on duty. New York City in 1844 had 548 watchmen on duty each night under the old system. By 1876 there were still only 769 policemen on the street each night, even though the city had grown enormously in the interim. The Chicago police department made a heroic effort in 1880 to patrol 600 of the city's 651 miles of streets, but the department had only 321 men available for patrol duty. Officers on the night shift had assignments that averaged three and one-quarter miles, while those on the day shift were expected to cover an average of four and one-half miles. The superintendent of the Chicago police observed that "It should not be surprising if the cry 'where are the police?' is occasionally heard." Leonard Fuld, in his 1909 textbook *Police Administration* pointed out that "it requires no elaborate demonstration to show that if a policeman's post covers three or four miles of streets, he is unable to keep himself constantly informed of what is taking place on every part of his post."[53]

There persists in the public mind, and in much of the folklore of police administration, the myth of the nineteenth-century patrolman as a man who knew intimately the residents of his beat. Unfortunately, a sober assessment of the situation cannot sustain such a romantic notion. The ratio of police to population suggests that there could have been only minimal contact at best. Morever, historians have now established that the rate of population mobility was far higher in the nineteenth century than today. In other words, the idea of stable neighborhoods is itself a romantic and nostalgic myth.

The perfunctory nature of patrol is further indicated by the fact that many police departments did not even attempt to patrol the entire city. Chicago did relatively well to patrol 600 of 651 miles of streets. The Cincinnati police patrolled only 300 of 402 miles, while the Minneapolis police patrolled only fifty of 200 miles. Madison, Wisconsin, had perhaps the best solution to the problem: the police did not patrol at all but remained in the station house and responded to specific calls for service.[54]

The limited technology of the period further reduced the ability of the police to respond to the needs of the public. In the twentieth century the telephone, in combination with the radio-dispatched patrol car, became the principal device for mobilizing the police. By the 1960s well over 80 percent of police activities were the result of citizen-initiated calls for service. In 1909 Leonard Fuld pointed out that "there is at present no satisfactory method by which a citizen can summon police assistance in cases of emergency." One would have to run to the nearest police station or hope to encounter a policeman on the street corner in order to obtain service. As August Vollmer pointed out, "The patrolman ... was almost completely isolated on his beat." He was isolated both from the public, who might need service, and from his supervisors, who might want to either mobilize him for emergency duty or simply to monitor his activity.[55]

The difficulty in mobilizing the police had an important effect on public expectations. Since there was no way to obtain services quickly, the public generally tolerated conditions that would not be tolerated today. Cities in the nineteenth century were generally characterized, if not by more crime, then certainly by more public disorder than would be allowed by contemporary standards. Public drunkenness, brawls, and domestic disputes were accepted as a normal part of city life—there was no effective way of eliminating them. The technological revolution of the twentieth century, rapid communications in particular, has effected a parallel revolution in public expectations. Because it is possible to mobilize the police for routine service calls (such as quieting minor disorders) the public increasingly thinks of this as a legitimate police function.

The relationship of the police to criminals in the nineteenth century was symbiotic and rather formal. As Mark Haller suggests, the police regulated rather than suppressed crime. The dynamics of the relationship between the police and criminals was fundamental to the nature of police work and remains relatively unchanged today. In order to detect crime, the police need information; the most useful information, of course, can be obtained from other criminals. Even today the police rely on a network of informants that includes prostitutes, drug dealers, ex-offenders, and individuals who are under arrest and awaiting prosecution. In the nineteenth century the police entered into formal relations with both pickpockets and prostitutes, among others. Many police chiefs preferred to tolerate prostitution in segregated districts rather than to suppress it completely. The prostitutes became valuable sources of information, and criminals, the police believed, tended to concentrate in the segregated districts.[56]

In some cities there developed an elaborate system of pickpocket regulation. Professional pickpockets in New York City, for example, established defined territories and insisted on a monopoly in that area. The police enforced this arrangement by chasing out unauthorized pickpockets in return for information and other services from the regular pickpockets. James Richardson offers an illuminating portrait of the activities of New York City Detective Thomas Byrnes. Relying on an organized network of informants, Byrnes could work miracles of crime detection when needed. If a wealthy banker lost his watch, or if a particularly valuable piece of property were stolen, Brynes could arrange for its return through his contacts in the underworld. Byrnes apparently profited immensely from this system. The Lexow committee investigation in 1894 discovered that Byrnes' personal wealth was in the neighborhood of $350,000, most of it in real estate held in his wife's name. The investigators did not probe too deeply into his finances, since it was clear that it would implicate a number of prominent figures, including bankers, with whom Byrnes had a working relationship. In short, Byrnes entered into a corrupt relationship with professional thieves to cement an equally corrupt relationship with the financial elite. Crime, as Daniel Bell once observed, was clearly "an American way of life."[57]

The image of the individual criminal had a very different character for most of the public in the nineteenth century. Unlike the highly sociological image of criminality that prevails today, with its emphasis on abstract socioeconomic or psychological forces, nineteenth century Americans thought of crime in terms of colorful individuals. A certain romanticism surrounded the reputed exploits of professional thieves, pickpockets, swindlers, and robbers. No one did more to popularize that image than Allan Pinkerton, the founder of the famous detective agency. Between 1874 and 1885 Pinkerton published more than eighteen books on crime and criminals. *Thirty Years as a Detective* was typical of the genre. In a chapter on "House Breaking as a Fine Art," Pinkerton wrote that "romance and tradition have for a long period of time accredited the cracksman with being the most expert in their profession." The police officer was expected to match wits with these expert criminals and the game of crime fighting took on the aspect of an heroic contest.[58]

Pinkerton helped to promote this view of criminality among the municipal police. His two sons, William and Robert, became honorary members of the International Association of Chiefs of Police (IACP). Annual conventions of the association usually featured an address by one of the brothers on the crime problem. The heroic view of crime detection can also be found in annual reports from the period and in the many histories of local police departments published before the turn of the century. John J. Flinn's *History of the Chicago Police*, for example, devoted long sections to the exploits of particular criminals and the efforts of the police to apprehend them. The biographical sketches of prominent members of the department, and even of lowly patrolmen, emphasized particularly spectacular or colorful arrests. Detective Thomas Byrnes of the New York police published in 1886 a book entitled *Professional Criminals of America*, which also presented the crime problem in very personal terms.[59]

Although the new police were established primarily to prevent crime, we have no solid data on the nature of their actual impact on the incidence of criminality. The only available official statistics, arrest and prosecution figures, are of questionable value even for recent years and wholly unreliable for more distant periods. Not only are the records themselves poorly maintained, but police arrest practices do not necessarily reflect the true incidence of criminal behavior. The issue is further complicated by the fact that there is an important difference between the incidence of major crimes and the level of public order which involves a host of lesser offenses. The writings on urban history and police history are filled with assertions that the crime rate was dramatically rising or falling at various periods. But, as historian Roger Lane cautions, we have no conception of a "standard level of disorder" by which to measure long term changes.[60]

Despite these methodological difficulties, a number of historians have argued that there has been a significant decrease in the incidence of crime over the past century and a general rise in the level of public order. Theodore Ferdinand, in a study of the crime rate in Boston since 1849, argues that the crime rate has declined by an astounding two-thirds since the 1870s. Roger Lane offers a more sophisticated analysis of the same phenomenon. Recognizing that the data is highly unreliable, Lane argues not simply that there was a decline in the crime rate, but that public expectations of what was acceptable in an urban society changed dramatically. "The machinery of justice was increased because of a felt need, a growing intolerance of behavior which had been earlier tolerated, coupled with a belief that the state and not the individual citizen was required to do the necessary job." Lane argues that rising public expectations were part of the urbanization process: "The move to the cities had, in short, produced a more tractable, more socialized, more 'civilized' generation than its predecessors." A similar argument is advanced by historian Samuel Warner in his study of Philadelphia, *The Private City*. He too finds a rising level of public order and argues that as urbanization progresses people develop an intricate network of formal and informal associations that provide structure and meaning for their lives and, in the process, raise the level of public order.[61]

The argument advanced by Lane and by Warner stands in sharp contrast to the popular view of the "urban crisis," in which urbanization is seen as a steady deterioration of the quality of life. The role of the police in this process, however, remains problematic. The evidence suggests that the police played a distinctly minor rather than major role in establishing higher standards of public order. Other institutions, particularly the schools and the discipline of the work routine itself in an urban-industrial society, were more pervasive in their influence. The police, while admittedly a "continual presence," were simply too few in number and too close to the populace to have had much of a coercive effect. The available arrest statistics should be viewed with caution. Even today police practices are characterized by a rather systematic underenforcement of the laws. Given the practical problems in effecting a simple arrest in the nineteenth century, it is reasonable to assume that there was even greater underenforcement. Police activity, even the arrest of drunks, was more a token gesture than a systematic effort to enforce moral standards. And we should not forget that if the complaints of the reformers had any validity at all, the police themselves spent an inordinant amount of time in the saloons, not overseeing the morals of the public.

As far as many nineteenth-century Americans were concerned, the problem of "lawlessness" involved not the incidence of major crimes but rather the failure of the police to enforce existing laws. The police, not professional criminals, were the problem. Theodore Roosevelt, who attempted to institute a full enforcement policy during his two years (1895-1897) as a New York City police commissioner, argued that the central issue in public life was "whether public officials are to be true to their oaths of office, and see that the law is administered in good faith." Roosevelt's concern was mainly a result of the rather systematic nonenforcement of the laws against drinking, gambling, and prostitution, and the corruption of the police that resulted from the mere existence of such laws. In the nineteenth century, the "crime" problem was largely one of the vice laws.[62]

As any number of investigations revealed—the 1894 Lexow investigation being the most extensive and most famous—police corruption was endemic. The police were involved in a systematic pattern of payoffs from drinking, gambling, and prostitution, and at the same time were often an important part of voting fraud. This system of corruption was inherent in the fact that the police were largely a political institution. As Mark Haller argues, the police were not oriented towards abstract legal norms. Rather, their activities were determined by the prevailing social and political mores of the community. Moreover, they were but one part of a larger criminal justice system that was equally fraught with politically influenced corruption. The political machines effectively nullified the intent of many of the laws. Even when the police did attempt to enforce the law, their efforts were frustrated by the lower courts. The complaint of the Cincinnati chief of police in 1882 was typical of a more general phenomenon. Cincinnati enacted a Sunday-closing law for saloons in 1882 and in the next three months the police arrested 313 saloon keepers for various violations. The chief of police reported, however, that "of this number but five were arraigned in court; these were tried and, with one exception, discharged. Under the existing jury system it became apparent that conviction could not be had. . . . " The chief concluded that "the law is now a dead letter, for public sentiment does not sustain it."[63]

Efforts to enforce public morals were episodic at best. Edward H. Savage, later police chief in Boston, described one famous antiprostitution raid in 1851 – apparently a widely publicized event and one of the keys to his later appointment as chief. For the "descent" on the red-light district, Savage mobilized the entire fifty-man police force (one wonders about police protection in the rest of the city) at 9:00 P.M. on April 23. Within a half hour they arrested 165 people, mostly women. The raid could not have had much more than a temporary effect on the practice of organized prostitution in Boston, however, for it was not followed up with any systematic attempt at suppression. By Savage's own account the next "descent" did not occur for another seven years. Clearly, the raids were more for show than anything else.[64]

The Politics of Police Administration

The "lawlessness" of the police–their systematic corruption and nonenforcement of the laws–became one of the paramount issues in municipal politics during the nineteenth century. Repeated reform movements arose with an eye to alter police practices. The heart of the matter was not the question of law enforcement itself but the social and political dynamics of the urban community. Police corruption was part of the political machine, a means by which party favorites were allowed to conduct illegal business and by which the cultural styles of different ethnic groups were preserved. The latter was especially important for both the Germans and the Irish who were the objects of a continuing antiliquor crusade by Protestant, native-born, and middle-class Americans. The liquor question and the police question were, in fact, inseparable. As Wilbur Miller argues, moreover, the liquor question was not a conflict between urban and rural America, as it has so often been portrayed, but rather a conflict between different elements of the urban community. At various times, each of these factions was able to draw upon support from rural areas to impose its particular standards on the city.[65]

The reform syndrome developed a rather predictable pattern. While corruption was rather pervasive and continuous, a particular incident could touch off a reform effort. The circumstances of the famous Lexow committee investigation in New York City was fairly typical. In 1892 the Reverend Charles Parkhurst of the Madison Square Presbyterian Church suddenly awoke to the existence of widespread illegal activities in the city. Parkhurst denounced the police and Tammany Hall from his pulpit. At first embarrassed because he lacked specific evidence, Parkhurst soon took to the streets to obtain it. Tammany Hall responded to charges of corruption with a wholesale shift of assignments for police captains, a game of musical chairs that fooled no one. Meanwhile, Parkhurst's campaign against vice coincided with the interests of the state Republican Party, ever on the lookout for an opportunity to embarrass the Democratic Party machine in New York City. When the GOP captured control of the state legislature in late 1893, the stage was set for a partisan investigation of the New York City police.[66]

The Lexow committee investigation exposed a pervasive pattern of voter fraud, payoffs for police protection, and bribes for promotion within the department. The major result of the exposé was a new state law in 1895 creating the bipartisan Board of Police Commissioners, to which Theodore Roosevelt was appointed. The change in the formal structure of control of the police department had little long-run effect on police practices—as Roosevelt discovered to his dismay. By 1900 the New York City police were again firmly in the grip of Tammany Hall and again the object of a major investigation by the state legislature. Once again the formal administrative structure of the department was changed: the board of commissioners was abolished and the department placed under the responsibility of a single commissioner.

The struggle among different political factions resulted in a continuing series of changes in the administrative structure of police departments in the nineteenth century. The sequence of events in New York City found its parallel in virtually every other city. Each faction sought to use a temporary political advantage to alter the administrative structure in such a way as to give it permanent control. Police departments became a major political football in local politics.

Developments in New York City marked the boundaries of a distinct era in police history: the age of the police commission. In 1853 responsibility for the New York City police was given to a Board of Police Commissioners, consisting of the mayor, the recorder, and the city judge. This move was designed to separate the legislative and executive functions and take administrative responsibility for the police out of the hands of city council. It was also hoped, in vain, that it would reduce partisan political influence in police affairs. For the next forty-eight years, the New York City police were governed by some form of multimembered police commission. Within a few years other cities began to experiment with commissions of their own. Changes were frequent and a truly kaleidoscopic variety of forms was devised. Only Philadelphia among major cities never experienced the police commission. Finally, in 1901, New York City again led the way with the abolition of its board of commissioners. Within the next few years other major cities began to follow suit and the police commission soon became a thing of the past.[67]

The experience of Cincinnati suggests not only the intensity of the struggle for control over the police, judging from the frequency of changes, but also the wide variety of forms that were adopted. Between 1859 and 1910 there were ten major changes in the administrative structure of the police department, most of them occurring between 1859 and 1886. From its inception in 1844 to 1859 the police were under the direct supervision of the mayor. In 1859 control was transferred to a four-member commission appointed jointly by the mayor, the police judge, and the city auditor. This experiment lasted exactly one year and in 1860 control was returned to the mayor. In 1873 a second commission was established, this one elected directly by the voters. Like the first, the second commission lasted only one year and control was again returned to the mayor in 1874. Three years later the state legislature intervened and created a five-member board appointed by the governor. This board survived for three years, but in 1880 it too was abolished and control again returned to the mayor. In 1885 and 1886 a major political scandal erupted in Cincinnati. First, a three-member board appointed by the Board of Public Works was created, but it was soon replaced by a four-member "nonpartisan" board appointed by the governor in 1886. The nonpartisan Board of Police Commissioners, which we shall examine in detail later, introduced an element of stability in the Cincinnati police department. It enjoyed a remarkable life span of sixteen years, during which it introduced a number of important reforms. In 1902, however, the board was abolished and control given to a four-member board appointed jointly by the mayor and the city council. Finally, in 1910 Cincinnati followed the lead of New York City by abolishing the idea of a board altogether and placing the police department under a single director of public safety.[68]

As the Cincinnati experience suggests, police commissions took a wide variety of forms. Raymond B. Fosdick's classic 1920 study, *American Police Systems*, offers the most thorough examination of the police commission phenomenon. Commissions were both elected and appointed. The method of appointment also varied widely: the mayor, the city council, the governor, or some combination of public officials had appointment powers at various times in different cities. The size of boards also ranged from a low of two to a high of twelve members. In their effort to limit the influence of partisan politics, many police commissions were officially bipartisan. The law creating the 1895 New York City Board of Police Commissioners specified that "At no time shall more than two such commissioners belong to the same political party, nor be of the same political opinion on state and national issues." Even where bipartisanship was not mandated by law there was often an informal understanding that positions would be divided between the two major parties. In Indianapolis the law went a step further and mandated that positions on the police force itself be divided equally along political lines.[69]

In many instances the state assumed control of the municipal police. Here again, New York led the way. The Metropolitan Police Board established in 1857 was the first example of state control of a municipal police force. Maryland followed suit in 1860 with a board to control the Baltimore police, while Missouri assumed control of the St. Louis and Kansas City police in 1861. The idea continued to spread and, by 1915, had been tried in twelve of the twenty-three largest cities in the country. In rare instances, state control was a distinct improvement. The state controlled board that ran the Cincinnati police from 1886 to 1902 was a remarkable success by any measure. More often, however, the assumption of state control precipitated political confrontation. The legitimacy of the New York Metropolitan Police in 1857 was openly challenged by the mayor and the old municipal police force. The result was a genuine police riot, featuring a pitched battle between the two police forces. When the state assumed control of the Omaha police in 1887, the city council refused to appropriate any funds for the department. A similar crisis hit St. Louis in 1899.[70]

The particular form that the administrative structure of a police department took, however, made little difference. Control of the police merely shifted from one partisan faction to another: the fact of the police as a partisan instrument remained constant. Even more important was the fact that effective control of the police remained at the neighborhood level. Reform-minded administrators, as Theodore Roosevelt soon discovered, could not translate their ideas into policy. They lacked both an ideological rationale that could counter the idea of the police as a partisan instrument and means of asserting uniform control over the rank and file. After the turn of the century, the professionalization movement would provide both the rationale (nonpartisan public service) and the means (administrative centralization and the techniques of efficient business management).

Social Control in an Urban–Industrial Society

Ultimately, the important questions about the police concern the role of the police in the development of society. It is not simply a question of who controlled the police and what they sought to do with them, but also a question of the impact of the police as an institution on the quality of life. English historians, for example, have argued that the London police had a major hand in improving the quality of life in that country. They argue that the high standards of professionalism that prevailed set in motion a "benign circle" of events that largely reduced the incidence of violence in English society. One might well argue with this overly romanticized view of the London police, but the more general question of the long-term influence of the police institution remains a challenging one.[71]

We have already suggested the main thesis of this history of the American police: that their impact, for good or ill, was minor rather than major. The ability of the police to either prevent crime or apprehend criminals was minimal at best. The role of the police as agents of high standards of public order is also questionable. It would seem that the public was more effective in socializing the police than vice versa. The police should be viewed in the full context of the social control problem. From that perspective, they played a distinctively minor role.

Even in terms of some of the more obvious law enforcement functions, the police were supplemented and in some instances supplanted by other agencies. The more extreme radical view that the police were the tools of a ruling class is belied by the fact that the wealthy and powerful in nineteenth-century America continually turned to alternative means to accomplish their ends.

Businessmen found private police a far more reliable means of protecting their property. They were free of political influence (that is, of influence from potentially antagonistic interests) and from a management perspective were more cost effective. A businessman could hire a private policeman and receive the benefits directly, a procedure they found much more attractive than paying higher taxes for municipal police of dubious reliability. Private policing took several different forms. Virtually every city made provisions for special police. Businessmen could hire their own guards and have them sworn in by the police department. Although they remained private employees, hired, paid, and directed by private companies, they were clothed with the powers of the municipal police. To add to the ambiguity of their status, the "specials" often wore uniforms that were nearly identical to those of the municipal police. The "specials" were generally only required to report to the police department once each month to renew their appointments. As municipal police departments began to develop a rudimentary professional identity, they sought to eliminate the "specials." The chief of the Cincinnati police in 1882 complained that the "specials" "constitute, to a certain extent, an irresponsible body of officers, who are lost sight of and liable to abuse their trust."[72]

In Pennsylvania the institution of private policing reached its most elaborate and notorious level. State law allowed private corporations to mobilize their own police forces. Railroad corporations first won this power in 1865; two years later it was extended to coal and iron producers in rural areas. Under the terms of the Coal and Iron Police Act, industrialists merely had to petition the sheriff of the county for permission to have a number of employees deputized. For the next seventy years (until the institution was abolished in the prolabor climate of the 1930s) the Coal and Iron Police operated as legalized vigilantes in many rural communities. They were used primarily to suppress the struggling labor movement. Because they circumvented popular control, they were far more reliable than either municipal police or even the state militia, which too often consisted of men who were sympathetic to the interests of workingmen rather than employers.[73]

No account of private policing would be complete without mention of the Pinkerton Detective Agency. Irony surrounds the career of Allan Pinkerton. He fled England in the 1840s as a fugitive from justice, wanted by the authorities for his participation in the radical Chartist movement. In the United States he switched sides ideologically and his detective agency became one of the most prominent antagonists of the labor movement. Pinkerton built his agency on the needs of businessmen which were not being filled by public law enforcement agencies. In 1855 he was hired by six midwestern railroads to provide them with police protection in a five state region. Railroad properties in rural areas were virtually without any protection. Pinkerton also engaged in investigation of railroad employees, with a particular eye to incipient labor union activity.

In 1858, Pinkerton extended his activities into areas nominally the responsibility of the municipal police. Cyrus Bradley, former Cook County sheriff and Chicago chief of police between 1855 and 1856, had previously formed a private security agency. Bradley offered his customers detective services and evening patrol in suburban residential districts. Recognizing an opportunity for expanding his own business, Pinkerton also began offering private security services to businessmen in the Chicago area. In its first year of operation, the Pinkerton Protective Police Patrol boasted that it had found 751 instances where the doors of private businesses were vulnerable to potential criminals. Through its spying operation, meanwhile, the Pinkerton agency identified 440 cases of employee misconduct. As historian Frank Morn suggests in his analysis of the Pinkerton services, "In the late 1850s and early 1860s, it seemed that private police were more modern than the modern public police." That is to say, they had more of the trappings of professionalism: a more tightly centralized command structure and a more serious orientation toward the business of crime fighting.[74]

With respect to the broader question of social control, a different private agency was far more important than the municipal police. Vigilante action, by which members of the elite of a community took the law into their own hands, was a frequent phenomenon in the nineteenth century. Historian Richard Maxwell Brown, who has examined vigilantism in detail, argues that "the first vigilante movement in American history occurred in 1767. From then on until about 1900, vigilante activity was an almost constant factor in American life." Brown himself identified and classified over 300 separate vigilante actions, and it is clear that many more went unrecorded.[75]

The case of the San Francisco Vigilance Committee of 1855–1856 offers an illuminating picture of the relationship of vigilantism to local politics and the municipal police. City government in San Francisco had fallen under the control of the Democratic Party, which in turn was dominated by Irish-Catholics. The San Francisco *Daily Evening Bulletin*, under the editorship of James King, launched a continuing attack on "Boss" David Broderick's Democratic Party. King found a cause celebre when Charles Cora, an Italian-American gambler accused of murdering a U.S. marshal, was set free because of a hung jury. King charged political interference and was then shot and killed by James P. Casey, a well-known Irish-Catholic political figure. Within a matter of days, King's associates mobilized a vigilance committee of between 6,000 and 8,000 members. The committee not only tried and hanged both Cora and Casey, but also executed two other men and deported twenty-eight people from the city. The committee, "dominated lock, stock, and barrel by the leading merchants of San Francisco who controlled it through an executive committee," broke the back of Broderick's Democratic Party machine. Although the committee formally disbanded on August 18, 1856, it was in reality replaced by the People's Party, which controlled city politics for the next few years.[76]

The San Francisco Vigilance Committee represented the dominant attributes of vigilantism. It was a means by which the elite could circumvent established law enforcement authorities by simply taking the law into their own hands. The police and the entire city government in their view had fallen into the wrong hands. Vigilance committees were generally dominated by the elite of the community and were used to apprehend particular suspects, to destroy opposing political organizations, and frequently to enforce public morals. In many cases, for example, men deemed lazy and shiftless were subjected to whippings and told to either find work or leave the area. Vigilance committees respected the trappings of legalism. They frequently had constitutions and bylaws, formal membership requirements, and mock trials for their victims. In short, vigilantism was not an expression of mob lawlessness; rather it was an ad hoc supplement to official criminal justice machinery. And it was a preferred method for the elite since it circumvented the popular political influence of the lower classes.

The municipal police, subject to political influence, were an unreliable instrument for social control. In many respects, reform was an attempt by elite groups—especially business and professional interests—to break the power of the working-class based political machines that dominated the police. Despite its claims to nonpartisanship, then, the idea of professionalization was itself a movement that served partisan ends. The attempt to remove the influence of politics was essentially an effort to supplant one political element with another. To achieve this end, however, the reformers undertook both a wholesale restructuring of police departments and a redefinition of the police role.

2 The Emergence of Professionalism

The idea of policing as a profession began to emerge slowly in the latter part of the nineteenth century. At first there was no formulation of a coherent idea of professionalism. That would not appear until the turn of the century. Reform ideas first appeared as a reaction to the corrupt and politicized state of the police. A small group of reformers, often independently and without reference to each other, began to search for a different approach. All agreed that partisan politics was the heart of the problem. Slowly, the idea of policing as a higher calling (higher than the concerns of local politics, that is), as a profession committed to public service, began to gain ground. From this initial impulse flowed a host of other reform ideas: the need for making police work a career, the need for formal training, the idea of a science of policing, and, finally, the idea that, as a profession, policing could contribute to the betterment of society.[1]

Almost immediately, different and often contradictory ideas of police professionalism appeared. One of the dominant motifs emphasized reform of the internal administration of police departments, placing a premium on managerial efficiency. For many reformers that was an end in itself. For others, it was a means to other ends. Two ideas about the proper role of the police in society also appeared. One emphasized improvement in the law enforcement role, especially the acquisition of scientific techniques of crime detection. An alternative view of the police saw them playing more of a social work role. Police officers, it was suggested, could reform society by preventing crime, by intervening in the lives of individuals so as to keep them out of the machinery of criminal justice. The advocates of this view were closely tied to the emerging rehabilitative ideal in correctional cricles. These various definitions of police professionalism made their first appearance in the late nineteenth century. Later, they would acquire a more complete conceptualization. Throughout the history of police reform, however, there would be a continuing tension between these alternative and often conflicting definitions of exactly what police professionalism consisted of.

The Beginnings of a Police Literature

The relative absence of any serious writings on police work testifies to the low level of professional consciousness in the nineteenth century. Prior to the mid-1880s there was virtually nothing in the way of a police literature. The first books that began to appear from the mid-1880s onward were either memoirs or partisan histories of local police departments. The appearance of these first books marked an important first step in the development of professionalism: at least someone was sufficiently committed to policing as an occupation to feel concerned about explaining and defending the police.

The development of professional consciousness among police chiefs can be understood as a passage through several stages. In his study of the career patterns of St. Louis police chiefs, John K. Maniha identifies three distinct stages. "Chiefs of Phase I," he writes, "were recruited on the basis of their status as minor community notables, or possibly through political patronage—in keeping with the high degree of politicization and other particularistic factors present in all urban institutions of the period." Police chiefs were recruited laterally, to use modern terminology, on the basis of criteria that had little or nothing to do with police experience. In the second phase of development, police chiefs began to be recruited from within the ranks of the department. This represented an important change, a symptom of the first glimmerings of policing as a profession. It meant that individuals who worked as police officers had at least made a commitment to policing as a career. Maniha points out that by the end of the century the St. Louis police department had formalized rules concerning the appointment of its chief. This represented not so much the advance of professionalization as of bureaucratization. The idea that police chiefs should come up through the ranks, and that lateral movement should be restricted, became a dominant characteristic of police bureaucracies in the twentieth century.

A glance at the careers of the first police chiefs in St. Louis suggests the amateurism that surrounded the job. James McDonough, the first chief, had been a master carpenter before his appointment in 1843. He held the job for three years and then served in a number of other elective and appointive political positions until being reappointed police chief in 1861. But this time he served only six months, being dismissed when the Republicans regained control of the St. Louis police and "he found himself on the wrong side." But McDonough was not finished with the St. Louis police. He served again as police chief between 1871 and 1874 and then again between 1875 and 1881. The other men who served as chief during this period had careers that were remarkably similar to McDonough's. All were essentially small businessmen who tried their luck in a variety of different ventures. Maniha comments about McDonough that "The police department was not a full-time career for him. He came back to it only when his other interests failed, and when he did come back, he reentered at the top."[2]

In New York City many of the early police officials were also small entrepreneurs with a number of outside business interests. The police department, in fact, was frequently a means of promoting these other interests. George Matsell served as police chief from 1845 to 1857 and then as superintendent from 1871 to 1875, losing his job in both instances because changing political fortunes.

Matsell was also the publisher of the *Police Gazette,* a popular journal that owed much to its publisher's connections with the police department and the Democratic Party political machine. In the 1880s, Detective Thomas Byrnes published the book *Professional Criminals of America* as a private business venture. The Lexow investigation, meanwhile, turned up evidence that clearly suggested that Byrnes used his position as detective to engage in real estate speculation using illegal payoffs as his source of capital. As Mark Haller suggests, the police were part of a larger criminal justice system that was essentially a form of systematic racketeering. The attractions of positions of authority lay primarily in the opportunities they offered for business ventures.[3]

Edward H. Savage, Boston police chief between 1870 and 1878, holds the distinction of having written the first book-length history of a police department. First published in 1865, *Police Records and Recollections, or Boston by Daylight and Gaslight For Two Hundred and Forty Years* was reprinted in an enlarged and revised version eight years later. Savage's account was quite different from the police histories that began to appear in the 1880s. In reality it was not a history at all. The first part consisted of a chronicle of the development of the Boston police, beginning with the earliest night watch system in the colonial era. Savage made no effort to organize this material into a coherent and interpretive history. The second part consisted of a random collection of essays on a wide variety of subjects. It included, among other things, the chief's "Advice to a Young Policeman," and short descriptions of notable events such as the cholera epidemic of 1854, the Civil War draft riot, and a famous antivice raid of 1851.[4]

More characteristic of the genre of nineteenth-century police histories was *Our Police Protectors,* Augustine E. Costello's richly detailed 1885 history of the New York City police. Because of its wealth of detail, including many original documents woven into the narrative, Costello's account is an invaluable historical source. *Our Police Protectors,* as the title suggests, was a partisan defense of the New York police. The author had been the police reporter for the New York *Herald* and in that capacity had developed a close relationship with the police department. In 1883 the police pension fund faced the prospect of imminent bankruptcy and Costello agreed to write his history as a fund-raising venture.[5]

Costello's *Our Police Protectors* set the model for police histories in other cities. Two years later John J. Flinn published his *History of the Chicago Police.* Flinn was also a police reporter and his book was published for the benefit of the Chicago Policeman's Benevolent Association. Howard O. Sprogel published his *Philadelphia Police: Past and Present* in 1887, and by 1890 there were similar histories of the Pittsburgh, Baltimore, and Cincinnati police departments. By the turn of the century there were histories of many other large city police departments.[6]

These histories marked the dawning of organizational self-consciousness among the American police. One hesitates to suggest professional self-consciousness since they were largely combative, partisan accounts, designed to defend the police against the attacks of political opponents. But they at least reflected the fact that the police did have a growing sense of collective self-interest. That alone was an important precondition to the development of a more professional outlook. Costello's view of the New York City police was typical of the genre: "Night and day, fair weather and foul, when his tour of duty commences, the Policeman, like the trusty sentinel, must go to his post and be prepared to meet all kinds of danger." It was, in short, the heroic view of the police that emphasized physical prowess and bravery. The accounts were generally anecdotal and devoted large amounts of space to spectacular crimes or major disturbances. Flinn, for example, devoted a total of six chapters to the role of the Chicago police in the labor disturbances of 1877 and 1886. He brooked no criticism of the Chicago police and vigorously defended their violent actions during the 1877 riots. "The manner in which the force conducted itself during the riot," he wrote, "won for it the highest public commendation."[7]

The picture of police departments offered in these histories was grossly inaccurate in some respects but extremely illuminating in others. Since most of the authors were closely tied to both the police and the political machines that dominated them, they said not a word about corruption, either in terms of payoffs for vice protection or bribes for promotions. For the most part they blandly asserted that only the most qualified men were selected for the job and that politics played little or no role. Only by reading between the lines of Costello's account, for example, which offered abundant detail about the many changes in the administrative structure of the New York City police, does one get a sense of the political controversies that engulfed the department. Much of the value of these police histories lies in the fact that they represent the point of view of those in power, rather than the views of the reformers who were generally not in power. Because reformers were more inclined to write, and write extensively, we know more of their views than of their opponents. Too much urban history has been written on the basis of this imbalance of source material. The police histories serve as a useful corrective.

These histories provide an illuminating and invaluable glimpse into some of the informal processes that governed police departments in the nineteenth century. The final chapters of both Flinn's history of the Chicago police and Sprogel's account of the Philadelphia police are devoted to detailed descriptions of the men in each of the different precincts. Nothing could better convey a sense of the decentralized structure of big city police departments. Flinn even offered a brief description of each precinct station house, the social characteristics of the precinct, and notable events in the history of crime in that area. The city and the police department was an aggregation of small units.

Flinn and Sprogel also focused on the individual officer. Policing was not a matter of impersonal law enforcement, but rather the exploits of individual men. Sprogel expressed regret that he had been unable to write more about each officer: "It can be said that in the following pages justice has not been done either officers or patrolmen; space would not permit it. Even the bare mention of each patrolman has expanded the book to almost unwieldly proportions." Nonetheless, he did manage to provide detailed biographical sketches of the more prominent members of the department. From Flinn's account it would be possible to reconstruct a systematic portrait of the Chicago police force in the mid-1880s, complete with nativity, place of residence, and previous occupation.[8]

The focus on the individual patrolman—his background and his exploits—represented the personalized style of nineteenth-century policing. This would be lost with the advent of the professionalization movement with its emphasis on impersonal, bureaucratic standards. To retain their dignity the rank and file first attempted unionization and, when that was defeated, retreated into an informal but tightly knit occupational subculture. Augustine Costello concluded his discussion of police morale with the comment, "The trouble with policemen is that they are men, and rather more of men than the rest of the community." In short, they shared the same human sentiments as other people and were no more or no less corrupt than people in other jobs. Although clearly a partisan defense of the police, Costello's observation contained an important element of truth. One of the tragedies of the professionalization movement would be that, in their zeal to elevate the police as an institution, the reformers often lost sight of the human material with which they had to work.[9]

New Ideas in Police Service

The new conception of police service, as we have already suggested, involved a number of different and often conflicting ideas. Some reformers sought merely to reform the administrative structure and processes of police departments. Others sought to improve the crime-fighting powers of the police. Still others saw the police as an agency of social reform, devoting its efforts to the prevention of crime. The conflict between these different ideas did not take the form of a full-scale debate in the nineteenth century. The ideas themselves had not yet developed fully. Furthermore, there was no law enforcement professional association that could serve as a forum for such a debate. The various reform ideas developed gradually and in isolation.

Chief Edward H. Savage of the Boston police department was perhaps the single most notable exponent of the crime prevention ideal in the mid-nineteenth century. As a captain he developed a particular concern about the problem of prostitution. He took special pride in his well-publicized 1851 raid on the vice district which resulted in more than one hundred arrests. Seven years later, when Savage planned another massive "descent" on the vice district, he had begun thinking in terms of rehabilitating rather than merely arresting the prostitutes. After consulting with the "kind hearted Judge Wells of the Police Court," he developed a program of probation. During the raid of October 22, 1858, fifty-one women were arrested. When they appeared in court the next morning "the judge was informed of the nature of their case, and asked if not inconsistent with the requirements of justice, to give all who were found guilty of the charges preferred against them, a good smart sentence, with a suspension, to enable them to leave the city for their parents and home." Savage had questioned the women the night before "to learn something of their history," in what was one of the earliest presentence investigations on record. The judge agreed with the proposal and forty-seven of the fifty-one women "gladly accepted the opportunity" for probation rather than incarceration.[10]

Savage continued to pursue his humanitarian efforts for more lenient treatment of criminal offenders. Finding the climate in policing unreceptive to these ideas, however, he eventually left police work altogether. In 1878, with the passage of a state probation law, he became the chief probation officer for the city of Boston.[11]

The rehabilitative ideal advanced by Edward Savage found its most complete expression in the work of the National Prison Association. Organized in 1870 as a professional association of prison officials, it became an important national forum for new ideas in policing. In this respect it simply filled the vacuum left by the absence of a professional association of police officials. After an abortive national convention in 1871, there was no permanent national organization until the founding in 1893 of what eventually became the International Association of Chiefs of Police. The lack of a national organization, in fact, stands as one of the most important indications of the retarded state of professional consciousness among the police.

Soon after it was organized, the National Prison Association established the Standing Committee on the Police. The reports of this committee represented some of the most advanced thinking about policing between the 1870s and the turn of the century. Because of the preoccupations of its parent organization, it was hardly surprising that the members of the standing committee defined police professionalism in terms of crime prevention and rehabilitation.[12]

Charles Felton, superintendent of the Board of Inspectors of the Chicago House of Correction, was the most eloquent member of the Standing Committee on the Police. Felton suggested that prison reform was best aided by crime prevention. "Of what use are reform schools," he argued, "if crime-creating, recruiting agencies among the children are allowed to exist." Felton suggested that the police actively suppress gambling and other vices in order to prevent the corruption of children. Other prison reformers suggested that the police were simply too concerned about making arrests. The Reverend Frederick C. Wines, one of the leading prison reformers of the period, argued that "we punish too much and do too little in the way of prevention." Studying the figures in the 1880 census, Wines calculated that American police officers averaged forty arrests per year, a figure that he found altogether too high. Zebulon R. Brockway called for a "closer marriage of police and prisons. . . . The police do not believe in the reformation of prisoners. They think 'once a thief always a thief.' When the police come to better understand the modern management of prisons for reformatory purposes and know more of their methods and results—they come into closer sympathy with them."[13]

The reformers in the National Prison Association recognized that partisan politics was the major obstacle to the improvement of the police. And it was in the forum of the association that the professional ideal of nonpartisan police service received its most consistent endorsement. The 1874 report of the Standing Committee on the Police complained, "At present, things are in the worst state possible. The worst aspect of our politics is not its bitterness or onesidedness, but its demoralizing tendency in this respect—that men, chosen to execute the law, will not do their duty because the law has been made by another party." The reformers placed much of their hope in civil service as a means of separating the police from politics. Charles Felton argued that "the entering wedge of police reform is civil service." The campaign for civil service, however, was a long and difficult one. The city of Brooklyn (then a separate municipality) adopted civil service for its police in 1883, but the idea did not begin to gain widespread acceptance until the mid-1890s.[14]

Civil service was only one means of upgrading the police. The reformers in the National Prison Association also argued in favor of formal training programs for police officers. The 1888 report of the Standing Committee on the Police argued that "no public police department can claim efficiency, if its members are not schooled in their duty." Voicing a complaint that would not become widespread until after the turn of the century, the committee pointed out that "it is the common belief that any man who is of proper height and weight, and who has fair intelligence, and the physical ability to protect himself and to make arrests, is competent for the duties of a policeman." This was unacceptable: "we need a preponderance of brain and character, and conscience as well. Every policeman should deem his calling a high one." The campaign for police training proved to be an even more difficult struggle than the quest for civil service. By 1915, when most large cities had placed their police under civil service, formal training programs were still more an idea than a reality.[15]

While the reformers associated with the National Prison Association concentrated their attention on the crime prevention ideal and means of upgrading the quality of patrolmen, others began to think about more efficient methods of crime detection. As we have already indicated, the prevailing view of crime and crime detection portrayed a battle of wits between shrewd criminals and resourceful detectives. The latter were to rely primarily on their own ingenuity. Gradually, however, the idea of scientific aids to crime detection began to win adherents. The earliest efforts hardly warranted the label scientific, however. By mid-century technological developments in photography made possible the famous rogues gallery, a collection of photographs of known criminals. But the rogues gallery was hardly an effective aid in crime detection. Pictures accumulated rapidly and there was virtually no system of classification. Nonetheless, they did permit the police to think that in fact they were making a serious effort in their work.[16]

By the early 1870s police officials began to think about the systematic exchange of information between different police departments. At the 1871 National Police Convention (about which we shall say more later) there was considerable attention given to the systematic exchange of both photographs and information about specific crimes and criminals. Since the 1871 convention was not followed by another for over twenty years, little was done until the end of the century. The idea of greater cooperation between local police departments, however, became one of the major goals of police reformers who were most interested in crime detection. Part of this program included a national clearing house for criminal statistics—a goal that was partially achieved in the late 1890s but not completely fulfilled until the development of the FBI's Uniform Crime Reports system in the 1930s. The latter years of the nineteenth century also witnessed the arrival of the Bertillion system of criminal identification, which relied upon a series of physical measurements of the individual's body. This was eventually replaced after 1904 by the more efficient fingerprint system.[17]

In the end, however, scientific policing remained rudimentary at best, even through the early years of the twentieth century. A more serious attempt to develop a science of policing did not emerge until the second decade of the century. This development was a consequence of professionalization in two respects. First, the very idea of policing as a profession implied that there was a body of scientific knowledge. Second, professionalization led to the creation of a more elaborate bureaucratic structure for police organizations. This included the development specialized tasks related to criminal investigation and the growth of more accurate record keeping about criminal activity.

The Reform of the Cincinnati Police

The reformers associated with the National Prison Association and individuals such as Edward Savage were for the most part voices crying in the wilderness. The American police remained firmly in the grip of partisan local politics and police officials had little time or inclination to think about long-term improvements. There were isolated exceptions to this rule. Perhaps the most striking instance was in Cincinnati where the police experienced genuine reform beginning in 1886. The process by which reform came to the Cincinnati police was little different in its origins from the political struggles that engulfed the police in other cities. For reasons that are difficult to account for, however, the outcome was significantly different. By the end of the century Cincinnati police were far in advance of those in other cities; they were the first professionalized police department.

Reform had its origins in a political scandal. In 1885 there were widespread charges of illegal voter registration. A nominally nonpartisan Committee of One Hundred was formed to clean up the city. "The Committee soon discovered that registration frauds had been committed to an alarming extent." Investigators compiled and circulated a list of over 1250 false registrations. "Warrants were obtained for the arrest of seven individuals suspected of particularly blatant offenses but," the report of the committee continued, "the Police Commissioners and their officers would not support the Committee in its efforts, but refused and neglected to arrest the offenders, thereby rendering the efforts of the Committee in this direction fruitless." The Committee of One Hundred also found that in many instances grand juries refused to bring indictments for obvious fraud, "but instead directed its efforts toward an attempt to intimidate the Committee of One Hundred."[18]

Frustrated at the local level by a criminal justice system that was pervaded by political influence, the Committee of One Hundred turned to the state legislature. In the spring of 1886 the legislature enacted a bill reorganizing the Cincinnati police. The bill itself had been drafted largely by members of the committee and it placed the police department under a four-member nonpartisan Board of Commissioners appointed by the governor. This was not the first time Cincinnati had experienced state control of its police department. Between 1877 and 1880 there had also been a gubernatorial-appointed board of commissioners. But neither that board nor any of the other forms of police control had made any significant difference in Cincinnati. There was no reason to suspect that the 1886 nonpartisan board would have any greater luck. But the board lasted for a remarkable sixteen years and effected a number of significant and lasting changes.

In keeping with tradition the new Board of Commissioners began by cleaning house. They dismissed 238 of the 289 patrolmen and eight of the sixteen sergeants. Most of the remaining fifty-one patrolmen, moreover, had only one- or two-years experience, so Cincinnati found itself in the spring of 1886 with an almost completely inexperienced police force. The commissioners selected a former Cincinnati police officer, Philip M. Dietsch, as police chief. The Bavarian-born Dietsch had served on the force between 1863 and 1873. Interestingly, he served only one month in 1863 before being promoted to sergeant and then, two months later, was promoted to lieutenant. Dietsch's career clearly suggests that promotions were the result of political and personal influence rather than a record of experience and ability. One suspects that his departure from the force in 1873 was also due to a change in political fortunes that year. From 1873 to 1886 he worked with the United States Revenue Service.[19]

Dietsch and the new commissioners began to institute changes immediately. They first ordered a public inspection of the entire police force and the April 30 parade was described as "a revelation to the citizens of the city." The physical appearance of the men and the obvious lack of discipline shocked much of the public. The commissioners then instituted regular military drill and required policemen to exercise at least one hour a week in the new police gymnasium. This development prefigured one of the dominant themes of police professionalization. In their effort to impose some kind of discipline over police officers, reformers repeatedly turned to the military for a model. Concern about the public image of the police also led to greater emphasis on uniforms (including weapons) and the appearance of discipline as evidenced by close order drill. The militarization of the American police would be one of the dubious accomplishments of professionalization.[20]

The physical and mental qualifications of police officers also concerned the new commissioners. In December 1886 all officers were required to undergo semiannual physical examinations. To implement this, the police commissioners established a permanent Board of Medical Examiners. The board consisted of two private doctors and the police surgeon, a full-time civilian member of the department. To improve the physical condition of patrolmen, the commissioners also instituted a major change in patrol practice. The traditional two-platoon system was replaced by a three-platoon system. This reform, which other cities did not begin to adopt for another twenty years, required patrolmen to be on duty only eight hours and lightened their burden considerably. In his first annual report, Dietsch proclaimed the three-platoon system "a great success."[21]

Equally important improvements were made in the area of training. The commissioners published a revised version of the departmental rules and regulations in 1887 and, the next year, inaugurated a school of instruction. At first the commissioners attempted to conduct training in the various precinct station houses, but "it soon became evident to the clerk of the Board . . . that the pupils from station houses held views widely different as to police laws and regulations. Some central point of instruction, therefore, was found necessary." The Cincinnati commissioners discovered early what other reformers would learn in the twentieth century: it was necessary to centralize the operations of the department if one were to achieve any kind of uniformity.

The program of the Cincinnati school of instruction was truly impressive for its time. Other departments in the country would not reach a comparable level for another twenty-five or even fifty years. Cincinnati required a total of seventy-two hours of instruction. New recruits began by taking four hours of classroom instruction during each of their first seven days on the force. This was supplemented by the more traditional on-the-street orientation during the rest of the day. For the remaining three months recruits were required to take two hours of classroom instruction twice a week. They remained on probationary status—itself an important innovation—for a total of six months and at the end of that period were required to take both mental and physical examinations. Those who scored below 70 percent were to be reexamined again in sixty days and if they failed again were suspended from the force.[22]

The Cincinnati police commissioners succeeded in stabilizing the membership of the police force. The nonpartisan board remained in existence until 1902 and the wholesale turnovers in police personnel became a thing of the past. This, however, only created a new problem which became acute by the end of the century. By stabilizing the membership and inculcating the idea of police work as a career—the first step in the development of a professional outlook—increasing numbers of policemen remained long enough to reach retirement age. (In St. Louis, for example, John Maniha could not find any policemen who left because of retirement in the pre-1900 period, although some died on the job).[23] Some provision had to be made for adequate pensions if the morale of the force was to be maintained. Most police departments developed pension funds of some sort, but for the most part they were actuarially unsound.

By 1900 Cincinnati had an extremely elderly police force and a crisis was in the making. The average officer was over forty-one years old and had served ten years, eight months and two weeks on the force. The pension fund regulations allowed a man to retire at the age of fifty with fifteen years of service. In 1900 there were ninety-three members of the 525 man force over the age of fifty and sixty-four had served the required fifteen years. Thus, the department faced the prospect of having heavy demands placed on the pension fund in the next few years. Expenditures had been rising steadily already, rising from $8,016.18 in 1890 to $17,934.95 in 1899. As a consequence, Cincinnati faced earlier than most other police departments one of the side effects of professional development: the necessity of providing a full range of ancillary services that were inherent in the idea of a professional career.[24]

The reform of the Cincinnati police department was restricted to matters of inernal management: centralizing the command structure, stabilizing and upgrading personnel practices, and the like. Apparently little thought was given to alternative roles for the police in the community. The Cincinnati experience proved to be a forerunner of the dominant motif of police reform in the twentieth century, an early manifestation of the gospel of efficiency.

The Frustration of Reform: Theodore Roosevelt as Police Commissioner

The Cincinnati experience was a fluke, a rare instance of reform that succeeded in an era when most efforts failed. More typical of the frustration of reform ideas was the experience of Theodore Roosevelt as New York City police commissioner from 1895 to 1897. Roosevelt's career is also important because it illustrates the intellectual links between police professionalization and the broader progressive movement that flourished during the first two decades of the twentieth century. The police reformers shared many of the same ideas and proposed many of the same types of changes that reformers in other areas of American life proposed. Roosevelt's career also highlights some of the less attractive aspects of police professionalization: the often jingoistic militarism, the soaring and self-righteous idealism, an implicit but deeply rooted contempt for the mass of humanity, and an excessive emphasis on rhetoric and imagery.

Roosevelt's career as a police commissioner was a natural outgrowth of his deep involvement in municipal affairs. He had served in the state legislature as a representative from the city from 1881 to 1884 and in 1883 was elected floor leader by the majority Republican Party. In 1886 he was the GOP candidate for the mayoralty of New York City in a bitter three-way election campaign. Between 1889 and 1895 he served as a member of the New York City Civil Service Commission. Throughout his career he had expressed deep concern about the problems of working men and women (although from an elitist perspective) and had maintained a steadfast opposition to Tammany Hall. Much of his knowledge about and interest in the police came from his good friend and associate Jacob Riis. Riis had begun as a police reporter and knew the workings of the police department intimately.[25]

Roosevelt's appointment to the Board of Police Commissioners had its origins in the reform crusade of the Reverend Charles Parkhurst. Parkhurst began by denouncing the police and Tammany Hall for openly tolerating vice in early 1892. Although his campaign was largely frustrated at the local level by a Tammany-dominated criminal justice system, Parkhurst's interests coincided in part with those of the state Republican Party. In the fall of 1893 the GOP captured control of the legislature and began to make plans for a major investigation of the New York City police. The Republicans welcomed any opportunity to embarrass the Democratic Party, even if party leaders did not share the moralistic outlook of Parkhurst and his allies in the City Vigilance League and the Society for the Prevention of Crime.[26]

At first the legislature passed a bill abolishing the existing board of police commissioners and establishing a bipartisan board. The Democratic governor, however, vetoed the bill. Then the Republicans appropriated money for the investigation of the New York City police, but the governor vetoed this bill also. The GOP was not without powerful allies, however. The New York City Chamber of Commerce donated the necessary $25,000 and the Lexow investigation was launched. Named after its chairman, Representative Clarence Lexow, the investigation lasted three months, issued over 300 subpoenas, heard over 600 witnesses, and eventually published over 10,000 pages of proceedings and supporting documents. It was the single most extensive investigation of any police department. The findings, however, were drearily repetitious and were not untypical of conditions in other large city police departments. The Lexow investigation concentrated both on voter fraud and internal corruption in the police department. It is particularly famous for having turned up a published scale of bribes that were required for promotion to higher rank.[27]

The upshot of the investigation was a new four-member, bipartisan Board of Police Commissioners for the City of New York. This represented a compromise. The moral reformers led by Reverend Parkhurst had demanded a single police commissioner—a more effective way of eliminating political influence they believed. The GOP leadership was reluctant to overplay its hand and settled for a bipartisan board. One half of the membership of the board, they believed, was better than the complete Tammany Hall control that had prevailed before.

Roosevelt was appointed one of the two Republican commissioners and became president of the board. His two years on the board prefigured his career as president of the United States. Although he had no more power than the other three commissioners, he simply proceeded to act as if he were the board. It was, in short, a "bully pulpit" from which he was able to expound his views on a wide variety of subjects. James Richardson comments that Roosevelt was "able to generate a great deal of noise and some action. . . ." It was a frustrating experience, for he had little ability to control effectively the police force. As Lincoln Steffens observed, "He issued formal orders, he made personal appearances, and nothing happened."[28]

Although Roosevelt was not as obsessed with the problem of vice as was the Reverend Parkhurst and other moral reformers, he was deeply concerned about the corruption of the police created by moralistic legislation. He viewed the problem in the abstract, in terms of public duty and respect for law. "The question at issue in New York just at present," he argued, "is much more important than the question of a more or less liberal Sunday excise law. The question is as to whether public officials are to be true to their oaths of office, and to see that the law is administered in good faith." Although he disagreed with many aspects of the liquor control laws, he remained steadfast in his belief that the laws, whatever they were, should be enforced. He soon discovered, however, that it was easy enough to issue orders but that in the end he had little effective control over policemen on the beat. Moreover, his full enforcement ideas encountered strong opposition from within his own party. GOP leader Thomas Platt and reform mayor William L. Strong were interested in reaching an accommodation with the liquor interests, if only to guarantee success at the polls. Parkhurst and the moral reformers, of course, were outraged by the compromises that were made.[29]

Roosevelt also devoted a great deal of effort to the cause of raising the quality of patrolmen. On the one hand he simply argued for enforcement of the existing mental and physical standards of the civil service law. Between May 1895 and February 1896 nearly 55 percent of the 3170 applicants failed the physical exam while another 30 percent failed the mental exam. More rigorous recruitment standards did have significant social and political consequences which Roosevelt undoubtedly favored. Of the last one hundred men hired by the Roosevelt-dominated board, ninety-four were native-born Americans. (The introduction of civil service in Chicago, as we have seen, served to reduce the number of black police officers.) The meritocratic standards of professionalism inevitably discriminated against the lower class and helped to break the power of the blue-collar-dominated political machines.[30]

Raising standards of police performance was another of Roosevelt's goals. To accomplish this he attempted to establish a new ideal of public service. And toward this end Roosevelt relied particularly on the military ideal. "In our present highly complicated civilization," he wrote, "there are a number of occupations which, even when carried on during a time of profound peace, call for the development in a very high degree of the prime virtues of the soldier— energy, daring, power of obedience, and marked bodily prowess." Roosevelt then began "systematically to acknowledge gallantry." Medals and certificates were awarded to patrolmen for specific acts of bravery. These generally included such things as the apprehension of a runaway horse and carriage, the rescue of a woman from a burning building, or the arrest of a particularly brutal murderer. Roosevelt commented, "I doubt if the average citizen, especially the average stay-at-home citizen, realized how often the man of the night-stick is called upon to display qualities which in a soldier would be called heroic." In reality, how- ever, the perception of the average citizen was probably more nearly accurate. Dramatic incidents requiring bold action were, and still remain, infrequent occurrences in the life of a patrolman. But Roosevelt was not interested in presenting a statistically accurate picture of police work. Rather, he was con- cerned about developing an ideal of service that could be used to motivate rank and file patrolmen. Unfortunately, however, he chose a model that had little to do with the realities of police work. The emphasis on "crime fighting" as a measure of police work would be further exaggerated by the professionalization movement, with unfortunate consequences.[31]

Roosevelt remained police commissioner for two years. Increasingly he was frustrated by his inability to effect any real changes and by the influence of party politics. The bipartisan board soon became deadlocked between its two Republican and two Democratic members. In his letter of resignation Roosevelt denounced the bipartisan form of control: "In this department we, as well as you, have been hampered by unwise legislation, and the so-called bipartisan law, under which the department itself is administered, is of such absurdly foolish character that it has been impossible to achieve the results which would have been achieved had you had your hands free with reference to your appointees and your appointees in turn possessed full and proper power over the force." He concluded with the comment that "it has been impossible to make of this splendid body of men all that could be made, if the board had one responsible head with complete power and absolute singleness of purpose to do right."[32]

Roosevelt's departure from the New York Board of Police Commissioners marked, in a symbolic way, the end of an era in American police administration. His career dramatized the frustration of reform efforts in the nineteenth century under the prevailing system. The advocates of police reform in other cities, encountering the same difficulties, drew the same conclusions that Roosevelt did. His attack on the administrative inefficiency of a multiheaded police com- mission became one of the dominant themes of police reform in the early years of the twentieth century. Raymond B. Fosdick's *American Police Systems*, the most extended analysis by a police reformer, carried Roosevelt's critique to its logical conclusion and was primarily an argument in favor of administrative efficiency by means of a single police executive. The achievement of the changes advocated by Roosevelt, however, had to wait upon the emergence of a very different social and political climate, one that did emerge after the turn of the century and one which Roosevelt himself, as president, helped to bring into being.[33]

The Emergence of Professional Associations

The promulgation of reform ideas required a national sounding board. One of the most significant indications of the lack of professional consciousness among the police was the absence of state or national professional associations. Prison officials were far ahead of their counterparts in policing. The National Prison Association was organized in 1870 and through the rest of the century served as a focal point for the nurturing of new ideas.

Police officials made a brave attempt to form a national organization in 1871, but it proved to be a still-born effort that was not followed up for another twenty-two years. The 1871 National Police Convention was in fact a rather impressive effort. Organized largely through the efforts of the chief of police and board of commissioners of the St. Louis police, the convention brought together more than 100 delegates, representing twenty-one states and the District of Columbia. It was a broad-based group of delegates which included not only police chiefs, but lower-ranking police officers, a few mayors and other public officials. Joseph Brown, mayor of St. Louis and president of the Board of Police Commissioners, welcomed the delegates by suggesting, "The principal object is to bring the united talent and experience of the police departments of the United States to bear upon the detection of crime." Expressing a primary concern with crime detection, Brown argued, "It is evident that unless these isolated forces are united by some well understood system of cooperation and communication, the effective prevention of crime, as well as the capture of criminals, are rendered extremely difficult and uncertain."[34]

The convention delegates, meeting from October 20 through 23 in St. Louis, devoted their attention to a remarkably wide range of subjects. While the committees on "Photography and Exchanges of Same," "Police Telegraphing," and "Detective Information" were primarily concerned with the apprehension of criminals, the committees on the "Social Evil" and "Abandoned Youth" advanced suggestions relating to a crime prevention role. A particularly vigorous debate took place over the question of prostitution. Advocates of both official toleration and suppression argued their respective points of view. With respect to juvenile delinquency, a number of delegates argued that the police should do something other than merely attempt to make arrests. These suggestions echoed those that were even more prominent in the discussions of the National Prison Association.

The St. Louis convention was an excellent beginning, but its promise went unfulfilled. Although a committee was appointed to make arrangements for another meeting, none was held. The reasons for this failure are not clear. There would not be another attempt for twenty-two years. On November 18, 1892, Chief Webber S. Seavey of the Omaha police department circulated a letter to his fellow chiefs. "I have the honor," he began, "to suggest for your considera-tion the advisability of organizing an association composed of the General Superintendents and Chiefs of Police of all cities in the United States and Canada having a population of 10,000 or more." He suggested that the meeting be held in Chicago the following year to coincide with the World's Columbian Exposition. Seavey argued that a national organization would "be the means of elevating our American police system to a much more proficient and high standard" and would be "the greatest stroke which has ever been made in this country against crime."[35]

The first meetings of the National Police Chiefs Union (later the Inter-national Association of Chiefs of Police) were not nearly as impressive as had been the 1871 meeting. There was virtually no discussion of any broad social problems and the delegates concerned themselves largely with the mechanics of establishing an organization. It was also evident that they were particularly interested in disposing of the official business as quickly as possible so that they could partake of the pleasures of Chicago. Chief Seavey himself was wary of the idea of reform. "To introduce and accomplish reform; to advance and promote the efficiency of the American police system is a grand and noble work," he argued. But he doubted the value of "the alleged 'moral wave' which has swept over our country, having for its object the disruption of the police departments in many instances."[36]

As an instrument of professional development, the National Chiefs of Police Union languished for about the first eight years of its existence. A second convention was held in 1895 and then annual conventions thereafter. But the level of discussion at these meetings was extremely low. The location of the next year's convention seemed to elicit the most vigorous debate. The turning point came in 1901 with the election of Major Richard Sylvester, superintendent of the District of Columbia police, as president of the organization. Sylvester had already achieved a national reputation for his administrative leadership in Washington. He helped to rename the organization the International Association of Chiefs of Police and infuse it with a truly professional spirit during his fifteen years as president. The creation of a national organization in 1893 was itself a major accomplishment; the advent of Richard Sylvester in 1901 clearly marked the dawn of a new era in American police administration.[37]

The last years of the nineteenth century marked another important organiza-tional development among the police. Just as police chiefs recognized the importance of a national organization to advance their interests, so rank and file patrolmen began to see the need for organizations of their own. This develop-ment was another expression of the growing commitment to police work as a career.

Fraternal and benefit societies among rank and file police officers had existed as early as the 1860s and perhaps even earlier. Like many of the early trade unions, they emerged as a response to specific economic needs. In St. Louis, for example, a Police Relief Association was organized in 1867 to raise funds for sick or disabled police officers or the widows of deceased policemen. Similar organizations appeared in most other police departments, but they were generally built on a very unstable financial basis. The Denver Police Mutual Aid Society, for example, was organized in 1890 but collapsed because of insolvency in 1894. The benefits offered by these early associations were extremely limited. The Denver Mutual Aid Society assessed dues of 50¢ per month and paid death benefits of $500. The New Orleans Mutual Benefit Society, organized in 1893, assessed the same dues but paid only $250 upon the death of a police officer and then only to those with one or more years of service.[38]

Police fraternal associations also organized a wide range of social events. The Denver police organized a baseball team in 1883, while the Cleveland police organized a rifle team in 1881 that engaged other clubs in regular competition. Gradually, however, rank-and-file patrolmen in some of the major cities began to recognize that their interests required political action. The New York City police, the largest in the country, were the first to take this step. The New York Patrolman's Benevolent Association (PBA) was organized in 1891 and the next year hired a lawyer to draft a pay increase bill for presentation to the legislature. In 1900 and 1901 the P.B.A. lobbied successfully for an eight-hour day. These activities represented not only a response to a relative decline in the economic status of police work (a decline that would culminate in 1919), but also a growing sense of organizational self-identity among police officers. While rank-and-file policemen did not yet think of thmselves as professionals, there was at least a growing sense of police work as a lifetime career.[39]

The development of organized rank-and-file self-consciousness, however, proved to be still born. Patrolmen became the forgotten men of the early professionalization movement, as reformers concentrated on internal administrative changes. Many of the reformers regarded the patrolmen only as so much clay to be molded as they saw fit. Meanwhile, the material rewards of police work steadily declined relative to other occupations. The final crisis was reached in 1919 when the Boston police strike delivered a fatal blow to the police union movement. This proved to have profound long-term consequences for policing. The rank and file were left without an effective, organized voice in police affairs. In its place developed an informal "subculture." Professional consciousness came late to the police, but it came even later to the rank and file than to police administrators.

Part II:
Professionalism Arrives, 1900–1918

3

Cleaning House: Professionalization as Administrative Reform

The turn of the century introduced a new era in American policing. Reform ideas that had enjoyed a fugitive existence at best over the previous thirty years suddenly coalesced around the idea of professionalization. The police reform movement partook of the energy and spirit of the larger movement of progressivism. Not only were many of the leading police reformers active in other social reform movements, but there was a shared set of assumptions and reform proposals. Police reform, however, remained more an idea than an accomplishment. Most departments resisted change and the achievements of the reformers remained limited at best. Nonetheless, the reformers succeeded in making the most important breakthrough: they established the intellectual and organizational base for continued reform efforts in subsequent decades.

The spirit of police reform soared highest in Detroit. The 1917 annual report of the police department, written as a textbook "for use of the public schools," captured better than any single document the aspirations of the police reform movement. "It is evident that the time has come in Detroit and elsewhere for a general change of methods in the administration of our institutions," declared the commissioner of police. The old methods were no longer adequate for modern society: "we have come to a 'parting of the ways' as between the old-time method of ruthless administration, catching and punishing crooks, and more modern, humane and effective procedures that require each officer to be an exponent of social service. . . ."[1]

Police professionalization was not a unified movement and the 1917 Detroit annual report reflects the divided spirit of reform. On the one hand professionalization meant streamlining the administrative procedures of the police department itself. Parker Sercombe, head of the statistical division of the Detroit police, argued that "there is no more reason why police departments or other public bureaus should run their BUSINESS in a haphazard manner, with no adequate standards for measuring results." Many police reformers believed that the managerial style of the modern corporation, with its emphasis on efficiency and the ability to demonstrate results, was the proper model for the police. To this end they believed that administrative control should be centralized within the department and that police executives should exercise more direct control over the work of patrolmen.

Other reformers put a different emphasis on professionalization. The police should play a major role in social reform; it was not so much a matter of how the department was run, but what it did. To this end reformers introduced a host of new police techniques, including women police officers, juvenile bureaus, and in some instances procedures to divert offenders from the criminal justice system. The idea that the police should do more than just arrest criminals, that they should seek to prevent crime and rehabilitate offenders, had been suggested years before. But it was not until after the turn of the century, when it enjoyed the support of similar reforms in other areas of American life, that it gained acceptance within police circles.

The two aspects of police professionalization—administrative efficiency and social reform—were not incompatible. In some cities they were closely linked; administrative reform was the means by which a group of reformers sought to capture control of the department in order to introduce social reform measures. This was particularly true in Detroit, for example. Professionalization, in fact, was an extremely diverse and fragmented movement. Some cities did not professionalize at all. Kansas City, for example, remained firmly in the grip of nineteenth-century-style politics until well into the late 1930s. Other cities adopted some of the trappings of professionalism and rejected the rest. New York and Chicago, if only because they had the largest police forces, adopted many internal reforms and yet remained pervaded with corruption. And finally, some cities instituted a number of reforms only to have them negated within a few years.

In short, it is difficult to generalize about developments in the many urban police departments. What does provide a sense of unity and offers a coherent framework for understanding this diversity is the *idea* of professionalization. The most important single achievement of the reformers was an ideological one. They succeeded in establishing the idea that the old system was inadequate and that professionalism was necessary. As a result, professionalism is the standard by which police departments have been measured throughout the twentieth century. And the specific terms of professionalism, particularly the idea of administrative efficiency, remained largely unchallenged. Only the major police crisis of the late 1960s served to raise new questions about the role of the police in society.

Not everyone, of course, agreed on the necessity of professionalization. Opposition to reform was strongest in the political machines, as they sought to retain their control and influence over the police. The reformers denounced the traditional political style as corrupt and portrayed themselves as disinterested and nonpartisan public servants. This was a self-serving definition of the situation, for the reformers had their own particular interests no less than their Tammany Hall-style opponents. Police reform was often an elitist movement, as a glance at the social backgrounds and connections of some of the leading reformers suggests. Raymond Fosdick's two books on European and American police, both major statements of police reform ideology, were sponsored by John D. Rockefeller, Jr. And many of the leading reformers in New York and Chicago had connections with the business, professional, and academic elite. Leonard Fuld, himself a lawyer and a scholar, put the matter in rather straightforward terms: "the control of the police force is subject too much to the influence of the class to control whose action the police force has been organized."

In other words, the elite and not the lower class should control the police. Many of the techniques of administrative reform, centralization in particular, were attempts to break the power of the lower class.[2]

Professionalization raised other problems as well. The two aspects of reform—administrative efficiency and social reform—were purchased at a price. Much of the history of the police in the twentieth century can be understood in terms of two dilemmas that continue to lie at the heart of the so-called police problem. Administrative efficiency was to be accomplished largely by means of centralization and impersonal management techniques. But efficiency had its price. Bureaucratic centralization resulted in police organizations that were both resistant to further change but also isolated from the public. By the 1960s a new generation of reformers faced the problem of *de*centralizing police departments and, in the process, challenged most of the precepts of traditional professionalization.[3]

The idea of the police as social reformers raised even more disturbing problems. To ask the police to play a social reform role, to seek to rehabilitate offenders rather than merely arrest offenders, is also to ask them to intervene more often and more directly in the lives of individual citizens. Like the juvenile court, the practices of probation and parole, and many other social reforms, this opened the door for often arbitrary and discriminatory actions by the bureaucrats charged with the responsibility of making decisions. The problem, in fact, is twofold. On the one hand there is the question of ensuring that decisions will be fair and equitable. At the same time, however, there is the question of whether this intervention into individual lives is justified in the first place. By the late 1960s there appeared a broad attack on the expansion of the power of the state to intervene, an expansion that had begun in the early part of the century and was inherent in the ideology of social reform. A dialogue runs throughout the whole of twentieth-century police history: should we ask the police to do more or to do less. Ironically, it has often been the police themselves who have asked to do less and who have resisted many of the social reform roles that others have sought to foist off on them.

A final criticism of the aspirations of the police professionalizers is in order. While they placed most of their hopes in organization—both new organizations and new forms of organization—they were extremely naive about the phenomenon of bureaucracy. To a certain extent they can be excused for this lapse; after all it is only comparatively recently that we have begun to recognize bureaucratization as a pervasive phenomenon in our lives and begun to attempt to understand and cope with it. Bureaucratization, however, raised particular problems with respect to the police—problems that the reformers did not always recognize. The professional ideal asks that the individual practitioner exercise considerable discretion, based on his own training and commitment to service. Police reformers, however, generally sought to limit the discretion of patrolmen, to bring them under control, and achieve a degree of uniformity in police practice. The dilemma of whether the police should be genuine professionals or simply bureaucrats also runs throughout police history in this century. The reformers generally used the rhetoric of the former ideal as they instituted changes that pursued the latter. In the end, it was the police chiefs who became professionalized, not the patrolmen.[4]

An Age of Organization

Historian Samuel Hays observed that the unwritten law of modern society became "organize or perish." Increasingly, the key decisions that affected economic and political life were made in the context of a "struggle for power among well-organized groups." The emergence of police professionalization was marked by the creation of national organizations that served as effective vehicles for reform ideas.[5]

The advocates of administrative efficiency developed a reform program that consisted of three basic components. They sought first to centralize authority within the department, second to rationalize the procedures of command and control, and third to raise the quality of police personnel. These ideas had circulated in police administration circles in the nineteenth century. The reform of the Cincinnati police after 1886 was certainly based on this basic program. Reform ideas, however, lacked a national forum, an organization that would serve as a vehicle for spreading them to other police departments. Such an organization did not even exist prior to the founding of the National Police Chiefs Union in 1893. And even then, it did not at first assume the traditional role of professional association for some years. The transformation of the National Chiefs of Police Union into the International Association of Chiefs of Police (IACP) was largely the work of Richard Sylvester.

Sylvester's career was a classic example of lateral entry. He never worked as a patrolman but entered policing through political patronage. Initially a journalist, he served briefly in 1882-1883 as an official of the Ute Indian Commission in Utah. When that job ended, he secured a job as clerk with the District of Columbia police. In that capacity he soon earned a considerable reputation. In 1894, for example, he compiled a history of the Washington police. The book apparently did as much to further the reputation of its author as its subject. In 1898 Sylvester was promoted to the rank of major (a title he used thereafter) and appointed superintendent of the District of Columbia police. Three years later he was named president of the IACP. He served as the head of both organizations until 1915. His seventeen-year tenure as the head of a major police department was truly remarkable for that era. In 1909 Leonard Fuld commented that the Washington police "under the able administration of Major Sylvester has in so many ways become the model police organization in the United States."[6]

The need for an effective professional association was recognized by a number of police executives. In 1896 J. C. A. Brannan, chairman of the Atlanta Board of Police Commissioners, declared, "This is a progressive age in which we live. It is a day of consolidation, of federations and organizations." The police were beginning to take their cues from other occupations. Benjamin Eldridge, President of the IACP in 1896, argued, "The time arrived a long while ago when most all kinds of professions, trades, and societies formed organizations for their special benefit and protection. Is it not the proper thing to do to have the heads of police departments meet in this manner . . . ?"[7]

Richard Sylvester was responsible for effecting the most important changes in the organization. The 1901 convention was significantly different from its predecessors; it featured, for the first time, serious presentations and debate upon a variety of topics ranging from crime prevention to the efficacy of probation and various strategies for the control of prostitution. Sylvester's annual presidential address was generally a statement of the ideal of professionalism and a summary of progress to date. "The world has attained its highest evolution in recent years," he told the delegates to the 1911 convention. Technology, he argued, had changed the nature of society and "The changed conditions have called for readjustments, many new features have had to be systematized and new methods invoked, particularly in the operating of municipal affairs which would meet with the modern situation." After reviewing some of the important changes to date, Sylvester suggested that "We look backwards over a path of progress made necessary to meet the extraordinary conditions of the age." Sylvester's rhetoric had an important political function: to inculcate the spirit of reform and to establish the intellectual hegemony of the idea of professionalism. "If there was a realization of what we have accomplished for the benefit of society," he argued, "there would be in evidence a more liberal spirit to promote recommendations."[8]

Once established, the idea of professionalism gained momentum within the IACP. Expectations continued to rise. In 1915 William Jannssen, the highly respected chief of the Milwaukee police, complained that there was insufficient discussion and criticism of the papers presented at the conventions. Others argued for an official journal. Chief C. G. Kizer of the Norfolk, Virginia, police argued in 1915 that the time had come "that police chiefs may no longer continue the only organization of any consequence from able seamen to zoologists—running the entire length of the alphabet—which does not have its official organ." It was an important measure of rising professional consciousness that police chiefs were concerned about their stature vis-à-vis occupations. The organizational style of other professions became the standard of measure by which police chiefs began to judge themselves.[9]

Rising professional consciousness also expressed itself in terms of increased concern about the public image of the police. Indeed, one of the major functions of professional associations is to serve as spokesman for and protector of the image of the occupational group. The IACP undertook this role and began to defend the police from various perceived threats. Particular attention was given to the young motion picture industry and its treatment of both crime and the police. Sylvester complained that "in moving pictures the police are sometimes made to appear ridiculous, and in view of the large number of young people, children, who attend these moving picture shows, it gives them an improper idea of the policeman." To say that the Keystone Kops made the police look ridiculous was an understatement. The popularity of those comedies, however, suggests a great deal about the popular image of the police, one that the movies reflected rather than one it shaped. At the 1914 IACP convention William Pinkerton argued that "any committing magistrate in the Juvenile Courts will tell you of the considerable and growing harm pictures of this character are doing among the very young." Previously, in 1910, the IACP had adopted a resolution to the effect that "this association deprecates and condemns the moving picture shows that are making false representations of the police, together with tragedy, burglary, and all immoral displays, as they tend to the encouragement of crime."[10]

The response of the police chiefs to the new film industry was a combination of several different factors. They, like other social reformers in the progressive era, voiced genuine concern over the potential impact of films on the morals of the young. Jane Addams, for example, was convinced that the "House of Dreams," as she called the nickelodeon, pandered to the worst aspects of human nature and was perhaps even a direct cause of juvenile delinquency. At the same time, however, the police were aroused by considerations of self-interest. In their quest for professional identity and public respect, they objected to the Keystone Kop image of the police projected in the movies.[11]

Another image problem for the police involved the so-called third degree, the forcing of confessions from suspected criminals. There can be no question but that coercive techniques were frequently used. As we have already noted, the police had little notion of the procedural guarantees of due process in this period. The Wickersham Commission report in 1931 documented widespread abuses of this sort. Concern about the third degree or police brutality has come in cycles. The first major period was in 1910–1911. The 1910 IACP convention was dominated by the question, and the delegates were moved to adopt a resolution complaining that "there has been recent unjust criticism of the police in the United States in a revival of the oft-repeated allegation that there prevails a practice of maltreating prisoners for the purpose of securing admissions of guilt. . . ." The chiefs mounted a scattershot defense. First they denied that it existed at all, suggesting that the third degree was a phrase "coined in a newspaper office"; then they suggested that private detectives were the guilty parties; finally, they argued that "all this belongs to the past . . . and we hear of such things no more." The third degree was genuinely a national issue and in 1910 there was a special Congressional investigation into abuses by federal law enforcement agents. That investigation appears to have been directed especially at the tactics of the then two-year-old Bureau of Investigation.[12]

The work of the IACP was supplemented by a network of state chiefs of police organizations. These organizations emerged at roughly the same time as the IACP; by 1895 there were associations in thirteen different states. The Ohio association was organized in 1901 and by 1912 claimed one hundred members; the New York association was organized in the same year. A Pennsylvania chiefs of police association had existed prior to 1895 but apparently collapsed and was reorganized in 1914. The Pennsylvania group was especially close to private industry. In 1919, for example, at least forty-eight of the 250 members represented corporation police forces. Garrett P. Roach, chief of the Bethlehem Steel Co. police, was a member of the executive committee. Police professionalism, as we later see, was closely tied to the interests of private industry. The Pennsylvania state police, organized in 1905 along highly professional lines, was a major antistrike agency. And Richard Sylvester, after stepping down as head of the Washington, D.C., police, took a position as director of security with the Dupont Corporation in Wilmington, Delaware.[13]

The most impressive state association was the California Peace Officers Association, organized in 1921. By the mid-1920s and through the 1930s, the California group far outclassed the IACP as a professional association. Papers presented at the annual convention grappled with police problems on a far more serious plane than those at the IACP convention. Undoubtedly the influence of August Vollmer was a major factor as the California association undertook intensive discussion of such issues as higher education, pension plans, and the like. Indeed, by the 1930s the IACP was eclipsed by J. Edgar Hoover and the FBI as the most prominent national voice of law enforcement.

While the IACP was an important forum for the advocates of professionalization, it lacked the organizational capacity to effect the change. The advocates of professionalism through administrative efficiency found a more effective instrument in the New York City–based Bureau of Municipal Research. First organized in 1906 to conduct research for the city, it eventually evolved into a consulting firm with a national outlook. The first year it operated with a staff of eight people and a budget of $12,000. By 1908 it has a staff of forty-one and a budget of $89,920. It was soon engaged in contract consulting for cities across the country, and in 1921 it was reorganized as the National Institute of Public Administration.[14]

The Bureau of Municipal Research introduced a new style of police investigation, one that would become the dominant style in the twentieth century. Previously, police investigations had been blatantly partisan in orientation. The 1894–1895 Lexow investigation of the New York City police was typical: it was conducted by a Republican-dominated legislature in an effort to embarrass a Democratic administration in New York City. The new approach styled itself as "nonpartisan" and "scientific." The directors of the Bureau of Municipal Research defined their role as "applying the test of fact to the analysis of municipal problems and the application of scientific method to governmental procedure." Both the claim of objectivity and the use of social science expertise became the dominant style of police investigations from the early surveys of the Bureau, through the 1931 Wickersham Commission, to the 1967 President's Crime Commission, and beyond.[15]

The claim of objectivity, however, was self-serving. It cloaked a more specific set of assumptions that had important political ramifications. The Bureau of Municipal Research accepted the principles of modern business management as its guiding idea. The gospel of efficiency, particularly as defined by Frederick W. Taylor in *Shop Management*, inspired the researchers at the bureau. One member proudly quoted Woodrow Wilson to the effect that "the field of administration is the field of business." A similar perspective was shared by many other police reformers. Arthur Woods, police commissioner of New York City from 1914 to 1918, argued that the police should be organized "just as an army or a big business organization is arranged so as to meet and conquer any difficulties that arise." And Parker Sercombe of the Detroit police argued that "There is no more reason why police departments or other public bureaus should run their BUSINESS in a haphazard manner" than for the Standard Oil Corporation to do so.[16]

Efficiency, however, was an extremely partisan idea. Centralized management and the use of experts struck at the heart of the power of blue-collar-based political machines. The political implications of the gospel of efficiency are clear when one considers the sponsorship of many of the surveys done by the Bureau of Municipal Research. Between 1913 and 1924 the bureau examined police departments in at least seventeen major cities, including Rochester, Richmond, New Orleans, Denver, Milwaukee, and San Francisco. The Denver survey was commissioned and financed by the Colorado Tax Payer's Protective League, while the San Francisco study was commissioned by the San Francisco Real Estate Board. Similarly, the Chicago Crime Commission, organized in 1919 around the same principles, was organized and supported by local business and real estate interests. Efficiency served the interests of those who not only wished to reduce local taxes, but also who wished to break the power of political machines they could not control. The claim of nonpartisanship was but an elaborate rationale for an intensely partisan struggle for control of the police.[17]

Not surprisingly, the experts at the bureau found essentially the same conditions in almost every city they examined. The one major exception was Milwaukee, where a tradition of nonpartisanship and efficient management had begun to develop even in the late nineteenth century. By the second decade of the twentieth century the Milwaukee police were continually cited as the model of efficiency. The 1913 report on the Reading, Pennsylvania, police was more typical. It began with the observation, "The police department has been a part of the political system, controlled by partisan affiliations, its appointments and policies influenced, its progress and efficiency impaired by political sentiment under the theory 'to the victor belongs the spoils.'" Thus, the Bureau of Municipal Research advanced the dominant theme of police reform: eliminate partisan politics from the police department, guarantee job security of tenure to the police chief, and cultivate a sense of nonpartisan public service.[18]

For Reading, San Francisco, and most of the other departments studied, the experts at the Bureau of Municipal Research recommended a strong dose of modern business management techniques. These recommendations comprised the litany of efficiency-oriented police reform. In its report on the Reading police, for example, the bureau "recommended that the tenure of office for the Chief of Police be made permanent by ordinance and that he be removable only upon charges." Moreover, "The Chief is without sufficient power . . . [and] he should have ample power in matters of routine police administration." Adequate supervision of patrolmen was impossible under the existing system: "The present number of sergeants is insufficient. With but six sergeants it is impossible to supervise the day patrol force." Also, "The present method of patrol is antiquated and obsolete . . . It leaves the city without a single patrolman on post for a total of four hours during each day . . . [and] The posts as laid out at present do not provide for an equitable distribution of the men. . . ." In short, the bureau recommended that the police be led by an experienced executive who would undertake rational, scientific planning.[19]

In a host of other areas the bureau found the Reading police deficient. The rules and regulations of the department were not clear, nor was there any procedure for updating them and informing all members of the force. A training school for recruits was urgently needed. There was no means of recording either the activities of individual patrolmen or of the collective department. The police station itself was inadequate and the jails unsanitary. In short, the experts from the Bureau of Municipal Research could not find anything to praise in the Reading police department. The entire operation required overhauling. The report on the Reading police was virtually a carbon copy of the reports on most of the other departments. These reports, moreover, established the model for the police survey that became a standard item in police administration by the 1920s.

Efficiency Applied: Reform in Philadelphia

The story of the Philadelphia police department between 1911 and 1915 represents a classic case study of the reform of a local police department in the Progressive Era. Reform was ushered in by a political upheaval that brought a reform-minded administration to power. The new city officials sought to clean up the police department by applying the precepts of efficiency advanced by the Bureau of Municipal Research. And in the end, the story of the Philadelphia police indicates some of the severe limitations of efficiency-minded police reform.

Prior to 1911 Philadelphia boasted one of the most notoriously corrupt city governments in the entire country. In his classic expose of municipal corruption, *The Shame of the Cities*, Lincoln Steffens cited Philadelphia as "the worst governed city in the country." "Other cities, no matter how bad their own condition may be, all point with scorn to Philadelphia as worse. . . ." Steffens argued that the most deplorable aspect of the situation was the fact that the people were so thoroughly contented. "If Philadelphia is a disgrace," he concluded, "it is a disgrace not to itself alone, nor to Pennsylvania, but to the United States and to the American character." Political corruption pervaded the city and, with the exception of a small group of reformers (Steffens was writing in 1903), most of the people did not seem to mind.[20]

The essential problem, according to Steffens, was not that Philadelphians voted for the "wrong" party as they did in other cities, but that "The Philadelphians do not vote; they are disfranchised, and their disfranchisement is one anchor of the foundation of the Philadelphia organization." The political machine controlled the electoral process from registration to balloting. Fraud was endemic and the police were among the most important instruments in sustaining the system. Steffens reported that "The police are forbidden by law to stand within thirty feet of the polls, but they are at the box and they are there to see that the machine's orders are obeyed and that repeaters whom they help to furnish are permitted to vote without 'intimidation' . . ." Steffens claimed that people who had attempted to identify repeat voters and put a halt to other irregularities had been attacked and beaten by the police—and then arrested themselves on trumped-up charges. Sustained in office by a fraudulent electoral system, the Philadelphia machine then proceeded to loot the public treasury in a systematic pattern of graft, payoffs, and kickbacks.

The so-called good government forces in Philadelphia waged a long and frustrating campaign against political corruption. For twelve years such groups as the Citizens' Municipal League, the Allied Reform League, and the Law and Order Society sought to throw the rascals out. They finally succeeded in 1911 with the election of long-time reformer Rudolph Blankenburg as mayor. Blankenburg promised reform based on the principles of business efficiency; he would "change the conduct of municipal affairs from a political to a business proposition," eliminate graft, and introduce sound business management techniques. After four years in office (he was not reelected), Blankenburg claimed to have saved the city a total of $5,000,000 which included a saving of $700,000 in garbage collection contracts alone and over $900,000 in the cost of operating the city water department.[21]

The Blankenburg administration took office in early 1912 and immediately began to clean house in the police department. Reform began at the top and Blankenburg appointed George D. Porter director of public safety. Porter then proceeded to force the resignation of superintendent of police John B. Taylor and appoint James Robinson in his place. Robinson at the time was drillmaster in the department, a "man with wide police and military experience." Porter also enjoyed the assistance of Martin H. Ray who served as an informal advisor in the reform effort. Ray was a lawyer with a West Point education. He was not paid from the regular departmental budget, but was "employed by the citizens from private funds." He served in this capacity for a year before leaving to take a similar position with the New York City police.[22]

Superintendent Robinson injected a strong dose of militarism into the Philadelphia police department. In his first annual report he claimed that "Military methods have been adopted and military discipline enforced." Regular physical exercise drills were instituted, with an emphasis on boxing, wrestling, and running. In the first year an average of 145 men attended the 295 separate exercise periods. Robinson reported that "The personal appearance and set up of the men show the benefit of this training, and the necessity of being civil and courteous to all persons has been impressed upon them with satisfactory results." To further enhance the public image of the police, the department obtained new uniforms and organized a sixty-five piece police band for ceremonial occasions. Looking back on his accomplishments after two years in office, Robinson boasted that "no city can show a police force more military in appearance or higher efficiency, or better uniformed men than the force of this city." Reform in Philadelphia followed the model established by Cincinnati nearly thirty years before. The first changes involved an infusion of militaristic values in an effort to impose a minimal amount of discipline in the department.

The new administration also took dramatic steps to raise the quality of patrolmen on the beat. It published a new patrolman's manual and introduced a School of Instruction. The old manual had not been revised since 1897 and it "covered only in a very general way the duties of patrolmen." Moreover, "there were only a few copies in existence, and none of the force appointed within the last few years were supplied officially with copies." The new manual, issued on May 1, 1913, served as the textbook for the new School of Instruction that opened two months later. Classes consisted of forty men and lasted four weeks. At the end of the session patrolmen were required to pass both written and oral examinations with a score of 70 percent or better. Those who did received a diploma to mark their accomplishment. By the end of 1913 the department reported that 125 officers had completed the course, while another 121 were still under instruction. This was a small but hopeful beginning in a police force of some 3,800 men. The school of instruction, moreover, was supplemented with weekly quizzes based on the new patrolman's manual. These quizzes were conducted in all of the precinct station houses.[23]

To raise the efficiency of the patrolmen on the beat, the new administration also introduced the three-platoon system of patrol. The two-platoon system was extremely onerous. During any forty-eight-hour period an individual patrolman was required to serve eighteen and one-half hours of street duty and eleven and one-half hours of reserve duty. That left only eighteen hours, or an average of nine hours a day of free time to spend at home. Under the new three-platoon system each officer was required to work only an eight-hour shift. Moreover, the new system allowed for greater flexibility in assignments and in most precincts each platoon was subdivided, with one section on street patrol and the other on reserve. Superintendent Robinson claimed that the greater efficiency of the three-platoon system helped reduce the crime rate. He told the 1914 IACP convention that there was a 20 percent increase in the number of arrests as a result of the new system. Robberies fell from 582 in December 1912 to 416 in May 1914. These claims had important long-term significance. The professionalization movement raised the level of expectations concerning the police. To justify their existence, to justify changes that were made, and to argue for additional changes, police administrators increasingly relied upon the official crime rate as a measure of efficiency. Willy-nilly, then, the mandate of the police underwent a subtle but important shift. The crime-fighting role moved steadily to the fore. This change was not entirely a conscious one, but was in many respects inherent in the efficiency ideal.[24]

The Blankenburg administration also sought to instill a sense of nonpartisan public service into the police force. Superintendent Robinson issued a list of "Ten Suggestions to Police Officers," which advised them to: "1. Remember that you are a paid public servant of the public; 2. Your first duty is to aid the citizen . . . ; 4. The detection of crime is important; the prevention of crime is more important . . . ; 6. Police efficiency is measured by the absence of crime rather than by arrests . . . ; 10. Remember, above all, 'PHILADELPHIA, MY CITY.'" Porter sought to enforce the long-standing but ignored prohibition on political activity by police officers. He issued a directive ordering that "any participation whatever in political activities of any nature whatever is in direct violation of the regulations of this department and the laws of the state." Political activity specifically included the marking of ballots for voters, the direct or indirect solicitation of votes, and "any participation in or attendance at any political meeting, other than in the performance of his duties." Porter also claimed that "one of the most important reforms instituted was the abolishment of the payment of assessments or 'voluntary' contributions for political purposes." The effort to eliminate politics from the department was sincere, but as reformers in city after city discovered, was not easily accomplished. One indication of success was the fact that between 1911 and 1912 the number of registered voters in the city declined by some 28,000. Previously, the police had been instrumental in maintaining the system of fraudulent registrations. Porter claimed that the November 1912 election, the first under the new administration, was "the most orderly the city has seen in years." Unfortunately, it did not help the reformers when they stood for reelection in 1915. Running on the reform ticket, Porter was defeated in his bid for mayor.

The regulations that Porter and Robinson issued concerning political activity were as significant for the form they took as for their substance. By putting departmental orders in written form and circulating them to all officers, the new administration sought to strengthen its control over the day-to-day conduct of the force. This was part of a general internal housecleaning instituted by Porter. He not only rearranged the physical layout of offices at police headquarters, but effected "a redistribution of duties on the basis of functions and qualifications of the several employees." Following the precepts of modern business and management, Porter also instituted a centralized system of records. Previously, the activities of the department had been compiled in reports from the five precincts. The reports were long, detailed, anecdotal accounts emphasizing the exploits of individual officers. This was the nineteenth-century style with respect to crime and crime fighting. Porter abolished this system and reduced the precinct reports to one-page statistical compilations. Efficiency demanded facts, presented in an impersonal manner, not colorful and episodic accounts of individual men.

The Blankenburg administration was not interested in streamlining the police department as an end in itself. It also intended to use the reformed police as an agency of social reform, and for suppressing vice in particular. In its first annual report, the department claimed to have closed 335 "bawdy houses" and 132 "assignation houses." The following year it intensified the antivice campaign. Porter announced that "All known houses of prostitution were on May 6, 1913, quarantined by the police. No one was permitted to enter such houses except those known to reside there." Moreover, "soliciting on the streets has been almost abolished." Private agencies worked closely with the police in the antivice crusade. The Law and Order Society assisted in the prosecution of saloon keepers arrested for violating the liquor laws. There was also increased concern about the proper handling of female offenders, whose numbers had increased significantly as a result of the antiprostitution drive. A "court-aid committee, composed of public-spirited men and women, was formed" to supervise female prisoners at night court. Private groups raised funds to hire a trained social worker for this task, a procedure that was repeated in many other cities in this period and, as we later see, helped pave the way for women police officers.[25]

The antivice campaign highlighted the extent to which police reform in Philadelphia was a movement by the city's elite. The attack on organized prostitution, gambling, and liquor law violations reflected the values of Philadelphia's middle class. The emphasis on efficiency and business management techniques, meanwhile, expressed the ethos of the business and professional groups, not the cultural style of the blue-collar-oriented political machine. And it was these relatively affluent groups that provided both the manpower and the financial backing for the civic-reform crusade of Rudolph Blankenburg, as well as the support for police advisor Martin H. Ray and the trained social workers to handle female offenders. To consolidate his political support, Public Safety Director Porter organized a "series of dinners in the various police districts . . . to promote harmony and good feelings among the men in the service." Prominent members of the business community, along with the top officials from the police department, attended the dinners and socialized with rank and file police officers.[26]

The Frustration of Reform

The reform of the Philadelphia police under the Blankenburg administration between 1911 and 1915 was an exciting event in the history of municipal government. Blankenburg, Porter, and Robinson succeeded in implementing many of the ideas of police reform and appeared to set in motion a continuing process of professionalization. Reform, however, proved to be an elusive goal. The traditional system of corrupt politics might suffer occasional setbacks, but in the long run it had enormous staying power. In New York City, for example, Tammany Hall was rarely out of power for more than one administration. Moreover, reform-minded administrators found it difficult to effect any significant and lasting changes in the police department. The abolition of the Board of Police Commissioners in 1901 proved to be a hollow victory. Between 1901 and 1918 eleven different men served as commissioner of police. Reformers such as Theodore A. Bingham (a retired brigadier general in the U.S. Army who served from 1906 to 1909) and Arthur Woods (Harvard educated and the former headmaster of an exclusive prep school who served from 1914 to 1917) were followed by machine-oriented commissioners who reestablished business as usual in the police department. Chicago reformers were even less successful than their counterparts in New York. Their sustained campaign for police reform was continually frustrated.[27]

Perhaps even more disturbing in its implications was the subsequent fate of the Philadelphia police department. Not only were many of the most important reforms abolished, but some of the most important techniques of reform were perverted and put to very different uses. In 1924 the Philadelphia police underwent a second "reform," one that was in many respects a grotesque parody of the 1911–1915 housecleaning.

W. Freeland Kendrick, elected mayor in 1923 on a reform platform, decided to clean up the police department by placing it on a "semimilitary basis." To accomplish this he recruited Brigadier General Smedley D. Butler of the United States Marine Corps as his public safety director. Over the objections of the secretary of the navy, President Calvin Coolidge granted Butler a leave of absence from the Marines for this assignment. Butler eventually served two years as public safety director and managed to undo much of the work of his predecessors.

Known as "Gimlet-Eye" Butler and the "Fighting Quaker," Butler was a man who believed in direct action. A veteran of the Spanish-American war and the Boxer Rebellion, he literally attacked his job in Philadelphia as if he were charging San Juan Hill. Sworn into office on January 7, 1924, he immediately ordered the police to rid the city of vice in forty-eight hours. Two days later an estimated 75 percent of the 1,300 saloons in the city had been closed and the "48 hour drive" became a regular feature of the Butler administration. General Butler was even more dramatic in his approach to crimes against persons and property. "Bandits?" he asked rhetorically, "shoot a few of them and make arrests afterward. The only way to reform a crook is to kill him." He then organized a special "bandit squad" consisting of 500 men armed with sawed-off shotguns and equipped with six armored cars. Presumably the bandit squad was to make a dramatic rush to the scene of any serious crime. General Butler took the idea of a war against crime literally and demonstrated remarkable disregard for the canons of criminal procedure in civil society.[28]

General Butler "cleaned up" the police department itself in an equally arbitrary and high-handed manner. He summarily abolished the School of Instruction, declaring that "from now on . . . every cop will learn his job right on the beat." Thus, in a single gesture, he destroyed one of the most hard won of all police reforms. Butler also threw aside established procedures for promotions in the department. He preferred to charge into a station house, locate a sergeant who seemed to have "leadership qualities," and announce "Here, you . . . I like your looks. What's your name? Well, you're lieutenant in charge of this district. Get busy." Presumably, getting busy meant imitating Butler's own style of furious and dramatic activity.

General Butler's comic approach to police administration had important implications for some of the most fundamental aspects of the police professionalization movement. The ease with which he could eliminate the school of instruction and cultivate a police style that emphasized arbitrary actions of dubious legality exposed the danger of placing too much reliance upon strong leadership. And yet, in their effort to transform the American police, the reformers did indeed overemphasize the personal qualities of the strong police executive. Raymond Fosdick's 1920 study, *American Police Systems*, stands as the most important statement of this aspect of police reform. Fosdick devoted crucial chapters to a sustained critique of police boards, indicting them for administrative inefficiency and arguing for a single, strong executive. "The character of the administrator is of far greater consequence in the upbuilding of a police force," Fosdick wrote, "than the kind of administrative machinery through which he works." "Vision and imagination are as essential to him as they are to any administrator. Above all else, he must be accustomed to *leading*." Transfixed by the charismatic personalities of such progressive leaders as Theodore Roosevelt and Woodrow Wilson, too many of the reformers believed that men could transform institutions. Contemporary experts on public administration, chastened by decades of experience with modern bureaucracies, recognize that administrators have relatively little ability to effect sweeping changes in complex organizations.[29]

Fosdick in particular misunderstood the lessons implicit in his own study of the European police, published as *European Police Systems* in 1914. There he found a form of police administration that impressed him as highly professional. He was particularly struck by the insulation of police executives from partisan politics and by their security of tenure. Moreover, European police administrators were recruited laterally and were often trained, professional civil servants, not former rank and file policemen or political operatives. Repeatedly, Fosdick held up the European system as a model for the American police. The comparison forms the dominant theme in his two books and helped to shape much thinking on police reform.[30]

Unfortunately, Fosdick did not sufficiently take into account the fact that the European style of police administration was built on a very different social and political tradition. It was not a style that could be grafted onto American society. European police administration was frankly based on an elitist social system where the civil service was a distinct caste of individuals recruited from elite backgrounds and trained for professional careers. It was incompatible with the informal tradition of participatory politics and the spoils system which had taken firm root in American society by the early decades of the nineteenth century. Fosdick's error had important implications for the entire movement for police professionalization. Neither he nor any of the other leading spokesmen for reform adequately reconciled their demand for expert leadership with the traditions of democratic politics. The tension between professional expertise and public control over the police forms one of the dominant themes of recent police history.

The idea of professional expertise was especially compatible with the interests of the elite in controlling the American police. Fosdick's own work was suggested and subsidized by John D. Rockefeller, Jr. through the American Social Hygiene Association, a Rockefeller-sponsored organization. When Fosdick entered private law practice in the 1920s his first client was John D. Rockefeller, Jr., and in the 1930s Fosdick served as president of the Rockefeller Foundation. Other prominent police reformers were also either members of the elite or else recruited laterally into police administration. Richard Sylvester, for example, had never worked as a patrolman, and became superintendent of the District of Columbia police through political patronage. August Vollmer, chief of the Berkeley, California, police, and by the 1920s the most famous spokesman for police professionalism, also entered laterally. He had held a number of miscellaneous jobs, including part ownership in a store, until he was persuaded to run for election as marshal of Berkeley in 1905. And in New York City, the most famous advocates of police reform, from Theodore Roosevelt to Arthur Woods, were members of the social elite.[31]

The progressive reformers assumed that positions of leadership would be assumed by good men, individuals with a commitment to the public interest. This assumption was naive for there was nothing that guaranteed what kind of person would assume power. In no city were the naive assumptions of the reformers more cruelly shattered than in Jersey City, New Jersey. There, the reform ideal was perverted by "Boss" Frank Hague who used the administrative mechanisms developed by the reformers to build one of the most corrupt political machines in all of American urban history. The fate of police reform in Jersey City deserves attention because of its implications about the assumptions of the police professionalization movement. Although the Hague machine reached its heyday in the late 1930s, its origins can be traced to pre-World War I urban reform.

Frank Hague's rise to power in Jersey City was originally based on the commission form of city government, itself a popular reform in the Progressive Era. The commission form of government was designed to place the administration of municipal affairs in the hands of a few officials, each of whom would specialize in a particular urban service function. It was assumed that specialization and expertise were the key to good government. Frank Hague proved that they could be the key to unchecked political power. In 1911 New Jersey passed the Walsh Act which allowed cities to adopt the commission form of government. Two years later Jersey City adopted the idea. Frank Hague and his associates welcomed the commission form of government, for they "saw that it would be easier to control a five-man commission than a large city council." In the 1913 municipal elections Hague campaigned as a reformer, condemning the old system for breeding "cheap politics." He placed fourth in the election and took his seat as one of the five commissioners. When the new administration met to organize city government, Hague became the director of public safety.[32]

Hague began to build his political machine by "reforming" the police department in a manner that, on the surface, bore a disturbing resemblance to the style used in Philadelphia and other cities. This meant centralizing authority in the office of the public safety director. In one of his first moves, Hague destroyed the budding alliance between the police and firemen's associations and the American Federation of Labor. He then arranged to have introduced into the legislature a bill that would have given him sole power to try officers for violating departmental rules. The bill failed when it encountered strong opposition, including some from police officers themselves. Hague lost that battle but won the war with another piece of legislation that slipped through almost unnoticed. An amendment to the Walsh Act conferred on city commissioners "all executive, administrative, and legislative power heretofore had and possessed by the mayor and city council. . . ." The net effect was that Hague as a commissioner gained the power to try members of the police department, since that had previously been the power of the mayor.

Armed with his new power, Hague proceeded to clean house. Hundreds of police officers were dismissed on a variety of charges; this was really no problem given the number of departmental rules and the fact that most of them had traditionally been ignored. Officers who were not dismissed outright were faced with stiff fines as an inducement to leave voluntarily. Captains and lieutenants who did not go along with the new system were ordered to do foot patrol and faced disciplinary proceedings if they refused. Rather quickly, Hague created a police department composed of men completely loyal to him. As a final step in the consolidation of his power, he established a special detective group whose main function was to spy on other members of the department.

Hague soon translated his control of the police department into higher political office. In 1917, after four years as a commissioner, he was elected mayor of Jersey City. He served as mayor until 1940 and developed one of the most corrupt municipal administrations in history. His philosophy of government was summed up in his famous statement, "I am the law." By the late 1930s Jersey City had one of the largest (relative to its population) and highest paid police departments in the country. It also had one of the worst percentages of patrolmen actually on the beat. The department was filled with political hacks who received high salaries for little or no work. To pay for this and similar practices in other branches of government, the residents of Jersey City paid one of the highest property tax rates in the country.

The Hague machine finally ran afoul of the CIO, the United States Constitution, and the Supreme Court in 1939. We shall examine that particular episode later in our study of the police in the depression. For the moment, however, it is sufficient to note that Hague's use of the Jersey City police exposed one of the major limitations of efficiency-oriented police professionalization. In the wrong hands, the instruments of reform could become the basis of despotism. Hague's use of the Jersey City police, in fact, prefigured J. Edgar Hoover's use of the FBI. As we shall see, Hoover's approach to law enforcement administration was also based on many of the ideas of professionalization; and he too succeeded in fashioning a secret police that he used for political ends.

Uplifting the Patrolman

Enhancing the power of police executives and installing centralized, rational administrative procedures were two of the three most important goals of the efficiency-minded professionalizers. The third involved improving the quality of police officer. To this end, reformers campaigned vigorously for formal training programs, procedures for evaluating the performance of policemen, and rational promotion guidelines. Civil service was also an important reform, but the leading spokesmen for professionalization had very mixed feelings about it. They preferred to give the maximum amount of power to police executives and chafed at the bureaucratic procedures that civil service entailed.

Prior to the turn of the century, formal training programs for police officers were almost unheard of. The elaborate program that Cincinnati developed after 1886 was a striking exception to the rule. As August Vollmer pointed out, "the only requirement necessary for appointment as policeman was political pull and brute strength . . . No preliminary training was necessary, and the officers were considered sufficiently equipped to perform their duties if they were armed with a revolver, club and hand-cuffs, and wore a regulation uniform." It was, Vollmer concluded, an "era of incivility, ignorance, brutality and graft." Police training became one of the great accomplishments of the professionalization movement, although it was a struggle that was still being waged as late as the 1960s. Nonetheless, the idea was firmly planted in the pre-World War I years, and August Vollmer became its most renowned exponent.[33]

The idea of formal training was inherent in the concept of police work as a profession. Arthur Woods, better than anyone else in those years, recognized the fact of police discretion. Writing in 1918, the former New York City police commissioner pointed out that "The policeman is in a very real sense a judge." He exercised an enormous amount of discretion and to a great extent determined the quality of criminal justice in any given American city. Consequently, it was important to train police officers in the complexities of criminal law and criminal procedure as well as other aspects of human and social behavior. At the same time, police reformers were conscious of the status of the police vis-à-vis other professions. If formal education was a sign of professionalism, then the police should have it too.[34]

Many police departments introduced formal training programs for the first time in the Progressive Era. Cleveland established a decentralized program in 1903. Once a week, captains in each of the thirteen precincts conducted classes that covered state laws, city ordinances, and departmental regulations. A few years later the school was centralized. In 1910 some of the officers organized the Forum Club on their own initiative. There they met to study law, sociology and other police-related subjects. The Forum Club, however, appears to have been the organizational base of opposition to Chief Fred Kohler whose autocratic style of reform had aroused hostility. Then, in 1914, the public safety director arranged a series of lectures "for the benefit of the force," to be given during the winter months. Lectures were given by the mayor, common pleas judges and prominent members of the bar.[35]

In Chicago, faculty members from Northwestern University offered to teach courses for the Chicago police. They sent a proposed curriculum to the mayor but received no response. Most of the enthusiasm for police training, in fact, originated with nonpolice individuals or reform-minded administrators who were sometimes replaced by men who were less excited about the idea. The Philadelphia School of Instruction, as we have seen, was summarily abolished by General Butler in 1924. The struggle for police training remained a long and difficult one.[36]

Also problematic was the quality of those training programs that did exist. A 1913 city council investigation of the New York City police academy uncovered deplorable conditions. According to the report the school was "defective because instructors, being members of the uniform force, are lacking in teaching experience." Moreover, "all recruits are passed from the school to policy duty, irrespective of intelligence or ability shown by them while under instruction." Recruits were not expected to take notes during lectures nor were they required to take any examinations. "No recruit is known to have been dismissed for academic failure." Partly as a result of the 1913 investigation, Commissioner Arthur Woods reorganized the academy in 1914; the fate of the program after his departure in late 1917, however, is uncertain at best. The implications of the New York City investigation were even more disturbing than the substance of the report itself. The New York City police academy was generally regarded as perhaps the best in the country. If this were the best, one can only imagine the quality of the early programs in other cities.[37]

Police academy training was but one aspect of the quest for higher standards. August Vollmer made an even more dramatic innovation in Berkeley, California, when he introduced the idea of college-level training for policemen. In an age when the majority of police officers lacked even a high school diploma, and many had difficulty with the English language, the idea of college education was truly startling. Through his efforts in this area, Vollmer soon established a national reputation as the most famous spokesman for police professionalization.

Vollmer came upon the idea in 1907 during the investigation of an apparent suicide. Suspecting that the death was in fact a homicide, Vollmer turned for assistance from a friend who taught biology at the University of California. Dr. Jacques Loeb's investigation of the case did not convince the grand jury to change its verdict, but it left an indelible impression on August Vollmer. Immediately, he began to explore the possibility of a more formal relationship between the university and the Berkeley police department. In 1908 he established the first official program, a series of semiformal lectures during the summer term. Members of the university faculty lectured on various aspects of the forensic sciences, while Vollmer himself and Inspector Walter Peterson of the Oakland police department lectured on practical police work. In 1916 Vollmer took another important step forward when he established a permanent three-year police training program with the university. Offered during the summer session and open only to members of the Berkeley police department, the curriculum covered the natural sciences, the social sciences, criminal law and procedure, and various aspects of police organization and administration.

Vollmer's program was essentially a police academy, but with an important difference. Whereas in other police academies the teaching was done by veteran police officers with no educational qualifications, the Berkeley program drew its faculty from the university. By the 1920s and 1930s the city of Berkeley was famous for its "college cops." Vollmer also made a concerted effort to recruit university graduates for the department. In the long run, Vollmer had an enormous impact on the development of police professionalism. Not only did he raise the level of expectations by introducing the idea of college education, but he also developed a cadre of disciples who carried on his work. The most famous of his followers was O. W. Wilson who, from the 1940s through the early 1960s, was the acknowledged leading authority on police administration. Vollmer's work also helped to put the state of California in the forefront of police professionalization. By the 1920s and 1930s the California Peace Officers Association, representing police chiefs in the state, was a professional association of the first rank. Its deliberations were perhaps even more impressive than those of the IACP for the same period. Finally, Vollmer's relationship with the University of California evolved into the first full-fledged School of Criminology in the United States. It was the first program to offer graduate degrees in police administration and helped to lend credibility to the new field of criminal justice education.[38]

August Vollmer's fascination with science had an important impact on another aspect of police professionalism. He became one of the leading advocates of scientific crime detection and helped to establish one of the first crime labs in the United States. The idea of policing as a science was inherent in the idea of professionalism. The first important innovations began to appear in the 1890s. In 1883, Alphonse Bertillion developed a system for identifying criminals that involved a set of measurements of various parts of the body. Using a set of calipers, the Bertillion method was complicated and time consuming. Nonetheless, it gained wide acceptance and began to spread throughout American police departments in the 1890s. It was soon replaced, however, by the far more efficient fingerprint system of identification. St. Louis claimed credit for being the first American police department to adopt the new technique. Members of the force learned the system in 1904 from a Scotland Yard officer who was in the city for the world's fair. The new technique was immensely popular and quickly replaced the more cumbersome Bertillion method altogether.[39]

The crime lab and the fingerprint system were more important for their public relations value than for their actual contributions to the apprehension of criminals. The aura of science was an important part of the imagery of police professionalism. Yet, as working detectives have long known and as recent studies have confirmed, crime detection represents a small but vastly overrated aspect of police work. It is difficult even under the best of circumstances to obtain even a single clear print from the scene of a crime. Moreover, detectives are most often successful in identifying a criminal when the name of a prime suspect is known at the time of the crime. The bulk of detective work consists of paper shuffling. But the public relations value of scientific crime detection proved to be enormous. In the 1930s J. Edgar Hoover would make a fetish of both fingerprints and the crime lab. Eventually, he would succeed in redefining police professionalism altogether, placing an undue emphasis on the image of the police as crime fighters.[40]

August Vollmer also sought to apply the social and behavioral sciences to police work. As he put it, he hoped to make every patrolman a "practical criminologist." We shall examine this idea and its consequences in the next chapter which deals with the crime prevention and social reform aspects of police professionalism.

In their effort to elevate the quality of policing, the reformers recognized the need for a formal system of evaluating the performance of individual patrolmen. The Cincinnati police began maintaining individual personnel records in 1900, but the St. Louis merit system, adopted in 1905, was perhaps the most elaborate system. Upon entering the St. Louis police department a patrolman received an automatic 750 points. He could then earn additional "merit" points for such things as an especially good arrest (twenty-five points), a display of bravery (twenty-five points), a record of "efficiency" (two points), and two points for each year of service. He could also lose points for any of nineteen different reasons and the range of penalties ran from five to fifty points. If an officer earned fifty merit points he was promoted to the next highest grade of patrolmen; and if he lost fifty points he would be demoted to the next lowest grade. When any patrolman's total sank to the level of 600 points, he was subject to a charge of general inefficiency and sent to the Board of Police Commissioners for trial.[41]

The St. Louis merit system was truly a pioneering effort, one that other departments did not copy for many decades. During the 1920s and 1930s, the Milwaukee police developed an equally elaborate system that also received wide recognition. The development of formal personnel procedures represented a recognition of the fact of bureaucratization—that in a large and complex organization it was necessary to develop impersonal and quantifiable measures to achieve uniformity. The demands of bureaucratization, however, often conflicted with the goals of the police professionalizers. As we have already noted, the reformers generally put their faith in the efficacy of strong executive leadership. They preferred to give executives a virtual free hand and chafed at the development of elaborate formal procedures, especially with regard to personnel matters.

Nowhere was the conflict between bureaucratization and the goals of the professionalizers more evident than with respect to civil service. On the one hand, civil service procedures represented one of the most important steps in the drive to eliminate arbitrary political influence in police personnel matters. New York City adopted civil service for its police in 1883. Chicago followed suit in 1895 and by the end of the century the idea had become widespread. A 1915 survey revealed that of the 204 largest police departments, 122 had adopted civil service. Even more significant was the fact that of the forty largest departments, only Kansas City, Indianapolis, Louisville, and Birmingham were without it.[42]

The reformers, however, had strong objections. Raymond Fosdick wrote that "the application to a police department of civil service had serious limitations." The problem was that "In the endeavor to guard against abuse of authority, it frequently is carried to such extremes that rigidity takes the place of flexibility in administration." He complained that "in trying to nullify the effects of incompetence and favoritism, we nullify capacity and intelligence too." The application of civil service procedures to the police raised one of the problems inherent in service-oriented bureaucracies. The formal procedures did not necessarily measure the qualities required for day-to-day work. Rather, they emphasized either abstract knowledge or negative criteria. Policemen in the twentieth century soon learned that the most important goal was simply to keep your nose clean. Arthur Woods observed that "In forces where promotion is made according to civil service systems, . . . a man attains promotion without any reference to the qualities of his day-by-day work."[43]

The reformers aspired to make the police professionals. While they succeeded in professionalizing police executives, the bureaucratization of police departments left the rank and file in an ambiguous situation. They were part professionals and part bureaucratic functionaries; they exercised an enormous amount of discretion in their daily work, as did other professionals, yet they were increasingly held accountable to specific procedural regulations that limited their discretion. The conflict between the competing claims of professionalism and bureaucratization remained one of the fundamental problems in the development of the police in the twentieth century.

New Approaches to Law and Order

Although this history is primarily concerned with developments in municipal police departments, the story of professionalization would not be complete without taking into account developments at the state and federal level. During the first decade of the twentieth century two entirely new law enforcement agencies appeared. Both of them embodied the central concepts of efficiency-oriented professionalization and both were attempts to circumvent the politically controlled municipal police. The creation of the Pennsylvania state police in 1905 and the birth of what eventually became the FBI in 1908 are important chapters in the history of police reform.

The Pennsylvania State Constabulary expressed in the purest form the values of administrative efficiency. It was a highly centralized agency and one that was far more militaristic in its ethos than any municipal police department. Pennsylvania introduced the modern state police idea. Previously, there had been a number of law enforcement agencies along similar lines, but the idea had never taken firm root. The Texas Rangers, for example, had been authorized by the Provisional Government of Texas in 1835. Massachusetts, meanwhile, created a few "state constables" in 1865 to aid in the suppression of vice. Fourteen years later these officers were reorganized into the Massachusetts District Police, a precursor to the state police created in 1920. Connecticut created a similar agency in 1903, while Arizona and New Mexico established agencies modeled after the Texas Rangers in 1901 and 1905, respectively.[44]

The Pennsylvania state police was a far more elaborate agency than any of its predecessors. Not only was it larger, but it was also given a broader law enforcement mandate. Although officially created to deal with the question of crime in rural areas, the Pennsylvania state police in reality dealt primarily with industrial strife. From the standpoint of industrialists, municipal police departments and the state militia were all too often unreliable in times of strikes. Either because of the social origins of the officers themselves or because of political influence, they were too sympathetic to the interests of workingmen. During the 1877 riots, for example, the militia had in many instances simply refused to oppose the workingmen. The Coal and Iron Police, created in the late 1860s, had served the interests of industrialists in some instances, but the state police was a far more systematic approach. The anthracite coal strike of 1902, which precipiated a national crisis and brought the intervention of the president of the United States, stimulated the birth of the constabulary.[45]

Officers in the Pennsylvania state police were uniformed, mounted, and assigned to barracks located throughout the state. In every respect it was a thoroughly militaristic agency. Consistent with the ideas of police professionalism, the commander was appointed by the governor and given broad executive powers. It was hardly surprising that efficiency-oriented experts repeatedly cited it as the most efficiently administered law enforcement agency. Bruce Smith commented approvingly in 1940 that state police forces "promise to continue as a proving ground for some of the latest adaptations of the theory and practice of public management to the severely practical task of police administration."[46]

Centralization had important political ramifications. It insulated the state police from the kind of political influence that the labor movement was best able to mobilize and made it far more responsible to the interests of industrialists. Not surprisingly, the Pennsylvania Federation of Labor bitterly denounced the actions of the men they preferred to call the "cossacks." In 1915 the federation published a major expose of the constabulary's role in labor disputes, denouncing it as "a body of cruel men, whose conduct stamps them as partial to the interests of the plutocracy; brutal in their dealing with the working class, generally of low character, and law-breakers when occasion requires." The fact that the constabulary was a mobile force, recruited statewide with roots in no particular community was, by design, an attempt to eliminate any possible sympathy between the state police and workingmen. Impersonality, one of the highest ideals of professionalism, did not serve the interests of working people. The Pennsylvania Federation of Labor concluded with the plea: "Let us get rid of them, that Pennsylvania may again return to the old-time peaceable condition, when it was 'a government of the people, by the people, for the people.'"[47]

The plea for abolition went unheeded in Pennsylvania, and other states eventually followed its lead. New York organized a similar state police in 1917, as did Michigan, Colorado, and West Virginia in 1919. Public fears about law and order during wartime was a great stimulus to the state police movement. Massachusetts consolidated its existing agency in 1920, while New Jersey and

Rhode Island created their state police in 1921 and 1925. The state police remained controversial, however. The Colorado Rangers, for example, became a major political issue in 1923 and were subsequently abolished.

Even more portentous for the future of law enforcement was the creation of the Bureau of Investigation in 1908. It marked the intervention of the federal government into the law enforcement picture in a manner that was without precedent. This, in turn, reflected rising national concern about the "crime problem," a development that has continued throughout the twentieth century. While the expansion of the federal role has been continuous, three periods are particularly significant. They are marked by the creation of the bureau in 1908, the dramatic expansion of the size, role, and public image of the bureau in the mid-1930s, and, finally, the "law-and-order" crisis of the mid-1960s with the creation of the Law Enforcement Assistance Administration. The long-term impact of the expanded federal role has been both to raise public expectations about the performance of the police and to subject them to national, and more demanding standards. The Bureau of Investigation also emerged as a national police force and helped to alter significantly the political meaning of the "crime problem." Whereas in the nineteenth and early twentieth century the political dimensions of the "crime problem" generally pertained to questions of vice and different cultural styles, the emphasis steadily shifted to one of national security, with an ideological rather than a cultural focus.[48]

The creation of the Bureau of Investigation prefigured its subsequent history. It was born amid political controversy, executive initiative, and questionable activities. Charles Bonaparte, Theodore Roosevelt's attorney general, asked Congress to create a permanent detective force within the Department of Justice in 1907. Previously, executive agencies had occasionally contracted for the services of private detective agencies, a practice that aroused controversy. Congress balked at the suggestion for several reasons. Two members of Congress had recently been prosecuted for fraudulent dealings in western lands, and Congressmen were sensitive about granting the executive branch additional law enforcement powers. Moreover, the idea of federal detectives conjured up images of the French secret police, an agency with a long-standing bad image in the English-speaking world. The fact that Attorney General Bonaparte was a grandnephew of Napoleon only reinforced the fears of many congressmen.

Congress, in fact, not only rejected the attorney general's idea, but moved to curb the law enforcement powers of the executive branch even further. On May 30, 1908, it passed a law forbidding the Department of Justice from borrowing detectives from the Secret Service or any other federal agency. President Roosevelt was enraged at this direct slap and retaliated as soon as Congress adjourned for the summer. On July 1, 1908, he simply established the Bureau of Investigation by executive fiat.

The first years of the Bureau of Investigation were as sordid as were its more recent actions with respect to civil liberties. Outraged that the president had circumvented its wishes, Congress launched an attack on the new agency as soon as it reconvened. Its fears of a secret police were soon confirmed when it discovered that agents of the bureau had opened the mail of Senator Benjamin R. Tillman, one of its most vocal opponents. Roosevelt's explanation set a worthy model for some of the tortured rationalizations of J. Edgar Hoover in later years. The president explained that "sometimes through the accidental breaking of such packages [U.S. mail!] the contents are exposed."[49]

The growth of the bureau was actually rather slow. Through the first two decades of its existence it remained a relatively small agency, although the publicity that surrounded its mismanagement and scandals gave it considerable visibility. The bureau acquired a more specific role with the passage of the Mann Act in 1910, although it used the law for political investigations of questionable legality, and, of course, it played a prominent role in the Red Scare of 1919. During the early 1920s the agency was headed by William J. Burns, more famous for his private detective agency. The Burns administration achieved a record of scandal and corruption that fit in well with the Harding administration generally. Finally, in 1924, Attorney General Harlan Fiske Stone brought in J. Edgar Hoover as director to clean up the bureau. Hoover had served quietly in the bureau from the beginning (although his role in the Red Scare remains a matter of controversy) and had established a reputation as an earnest and dedicated public servant. Ironically, Hoover's appointment was supported by the American Civil Liberties Union, who saw him as a considerable improvement over previous directors. Under Hoover the bureau languished for nearly a decade. The transformation of the FBI (along with the change in its name) was a product of the 1930s and, as we later see, was directly related to the general expansion of federal powers under the New Deal.[50]

The creation of the Bureau of Investigation was a significant expression of the police professionalization movement. First, it reflected rising public concern about the "crime problem." Policing was no longer a business that could be left to amateurs. The problem demanded not only the reform of existing agencies, but the creation of new ones as well. Second, the bureau, like the state police, was a highly centralized agency. Both were attempts to circumvent the legislative branch (whether at the state or federal level) and marked a significant expansion of executive authority. Finally, both the bureau and the state police, embodied the ideals of administrative efficiency. Executives were granted almost complete discretion to run the agencies as they saw fit. While rank-and-file officers were well trained (another goal of professionalization) they had little input into policymaking. The subsequent history of the FBI stands as monumental commentary on the ideals of the police professionalization movement. Like General Butler in Philadelphia and "Boss" Frank Hague in Jersey City, J. Edgar Hoover proved that the techniques of professionalism and efficiency could easily be perverted. In the end, the achievement of the police professionalization movement was an ambiguous one. Genuine improvements in the administrative efficiency of law enforcement agencies were matched by the disturbing potential for the misuse of police power.

4

Reforming Society: Cops as Social Workers

The second thrust of police professionalization in the Progressive Era came from the idea that the police should play a positive role in the general reform of society. Particular emphasis was given to the role of the police in relation to juveniles, women offenders, adults who had committed minor offenses, and the problems of drinking and prostitution. Although they did not use the terminology that we are familiar with, police reforms in the Progressive Era were attempts to experiment with rehabilitation, diversion, and decriminalization.

This group of police reforms was part of a more general reform of the American criminal justice system during the Progressive Era. The first two decades of the twentieth century represented a high point in the belief in the possibility of rehabilitating offenders. One of the most notable innovations was the juvenile court, first established in Chicago in 1899. Within the next two decades, virtually every state adopted a juvenile court of its own. The Progressive Era also witnessed significant innovations in the handling of adult offenders. Probation, for example, had been instituted in Massachusetts in 1878. By 1900 it had spread to six states. Between 1900 and 1915 it spread to another twenty-seven states. The founding of the National Probation Association in 1907 marked a step forward in the professionalization of probation. The indeterminate sentence, a feature of the juvenile court, was also extended to adult offenders. Between 1900 and 1915 the number of states with indeterminate sentencing laws grew from five to thirty-one. The practice of parole also spread rapidly, from three states in 1890 to forty in 1920.[1]

The social-work-oriented police reforms existed in an uneasy relationship with those directed toward managerial efficiency. The experts at the New York Bureau of Municipal Research, for example, stressed administrative reform with little concern about the role of the police toward social problems. In some cities, however, the two concerns were closely linked. In both Philadelphia and Detroit internal reform was seen as a necessary precondition to reorienting the role of the department in society. In still other cities, however, social reform was attempted with little or no concern for administrative efficiency. Chief Fred Kohler in Cleveland, for example instituted a number of social work-style police reforms without attempting any significant changes within the department.

It is important to examine the social-work-oriented police reforms for two reasons. First, this aspect of police history has been lost from view. Police professionalization eventually came to be defined almost exclusively in terms of administrative efficiency. By the 1930s, under the influence of August Vollmer, O. W. Wilson, and J. Edgar Hoover, the crime fighter became the ideal police type. The alternative model, the social work role of the police, fell into almost total eclipse.[2]

A second important reason for examining this aspect of police reform is the fact that it dramatizes some of the most fundamental dilemmas of police administration. The central problem is inherent in the idea of rehabilitation and, in this respect, has received considerable amount of attention in the areas of corrections and juvenile justice. The idea of rehabilitation, in brief, is founded on the belief that treatment should be individualized. To achieve the proper treatment it is necessary to rely on an enormous amount of discretion. The treatment approach has now come under heavy attack for, among other things, the fact that it opens the door to wide disparities of punishment and is in many respects inconsistent with standards of due process.[3]

A similar dilemma confronts those who would have the police play a social work role. The law enforcement mandate of the police conflicts with the idea of individualized treatment inherent in the rehabilitive approach. At the same time, to ask that the police involve themselves in the handling of noncriminal social problems is also to ask for a broad extension of their power to intervene in the lives of citizens. As a number of critics have argued, the rehabilitative ideal has indeed resulted in an extension of state power of the individual. All of these issues were confronted by the social-work-oriented police reforms of the Progressive Era. This chapter of police history provides valuable perspective on more recent proposals to expand the social service role of the police.[4]

Cops as Social Workers: August Vollmer Reconsidered

By the second decade of the twentieth century, August Vollmer had clearly emerged as the leading national spokesman for police professionalism.[5] Building upon the pioneering work of Richard Sylvester, Vollmer greatly expanded the concept of police professionalism. As chief of police in Berkeley, California, he achieved fame for his pioneering efforts to raise educational standards, his interest in scientific crime detection, and his emphasis on automobile patrol. Over the course of his long career, Vollmer's ideas underwent a subtle shift. In the early years he emphasized both the social work aspects of policing and the importance of technological innovations (the automobile, the two-way radio, the crime lab, the lie detector). By the end of his career in the late 1930s, however, the social work emphasis had fallen into eclipse. This shift toward a greater emphasis on crime fighting was part of a pervasive redefinition of the meaning of police professionalism—a change that Vollmer's thinking contributed to significantly. One needs only compare his speeches to the IACP in the early 1920s with his 1936 book, *The Police and Modern Society*, to sense the difference. It is significant, moreover, that Vollmer's principal disciple, O. W. Wilson, also emphasized the administrative and technocratic aspects of policing at the expense of the social work aspects.[6]

In the early 1920s there was no more articulate advocate of the idea that the police should function as social workers than August Vollmer. The belief that police officers should do more than merely arrest offenders, that they should actively seek to prevent crime by "saving" potential or actual offenders, was an important theme in police reform. It was an essential ingredient in the notion of professionalism. The members of the National Prison Association and such isolated individuals as Edward Savage in Boston had been toying with these ideas in the nineteenth century. An intellectual revolution—the rise of the rehabilitative ideal—and a host of reforms in other aspects of the criminal justice system (probation, parole, the juvenile court) gave impetus crime prevention-oriented police reforms after the turn of the century.

The spirit of reform generated wildly expansive views of the role of the police. Arthur Woods, commissioner of the New York City police, wrote that "the power of the policeman for good or for evil is great . . . In this aspect of his duties the policeman is an educator, just as truly as is the president of one of our large universities." Woods continued, suggesting that the policeman "becomes a teacher of cleanliness, an educator of good habits; . . . he plays the part rather of helpful friend and guide than of avenging, implacable autocrat." Josephy M. Quigley, chief of the Rochester, New York, police, told the 1912 IACP convention that "The police chief should be the moral physician of the community." In an article entitled "Police Work as a Profession," social worker and reformer Graham Taylor argued that "every beat should be something like a parish if the policeman who travelled it were taught to mix more gospel with the law."[7]

In a series of addresses to the IACP, August Vollmer advanced his own ideas of the proper role of the policeman in crime prevention. "The Policeman as a Social Worker" in 1918 and "Predelinquency" in 1921 contained the heart of Vollmer's message. He began by arguing that the "old methods of dealing with crime must be changed, and newer ones adopted." Like so many other reformers in the period, Vollmer was moved by an urgent feeling that traditional institutions and practices were no longer adequate for a modern and complex industrial society. Through his contacts at the University of California he began to study the emerging science of criminology. Although he recognized that "criminology as a science is still in its infancy," he believed that it could make a positive contribution to police administration.[8]

Essentially, Vollmer accepted the idea that it was possible to identify the social and pyschological roots of crime. "The policeman is learning that dependency, criminality and industrial unrest have a common origin, and that upon him rest far more important and far greater obligations than the mere apprehending and prosecuting of lawbreakers." It was pointless merely to arrest offenders, for then it was too late; the individual's attitudes and behavior patterns had already been formed. Vollmer argued that the policeman, "if he would serve his community by reducing crime he must go up the stream a little further and dam it up at its source. . . ." In short, Vollmer asked that the police intervene in individuals' lives before they entered lives of crime. This idea, noble as it seemed, raised a number of important questions.

In his 1921 address on "Predelinquency," Vollmer explored the social work aspects of policing in more detail. Drawing upon recent social science research he pointed out that adult offenders generally manifested antisocial behavior as children. Thus, he argued, it was possible to develop a typology of behavior patterns which would allow police, social workers, teachers, and others to identify potential criminals, whom he called "predelinquents." But Vollmer was extremely vague when it came to suggestions for specific police action. For the most part he merely suggested that they work closely with the schools and other social welfare institutions. In their social work role the police were to be largely a referral agency. Vollmer painted a glowing picture of the patrolman as social scientist. He suggested that the department maintain a map with pins indicating the residence of troublesome children, with different colored pins indicating different social problems (for example, parental alcoholism, and unemployment). "Thus armed with facts, not fancies, and with a constructive program for the mental, physical and moral health of the subject," Vollmer concluded, "the policeman is in an enviable position in so far as the future of the child is concerned."

But beyond making routine referrals, Vollmer indicated no positive steps that policemen could take to utilize their accumulated knowledge. Even the practice of referrals raised a problem that Vollmer ignored. The coercive powers of arrest that are implicit in the police role created a disturbingly ambiguous situation: in making a referral was the policeman merely suggesting that the individual undergo some form of treatment, or was he implicitly ordering treatment as an alternative to arrest? Vollmer chose not to consider the issue, nor has it generally been discussed by those who would expand the role of the police. The civil liberties question was compounded by a more mundane practical problem. How, in practice, could policemen apply the new social science theories of criminal behavior? Vollmer's passionate belief that each patrolman could become a "practical criminologist" was advanced with an excess of rhetoric and a shortage of practical suggestions. The traditional complaint of the nonprofessional police contained an important, though slighted, grain of truth. Jerome E. Richards, chief of the Memphis police told the IACP in 1900, "While I would not deprecate intelligent study and close investigations by policemen into scientific data relating to crime . . . our business is with conditions and not with theories."[9]

As police professionalism advanced, the gap between the self-styled practical policemen and the academically-oriented professionalizers remained. Social science theories of criminality, apart from their practical application, served other functions. They were an important part of the public relations aspect of professionalism. Those who sought to elevate police work as a profession were sensitive about the public image of the police. By associating themselves with advanced academic thinking, the reformers hoped to cultivate an image of the police as modern, up-to-date, and scientific. The forensic sciences, the crime lab, and technological developments in weaponry and communications were used in a similar fashion.[10]

August Vollmer's arguments in favor of a social work role for the police raised another important problem. To help prevent crime he not only suggested that they work closely with existing social welfare agencies but argued that they should become advocates of additional reform proposals. "You will ask what the policeman can do, and how shall he proceed to get the best results. My answer is—fight for everything which helps to decrease crime and dependency, and in this connection a few suggestions are offered for social service work in the community and state." Frequently, schools were overcrowded and Vollmer suggested that "the policeman can do his share to correct this condition by stating the facts to the voters whenever an opportunity is afforded."[11] He also recommended that they support expansion of recreational facilities, community social centers, and other antidelinquency agencies.

In short, Vollmer was suggesting that the police play an active and partisan role in the political life of the community. As a professional, an expert in his chosen field, the police administrator should be an advocate of what he deemed the proper policies. Yet, the major thrust of police professionalization had been to insulate the police from politics. This contradiction illustrated one of the fundamental ambiguities of the whole notion of professionalism. Professions sought insulation from the public to give themselves a free hand in the determination of public policy. The rhetoric of professional expertise and autonomy was a useful device to deflect suggestions that the public should have a more direct voice in important policy decisions.[12]

In yet another respect the idea that the police should function as social workers contradicted other objectives of police professionalization. Those who defined professionalization in terms of administrative efficiency generally sought to narrow the scope of police responsibilities. In particular they sought to relieve the police of responsibility for numerous miscellaneous duties that had accumulated over the years. The range of these activities was truly remarkable. A 1915 Census Bureau survey of municipal police departments offered a catalogue of these assignments. In many cities the police were responsible for enforcing the building codes. Philadelphia had ten fire escape inspectors in its police department; New York had thirteen boiler inspectors; Washington, D.C., had one pharmacy inspector; Buffalo, New York, had eight "market masters." The police were also responsible for child welfare in many cities. Washington, D.C., had two child labor inspectors; Seattle had three truant officers; Rochester, New York, had six school census officers. Police departments also acquired other moral reform assignments during the Progressive Era: a 1907 law gave the Chicago police department responsibility for censoring motion pictures. And, of course, in most police departments, uniformed officers were assigned to jobs that could easily be handled by civilians.[13]

Raymond Fosdick argued that "the tendency to load the police force with irrelevant functions is largely a matter of careless and untidy governmental housekeeping. The department has been made a sort of catchall for such miscellaneous activities as cannot be easily accommodated elsewhere." Fosdick and other spokesmen for professionalism argued that these miscellaneous assignments took uniformed officers away from the critical function of law enforcement. The efficiency-minded Fosdick proposed "building an organization around the single duty of maintaining law and order." Responsibility for miscellaneous social welfare tasks compromised the authority of the police—the public did not see them primarily as law enforcement officers.[14]

Nonetheless, many social reform-minded police reformers sought to add additional assignments to the police department. The Los Angeles police department, for example, established an "anticigarette clinic" in 1915. Under the supervision of Dr. T. H. Trinwith, who volunteered his services, the clinic "treated" over 2300 people in its first month of operation. Particular attention was given to persuading juveniles not to smoke. In Toledo, Ohio, the police conducted a survey of coal supplies in the city during the 1919 "coal famine." And in a variation of the police-lodging practices which had begun to disappear, the New York City police raised money for destitute men during the winter of 1915-1916. According to Arthur Woods, police officers themselves contributed $1900 of the $2800 raised. The money was distributed in the form of ten cent tickets that were honored at various restaurants. A decent meal, Woods explained, would hopefully deter some of these men from lives of crime.[15]

Antidelinquency efforts in some cities led to experiments with juvenile police. In Cincinnati, for example, one boy, whose salary was paid by a city councilman, was assigned to keep other children from damaging trees on city property. The Council Bluffs, Iowa, "Boy Police" consisted of about 250 boys who actually had the authority to make arrests. In New York City, Arthur Woods created the "Junior Police" which enrolled as many as 6,000 boys between the ages of eleven and sixteen; the boys were given uniforms and required to take both military drills and first aid training.[16]

Adding juveniles to the police force, and giving them powers of arrest as was done in some instances, contradicted the main objectives of professionalization. It encumbered the department with a contingent of untrained amateurs who as yet had no definite career aspirations and could not be expected to take their assignments completely seriously.

The Introduction of Policewomen

One of the most significant innovations in the Progressive Era was the introduction of policewomen. Previously, police work had been an exclusively male occupation, pervaded by a masculine ethos of physical strength. The fact that police officers spent many hours in the station houses on reserve duty, and often slept there in dormitories, further reinforced the sense of a male fraternity. Women were not even considered for clerical jobs in the department; these and other soft assignments were reserved for the aged, the injured, and political

favorites. The introduction of women police officers was part of the crime prevention movement. Once the police began to think in terms of preventing juvenile
delinquency, they responded to the traditional argument that women had a
special capacity for child care. The first woman police officer was appointed
in 1905 and by 1915 there was a self-conscious and well-organized national
policewomen's movement. The history of the policewomen's movement provides
insight into the convergence of both the movements for police reform and
women's rights. The ultimate fate of the policewomen's movement also illuminates some of the most important problems in the police-as-social-workers idea.[17]

Women began to gain a small foothold in police departments in the nineteenth century as matrons in local jails. The police matrons movement prefigured
the subsequent policewomen's movement in its most important aspects. Both
were based on the idea that women were necessary for the proper handling of
female and juvenile offenders. In both cases, the primary impetus came from
private women's groups, not from police departments. Private groups provided
most of the initial personnel and, in some cases, paid their salaries. The earliest
recorded appointment of a police matron occurred in New York City in 1845.
The American Female Reform Society demanded and obtained the appointment
of matrons in the various city jails. The matron idea gained the status of a full-
fledged movement in the 1870s, largely under the leadership of the Women's
Christian Temperance Union (WCTU). The local chapter of the WCTU obtained
the appointment of police matrons in Portland, Maine, in 1877. At first the
WCTU paid the matron's entire salary; later the city paid half and eventually her
full salary. Through the 1880s the movement gained momentum. Matrons were
first appointed in Chicago in 1881, Boston in 1883, Philadelphia, Baltimore,
St. Louis and Milwaukee in 1884. By the 1890s police matrons were a feature
of most large city police departments. While in some cases women with social
work backgrounds were hired, in many cities (Chicago for example) the job was
reserved for the widows of deceased policemen.[18]

Gradually, the police matrons began to acquire wider responsibilities than
merely supervising female prisoners. The Baltimore police matrons, for example,
returned seventy-five lost children to their parents in 1885. And in 1893 Mrs.
Marie Owen, widow of a former policeman, was appointed to the detective
bureau of the Chicago police.

The first woman known to have held full police powers was Mrs. Lola
Baldwin in Portland, Oregon. Portland was the host city for the Lewis and
Clark Exposition in 1905. A number of women's civic organizations who were
increasingly active in the area of juvenile delinquency prevention expressed concern that the event would offer too many temptations for the children of
Portland. Consequently, Mrs. Baldwin, an official with the Traveller's Aid
Society, was given a temporary assignment with the police department. She
was responsible for organizing a Department of Public Safety for the Protection
of Young Girls and Women that was staffed by volunteer social workers. At the

request of Mrs. Baldwin these volunteers were to be called "operatives" or "workers" rather than police officers. Their crime prevention role was viewed as a distinct departure from the traditional police role.[19]

The experiment proved to be a success, as far as those involved were concerned, and when the Lewis and Clark Exposition ended, Mrs. Baldwin received a permanent appointment with the Portland police department. In 1909 the office was renamed the Women's Protective Division with a staff of three full-time operatives. Significantly, the division maintained its offices in the YMCA rather than at police headquarters until 1912, a practice that further enhanced the social work rather than the law enforcement image of these first women police.

Between 1905 and 1910 a small number of other police departments across the country copied the example set by Portland. The policewomen idea achieved the status of an organized and self-conscious movement in 1910 with the appointment of Mrs. Alice Stebbins Wells to the Los Angeles police department. Like Mrs. Baldwin, Mrs. Wells had a background in social work. She had attended a theological seminary in Connecticut and had held several church-related social work positions prior to her appointment in Los Angeles. The idea originated with several women's groups in the city who then presented the proposal to the police department. The department was then in the hands of a reform-minded administration and it accepted the idea of policewomen immediately. Mrs. Wells was assigned to care for young women in trouble with the law and to prevent delinquency among juveniles of both sexes. Although at first there was no separate women's or juvenile division, she was to report directly to the chief of police.[20]

Alice Stebbins Wells' most important activities were national rather than local in scope. Immediately after her appointment she emerged as the leader of the policewomen's movement. Her main interest was in spreading the idea of policewomen through an intensive speaking campaign. In 1911, for example, she delivered speeches in thirty-one cities in one thirty-day tour organized by the WCTU. She also carried her message to the conventions of national professional associations. She requested and was granted an opportunity to speak to the IACP in 1914 and also appeared before the National Conference of Charities and Corrections in 1914 and 1915. By 1916 at least sixteen cities had appointed policewomen. At the 1915 convention of the National Conference of Charities and Corrections, women representing twenty-two states organized the International Association of Policewomen. Not surprisingly, Mrs. Wells was elected president of the new organization which was designed to "act as a clearinghouse for compilation and dissemination of information on the work of women police, to aim for high standards of work and to promote the preventive and protective service by police departments." The following year, police matrons established their own organization, the International Association of Police Matrons, in a parallel drive for professional status.[21]

As had been the case with the appointment of the first police matrons, the policewomen's movement originated with private women's groups. On the national level, important support was given by such organizations as the National Conference of Charities and Corrections and the American Social Hygiene Association. The response of police departments varied widely. In some cases, Los Angeles for example, the idea was welcomed immediately. In other cities, however, the response ranged from ambivalence to outright hostility. Nor was it always the police department itself that led the opposition; frequently mayors and city councilmen were among the strongest opponents. The variety of the response was due to the fact that the policewomen's movement challenged a number of different established ideas and practices. On the one hand there was widespread opposition to creating such a new role for women. At the same time many police departments were not yet ready to undertake specialized anti-delinquency efforts.

For the most part, the policewomen's movement drew its strength from established reform movements and organizations. Such was the case in Chicago where the appointment of the first policewomen was a direct outgrowth of the juvenile court movement. In 1910 the chief justice of the Municipal Court appointed a committee of women social workers to explore further the problem of delinquency. The committee eventually recommended the appointment of policewomen and this suggestion was quickly adopted by both the mayor and the city council. The necessary legislation was passed in late 1912 and the first Chicago policewomen appointed in 1913.[22]

The appointment of the first policewomen in Cleveland, however, came only after an eight-year struggle. The campaign had its origins in two antivice efforts that began in 1910. Mayor Tom Johnson set out to eradicate prostitution and in 1915 finally closed the city's semiofficial vice district. The drive against prostitution resulted in a significant increase in the number of women arrested and this in turn stimulated interest in developing new procedures for handling female offenders. In a parallel development, a group of civic reformers began in 1911 to inspect the dance halls in the city. This was part of a growing national concern about dance halls as the centers of vice and the breeding grounds of delinquency. A team of volunteers, many of them protestant ministers, systematically inspected the Cleveland dance halls. The effort received indirect official support; funds were provided by the mayor's office and some of the volunteer inspectors were eventually deputized by the police department.[23]

A highly publicized murder in 1916 aroused public opinion and launched the policewomen's movement in Cleveland. A sixteen-year-old girl was strangled to death by an employee of a well-known men's club. Civic reformers used this incident to dramatize their argument that there should be some means of protecting young women from the dangers that lurked in the city. They soon organized a Women's Protective Association and raised funds to employ a "Special Investigator." The investigator was assigned to "protective" work which meant seeking out young women and offering them counsel and guidance. The association deliberately chose the title of Special Investigator out of fear that "policewoman" would arouse too much opposition.

When the Women's Protective Association subsequently petitioned city government for the appointment of regular policewomen it encountered strong opposition. In 1917 the city council rejected a bill to create a separate Women's Bureau in the police department and to employ twenty-nine policewomen. Agitation lapsed during World War I but resumed again in 1921. The mayor expressed some interest in employing policewomen that year but left office without taking any action. Two years later the Women's Protective Association intensified its campaign and brought in representatives from the American Social Hygiene Association to help lobby. Finally in 1923 the city council authorized the employment of policewomen. But the public safety director opposed the idea and refused to make any appointments. Later that year the Mayor appointed the first four policewomen on his own authority.

Even in reform-minded Cleveland, then, the struggle for policewomen took eight years. As was the case in many other cities the campaign was largely the work of private women's groups and was intimately related to efforts to eliminate prostitution and delinquency. Opposition arose not only from within the police department, but from elected public officials as well.

The movement in Boston took almost as long. In 1912 the White Slave Traffic Commission recommended the appointment of policewomen in a report to the legislature on the prostitution question. Policewomen, it was believed, would help prevent young women from becoming prostitutes. Two years later, after a concerted lobbying effort, the legislature authorized cities in the state to hire policewomen. World War I intervened, however, and apparently no action was taken. As in Cleveland, the campaign revived after the war. In 1920 the legislature passed the Boston Policewomen's Act and the first six women were appointed in early 1921.[24]

Policewomen were obtained for Baltimore rather easily. Lobbying began in 1912 and the leader of the movement presented a bill she had drafted to both Republican and Democratic leaders in the legislature. At first, neither side was willing to sponsor the bill. Some legislators were "shocked and astonished" at the idea of women wearing police uniforms, patrolling the streets and "arresting negroes and drunken men." The spokeswomen for the policewomen's movement quickly indicated that this was a misunderstanding. They explained that "the women would not be uniformed, not have 'beats,' but that women and children in the community would be in their care." Thus reassured, the legislators quickly passed the necessary legislation.[25]

The policewomen's movement was a struggle on two fronts. It was both an effort to create a new specialized function for the police and to create a new role for women. The Baltimore episode indicates the extent to which leaders of the movement stressed the traditional image of the woman as guardian of children in their effort to overcome opposition. The entire movement, in fact, based itself on a rather conservative ideology. Mary Hamilton, the first police-woman in New York City and the author of an important book on the subject, argued that "in many ways the position of a woman in a police department is not unlike that of a mother in a home. Just as the mother smooths out the rough places, looks after the children and gives a timely word of warning, advice or encouragement, so the policewoman fulfills her duty." Louis Brownlow wrote in the *Policewoman's International Bulletin* that "The policewoman after all is a woman and she believes in house cleaning." Even this traditional point of view was not sufficient to overcome all opposition. Mary Hamilton reported that in at least one large Connecticut city conservative women's groups successfully blocked the policewomen idea.[26]

As a new venture for women, the policewomen's movement was an exciting concept. Mary Hamilton argued that it was a "chance for women with ideas and initiative to do constructive, pioneer work—to make history in fact." The policewomen's movement was indeed an important chapter in the history of the American police. It was an important expression of the new idea of crime prevention and the first step towards the creation of specialized juvenile bureaus in most police departments. The antidelinquency effort provided the entering wedge for women in police work. As Mary Hamilton pointed out, it was not until the crime prevention idea came to the fore that "the need for policewomen arose." The reliance upon the traditional child-raising role of the woman, while an opportunistic stroke at first, eventually proved to be a mistake. As we later see, it relegated policewomen to a narrow role and eventual second-class status in police work.[27]

The actual duties of policewomen differed significantly from those of male police officers. Alice Stebbins Wells sought to reassure the delegates to the 1914 IACP convention by advising that "we should understand thoroughly that the policewoman is not going to take the place of the policeman." Policewomen were assigned to patrol places of amusement where juveniles gathered. "Her chief duties," according to Chloe Owings, "comprised the supervision and the enforcement of laws concerning dance halls, skating rinks, penny arcades, picture shows and other similar places of public recreation. Among her activities were the suppression of unwholesome billboard displays, searching for missing persons, and the maintenance of a general information bureau for women seeking advice on matters within the scope of police departments." Policewomen did not wear uniforms for two reasons. On the one hand it removed any suggestion that they were usurping the traditional police role and, at the same time, it facilitated their investigative work.[28]

The mandate given policewomen was extremely broad and vaguely worded, opening the door to a number of legal problems. Eleanor Hutzel, director of the policewomen's unit in Detroit and the author of an important manual of instruction, defined the policewoman's responsibilities in the following terms:

"a patrol problem may be defined as any situation, arising in a public place, that is potentially harmful to a woman or child." This, of course, called for the broad exercise of discretion on the part of the policewoman. The policewoman's movement, meanwhile, was pervaded by a strongly moralistic and middle-class ethos. Frequently, pleasure itself was equated with vice. Mary Hamilton wrote, "Danger lurks in parks, playgrounds, beaches, piers, and baths unless there is someone to watch over these pleasure haunts experienced enough in recognizing a devastating evil, however well disguised."[29]

The result was an enormous extension of the power of the police to intervene in the lives of children and young women. Eleanor Hutzel, describing patrol duty, argued that "one of the most important crime prevention functions of the policewoman is to discover young girls who are in hazardous situations and to take appropriate action before they become a problem to the community." In actual practice this meant taking the child into protective custody. Assuming custody over a child who had not committed an actual offense raised a legal problem. In 1925 Mina Van Winkle of the District of Columbia police was taken to court over the detention of a minor. The court ruled in her favor, however, and thereafter, policewomen felt confident that their actions were justified. A 1945 manual of instruction, for example, declared unambiguously that the policewoman "should not hesitate to take such action through fear of any violation of civil liberties. Her legal right to follow this procedure has been upheld by the courts." This aspect of the policewomen's movement was the most explicit statement and justification of the expansion of social control inherent in the crime prevention idea.[30]

The policewoman's patrol duties were seen as an alternative to traditional police work in several respects. Many women argued that the policewoman would lend a gentler and more attractive image to the police department by offering counsel and guidance in situations where male police officers might make arrests. Mary Hamilton described a situation where young boys were playing baseball in the street. Rather than make an arrest, or chase them away with his billy club, as the male police officer might do, the policewoman would take the boys aside, point out the dangers of playing in the street, and perhaps suggest some other more constructive activity. At most, she would issue a strong warning. This view of police work carried a high presumption about the efficacy of such advice in changing the habits of young boys. The leaders of the policewomen's movement, however, were anything but modest in judging their potential for good works.[31]

Many police officials were attracted to the idea of policewomen because they felt they would greatly assist in traditional criminal investigation activities. Female victims and offenders alike were more willing to talk with a policewoman than a male officer. The Los Angeles police department reported that because policewomen reduced the embarrassment of discussing "matters of an immoral nature . . . many more such cases are reported to this department than formerly." At the same time, policewomen could interrogate females without raising any questions of possible improper conduct by the department. It relieved male officers of responsibility for delicate investigations and was, therefore, "a protection to the department."

The new crime prevention role of the policewoman also dramatized the issue of training. Mrs. Wells pointed out that "when we realize that police work is unlike any other work previously done by women, we at once realize that there is not a ready-made body [of knowledge and experience] from which to draw." She might have added that there was no body of knowledge and experience among male police officers either. The crime prevention role and juvenile delinquency work were both new activities for the police. Because of its close association with the social work profession, which was undergoing a vigorous professionalization process itself at that time, the policewomen's movement set rather high standards of education and training. The Committee on Qualifications of the International Association of Policewomen proposed that women police officers should have at least a high school diploma, with additional college-level training, preferably in "recognized schools of social work." Moreover, "women police should have at least two years of social casework experience in a recognized agency with preference given to those who have had, in addition, administrative or executive responsibility in social service, in public affairs, or in business."[32]

The result was a clear double standard for policewomen. Except in isolated instances such as Berkeley, California, college education for male police officers was unheard of. Most police officers lacked even a high school diploma, and in the mid-1920s leaders of the IACP were still seriously proposing that the minimum entry requirement for police officers be merely the ability to read and write English. A number of college and university programs, often associated with schools of social work, began to appear to offer training for policewomen. In 1918 the Southern Division of the University of California (the future UCLA) offered a special summer session organized and directed by Alice Stebbins Wells. In October 1922 the Boston School of Public Service, in association with Simmons College, offered a regular five-month curriculum for policewomen. That same year, the New York City police academy became the first police unit to offer specialized training for policewomen. This program supplemented the offerings of the New York School of Social Work which had been organized with the aid of the American Social Hygiene Association.[33]

The careers of the leading policewomen suggest that they did far exceed male police officers in terms of educational qualifications. Mrs. Wells had attended a theological seminary while Mary Hamilton had attended the New York University School of Philanthropy prior to her appointment as the chief policewoman in New York. In the mid-1930s, meanwhile, five of the top six officers of the California Policewomen's Association had some college education. One held a law degree, two were trained nurses, and two others had at least attended college.[34]

The double standard that developed for policewomen meant not only that they were expected to have considerably higher educational levels, but also that they could expect to be paid less than the average male patrolman. The 1915 survey by the U.S. Census Office indicated that most of the cities with policewomen specified a separate and lower pay scale for them. In Chicago, for example, male patrolmen began at $900 a year and eventually rose to $1320, while policewomen remained fixed at $900. The three San Francisco policewomen were paid $1200, compared with the $1464 paid the 765 male patrolmen. In a few cases, Baltimore for example, salaries nearly approximated the top salaries of patrolmen.[35]

The policewomen's movement enjoyed a period of vigorous growth from 1910 until the mid-1920s. At that point, however, it stagnated and gradually fell into almost total eclipse. The decline of the movement was the result of several factors. In part it was the result of the ideological limits that the leaders had imposed from the beginning. At the same time, the dominant definition of police professionalism underwent an important change. The social work emphasis of policewomen's work fell steadily out of touch with the rising emphasis on the crime-fighting orientation of professionalism. The decline of the policewomen's movement provides insight into the difficulties of giving a specific definition to social work-oriented police work.

By 1916 the number of police departments with policewomen was at least sixteen and perhaps as many as forty (the various available surveys differ). By 1919 the figure had risen to about sixty. A comprehensive survey in 1925, meanwhile, revealed that 145 cities had at least one policewoman. The International Association of Policewomen continued to thrive. With the aid of a number of wealthy benefactors it published its *Bulletin*, an impressive professional journal with extensive articles on the state of policewomen's work. In the mid-1920s, however, the movement lost its momentum and experienced almost no growth for the next four decades.[36]

Events in New York City provide some insight into the decline of the movement. As early as 1924, Mary Hamilton sensed an emerging "crisis in the history of policewomen's endeavors." The heart of the problem was simply that of defining the specific duties for policewomen. The location of the policewomen's unit in the police department bureaucracy was an important part of the problem. In 1921 the New York City police opened a special Women's Precinct, the first of its kind in the country. An old police station house at 434 West 37th Street was renovated for the purpose and redecorated to look "more like a charming club house for girls than an old-time police station." Mrs. Hamilton pointed out that this non–law enforcement image represented "the very essence of the principles for which the modern policewoman should stand." The isolation of policewomen's activities, however, created a major problem. The Women's Precinct soon "became more or less of a routine complaint bureau, to which men and women alike were assigned." Henrietta Additon of the Philadelphia Big Sisters Association also complained in 1924 that the precise role of the policewoman "has always been undefined and vague and as a result, the office of the policewoman has often been the dumping grounds for an assortment of miscellaneous duties."[37]

The creation of separate units within the police department for policewomen had been one of the main goals of the movement. At its 1923 convention the International Association of Policewomen adopted a resolution to the effect that "where women are employed in a police department they shall function in one unit as a Women's Bureau and shall have a woman in charge who shall be known as the Director of the Women's Bureau and shall be immediately responsible to the Chief of Police, . . . and shall have rank equal with other such officers as are immediately subordinate to him." By 1925 at least eight cities, including New York, Detroit, Cleveland, Indianapolis, and Washington, D.C., had created women's bureaus. The alternative approach was simply to assign the policewomen to another unit in the department—in most cases this was the detective bureau. Both approaches had their pitfalls. The separate women's bureau, as Mary Hamilton discovered in New York, easily became a miscellaneous complaint bureau. To place the policewomen in the detective bureau, or some other unit, however, risked losing the special identity of policewomen's work.[38]

The decline of the policewomen's movement was also the result of an ideological stagnation. By emphasizing a traditional child-rearing role for women police the leaders of the movement created an intellectual trap: policewomen became permanently assigned to a second-class status within the police department. Significantly, no new leaders emerged in subsequent decades to challenge the ideas of the founding generation and to demand a broader role for policewomen. Indeed, a process of bureaucratic ossification seems to have set in. By the 1930s women police officers seemed content to preserve rather than attempt to extend their special niche. The idea of juvenile protective work itself lost much of its intellectual excitement. What had been a bold and innovative idea in 1910 had become a routine, bureaucratized activity by the mid-1920s. Moreover, the social base of support for the policewomen's movement also changed significantly in the 1920s. The pages of the *Policewomen's International Bulletin* clearly indicated that the movement was increasingly sponsored by wealthy and conservative women's groups such as the Daughters of the American Revolution. The *Bulletin* itself was supported by one wealthy individual and, when she died, publication ceased.[39]

By the 1930s the policewomen's movement was not merely stagnating, it was actually losing ground, intellectually and organizationally. The intellectual problem was the fact that police professionalism acquired a new meaning. Under the leadership of August Vollmer (whose perspective began to change), O. W. Wilson, and J. Edgar Hoover, professionalism came to mean a combination of managerial efficiency, technological sophistication, and an emphasis on crime fighting. The social work aspects of policing—the idea of rehabilitative work—which had been central to the policewomen's movement fell into almost total eclipse. The result was a severe identity crisis for policewomen as they were caught between a social work orientation and a law enforcement ideology.

The reports of the Philadelphia police department's juvenile division in the 1950s offer a vivid picture of this identity crisis. The *Philadelphia Policewoman* argued that "policewomen need not, perhaps should not be, social workers as was stated. Police duties are clearly defined by law, and the primary responsibility of policewomen involves law enforcement." Yet, the activities of the division were clearly social work in orientation. Women officers were described as having "case loads" of between ten and sixty juveniles, while the division's director relied heavily on moralistic rhetoric with frequent citations from Biblical scripture.[40]

An extensive survey in 1946 revealed that only 141 out of 417 major cities employed policewomen, a figure that represented almost no growth whatsoever in two decades. Policewomen had not even made any significant gains during the World War II manpower shortage. Matters worsened even further in the 1950s and early 1960s. What can only be characterized as a male counterattack challenged the idea that policewomen should be supervised by a female officer. The two most important police administration textbooks from the period barely even mentioned women police. O. W. Wilson's *Police Administration*, widely regarded as the bible on the subject, advanced a blatantly antifemale argument. In the 1963 edition Wilson argued that while women could be of some value in juvenile work and other specialized tasks, a woman was not qualified to head the juvenile unit. A male police officer would have wider experience, would understand the activities of the other units and, therefore, would be better able to secure their cooperation. Moreover, men were "less likely to become irritable and overcritical under emotional stress" and were more effective as administrators.[41]

By the early 1960s, then, policewomen occupied an extremely marginal place in American policing. The policewomen's movement as such was completely exhausted. Not until the late 1960s did the policewomen's movement revive. For reasons that had almost nothing to do with the earlier movement, women police officers began to demand and win an equal role as patrol officers. We shall examine that development in the context of the upheaval in police administration in the 1960s. The earlier history of the policewomen's movement stands as a case study of the high hopes and ultimate frustration of social work-oriented police reform in the Progressive Era.[42]

Rehabilitating Adults: The Golden Rule Policy and the Sunrise Court

Juveniles were the major focus of the crime prevention idea, but police reformers also devoted attention to the job of rehabilitating adult offenders.

Fred Kohler, chief of the Cleveland police, became the leading advocate of two significant innovations in police procedures in the first decade of the twentieth century. Both the golden rule policy and the sunrise court were humanitarian-based attempts to divert adult offenders from the criminal justice system. Although Kohler did not use the contemporary terminology of *decriminalization* and *diversion* his innovations reflected an identical orientation. Kohler's reforms raised many of the same problems raised by other rehabilitation-oriented innovations. They called for the exercise of considerable discretionary judgment and opened the door for arbitrary and discriminatory action.

Fred Kohler was a colorful and fascinating character. Among the leading police reformers he was one of the few who had risen from the rank of patrolman to a position of executive responsibility. The son of German-born parents, he entered policing only after several attempts at small business ventures had failed. At age fourteen he became apprenticed to his father as a stone cutter. When his father died six years later he assumed control of the business. It eventually failed, as did a grocery store a few years later. Then at age twenty-five, in 1889, he used his political contacts in the local Republican Party to obtain a job with the Cleveland police department. He was promoted to sergeant in 1897, lieutenant in 1898, and captain in 1900. In 1903 Cleveland's reform mayor Tom Johnson appointed him chief of police.[43]

Even as a sergeant, Kohler established a reputation for vigorous, often arbitrary, and partisan activity. During an 1896 strike, for example, he personally escorted nonunion workers to and from their jobs. In 1897 and 1898 he served as a major campaign worker for a Republican aspirant for the Senate and even used patrolmen under his command to break up political meetings of his opponents. Kohler also established a reputation for vigorous opposition to prostitution and gambling. He was regarded an "uncontrollable" in the police department for his sudden and frequently unauthorized raids on vice dens. Fred Kohler brought the same attributes to his job as police chief. He acted from an instinctive, common sense notion of justice and rarely bothered to consult with the proper authorities when he effected a major change in police policy. Needless to say, his career as chief was stormy and he was eventually removed amid charges of corruption.

Kohler inaugurated his golden rule policy in 1908. As he explained it to the IACP delegates, he was troubled by the high volume of arrests that the police made each year: "I couldn't see that these wholesale arrests did any good. The number of them did not diminish; it increased. And I found not only that the arrests did not produce good results; they did harm. They brought disgrace, humiliation and suffering to countless innocent persons in no way responsible for the acts of a thoughtless, careless, mischievous, or even, if you will, a malicious first offender." Kohler expressed particular compassion for the families of offenders. "I found daily at police stations relatives and friends in tears seeking the release of some prisoner. . . . In Police Court next day I saw old and feeble parents, weeping wives with crying babies in their arms, and very often children clinging at their sides—all there to witness the degradation of those they loved. And what was the result? A hasty trial, and since the offense was usually trivial, the prisoners was discharged. Good! But all that suffering was in vain."[44]

Meeting with the various captains in the department, Chief Kohler set forth the principles that would guide the new golden rule policy. "First—juveniles were never to be placed in prison. They were to be taken home or the parents sent for and the child turned over to them for parental correction." Police officers were also directed to try to resolve domestic disputes without resorting to arrest: "Second—the members of the force were to use their kindly efforts in easing the friction and ill-temper between man and man, wherever and whenever it made itself manifest." The heart of the golden rule policy was found in the fourth recommendation: "That some men fall through some unfortunate circumstances and are not criminal at heart, and should be treated accordingly, in which case the best results might be accomplished with a well-applied reprimand." The Cleveland police, using "the least show or display or authority," should treat many adult offenders in the same manner that policewomen were to handle juveniles: to detain them and release them with perhaps only a mild warning.

To use contemporary terminology, Kohler simply decriminalized a number of offenses in the city of Cleveland. The golden rule policy which went into effect on January 1, 1908, dramatically reduced the number of people arrested for drunkenness and disorderly conduct. The total number of arrests dropped from 30,418 in 1907 to 10,085 in 1908, a decline of 66.8 percent. Kohler argued that the policy was not only more humane but that it enhanced the efficiency of the department. Since they did not bother with trivial offenses, there was more time to concentrate on serious crime. "Don't you think it was better to devote more time to the habitual criminal," Kohler asked, "and the more serious violators against the law, as we have done?" Based on his calculation that it cost the city over $52,000 to process the 10,085 arrests in 1908, he claimed to have saved the city an enormous amount of money.

The golden rule policy of merely issuing warnings to certain offenders was accompanied by the so-called sunrise court. First introduced in 1905, the sunrise court was designed to release "at an early hour all honest working people." Offenders who had been detained overnight were "released on waivers so they could return to their homes in plenty of time to prepare for, and be at their work on time, and not have to appear in court to be humiliated and embarrassed, causing them to lose their day's pay and perhaps their positions, which would mean a hardship to their innocent wives and children." To obtain his release the individual was required to sign Police Department Form #15 which stated: "Having been arrested for _____ I hereby admit my guilt of the violation charged against me and I request that I be immediately released from custody without being held for trial, that no affidavit be fixed or warrant issued against me. I sign this of my own free will and under no duress."[45]

Although Fred Kohler was the most prominent advocate of the golden rule and the sunrise court, enthusiastically describing it in addresses to the IACP, Cleveland was not the only city to experiment with them. Toledo, Ohio, under reform mayor "Golden Rule" Jones, went a step further by taking billy clubs away from police officers during the daytime. Along with the golden rule policy this was designed to improve the public image of the police department. In Detroit, under reform mayor Hazen Pingree, the "golden rule drunk" policy effected a drop in the number of arrests equal to that in Cleveland. The Los Angeles sunrise court, meanwhile, was run by private citizens, notably the temperance leader Tom Murphy. Drunks were provided with a sanitary fountain for washing and offered hot black coffee. Murphy claimed that it was "a big step toward the progressive advancement of educational temperance." Chicago under Mayor Carter Harrison in 1912 offered a somewhat different version of the golden rule: "vagrants and panhandlers were given so many hours in which to get out of town" or face arrest.[46]

Although well intentioned, the golden rule and the sunrise court both raised obvious problems. First, Kohler was criticized for arbitrarily changing public law enforcement policy without consulting any elected officials. One city official complained that "the Chief of Police, without consulting with us, has seen fit to modify the policy of the department in respect to the arrest of those charged with minor offenses." "A radical change should not have been made without at least holding consultation with us," argued a member of the Board of Public Safety. But that was Kohler's style of administration: to make a decision based on his own instinctive feelings and to put it into effect immediately; he was not one to be troubled with the formalities of bureaucratic procedure.[47]

To a certain extent Kohler's golden rule policy was nothing more than an effort to formalize the exercise of discretion that is inherent in police work. Kohler said, "I determined to have my policemen use their best human instincts. I proposed that my men should exercise that discretion which the judges did not always exercise." Having brought the issue of discretion to the level of public debate, however, Kohler encountered some criticism. In a thoughtful critique published in *The Outlook*, William J. Norton pointed out that despite the obvious virtues of the policy, "there is another side to the argument, of course. . . ." Norton pointed out that the courts operated under a system of formal guidelines and procedures. But under the golden rule policy, "the Chief of Police and his assistants supplant [this] without any system. . . ."[48]

Norton's point was well taken. There was nothing to prevent the exercise of discretion from becoming wholly arbitrary (although this criticism was equally applicable to the courts and to traditional police practice). The sunrise court was particularly troublesome. The waiver form in effect meant that the individual admitted his guilt without the benefit of trial. Morover, the accumulated waiver forms in the desk of the chief of police were a source of potential trouble. Norton conceded that Kohler was "one of the ablest Chiefs of Police in America," but pointed out that "one may readily see how, in the hands of a less scrupulous man than Chief Kohler, it might become an agent of blackmail." The political uses that J. Edgar Hoover in later years made of confidential FBI information suggests that Norton's fears were not unfounded.

That the golden rule policy was enforced in a discriminatory manner was clearly evident in Kohler's attitude toward vagrants. In Cleveland, as in Chicago, many individuals who were deemed "undesirable" were simply chased out of town. In the summer of 1908, for example, Kohler had the police round up "habitual mendicants and vagrants" and transported out of town. In one particular raid more than 300 men were rounded up, taken to police headquarters, and they "informed us where their homes were and promised, that if allowed to go, they would return to their native cities. The police conveyed them out of the city in the direction of their homes." Vagrants who were dumped in the neighboring villages of East Cleveland and Lakewood, however, were often rounded up by the police there and simply shipped back into Cleveland. Kohler's compassion was defined by a social class bias. The "deserving" poor and those regularly employed qualified for better treatment—the sunrise court, after all, was designed primarily for men with jobs and families. The unemployed man, however, risked either jail or deportation from the city.[49]

Suppressing the Social Evil

In his effort to use the police as an instrument of social reform, Chief Kohler also attacked the problem of prostitution, or as it was generally called, the "social evil." In this endeavor Kohler acted in his characteristically dramatic and arbitrary manner. The significance of Kohler's actions lay in the fact that it was part of a nationwide campaign against prostitution in the second decade of the century. An important but neglected aspect of that struggle was the role played by police departments in determining public policy. In city after city police chiefs were deeply involved in the policymaking process. The annual conventions of the IACP, meanwhile, featured vigorous debates between the advocates of toleration and suppression. The antiprostitution crusade which climaxed during World War I years forms an important chapter in the history of the police and their relationship to social problems.

As historian Roy Lubove has argued, "In the decade following 1907 urban America engaged in a spectacular vice crusade. Prostitution in general and 'white slavery' in particular became the objects of a nationwide campaign of expose and repression." The antiprostitution effort was intimately related to many other Progressive Era reforms. The leaders of the movement saw themselves helping to conserve the nation's resources and they directed much of their attention at the related problems of low wages, poor housing, and the lack of adequate recreational facilities in the city. Lubove observes that "the vice crusader tended to support a wide variety of liberal reforms." The final report of the Chicago Vice Commission, for example, stressed the fact that young women could not earn a decent living on the prevailing wages for domestic work.[50]

The extent of open prostitution in American cities at the turn of the century was truly remarkable by today's standards. In most large cities there were as many as several hundred known houses of prostitution. Richard Sylvester reported at least 200 in the District of Columbia; there were an estimated 247 in Pittsburgh and nearly as many in Cleveland. The Chicago Vice Commission estimated that there were at least 5,000 prostitutes working full time in the city, and that the business generated profits in excess of $15,000,000 annually.[51]

Prostitution flourished openly because most cities through the nineteenth century adopted a policy of toleration, either officially or unofficially. The protection of prostitution, meanwhile, comprised one of the most important aspects of police corruption. Whatever the intent of the law, the police tolerated and drew sizeable payoffs for organized vice. Some cities made toleration official policy and attempted to segregate prostitution in a particular sector of the city and to regulate it. In Cincinnati, for example, prostitutes were examined by physicians and licensed to practice their trade by the city. Each woman was inspected once a week and either granted a certificate of health or referred to the hospital for treatment. The proprietors of houses, meanwhile, were required to report new women to the police immediately. Liquor was permitted, but there was to be no music after midnight. Philip Dietsch, chief of the Cincinnati police, defended his policy before the IACP in 1901. He suggested that they "locate all houses in certain parts of your city and place them under strict police surveillance." He questioned whether the police could deal with the broader social problem of vice: "Do you, gentlemen, think the police may solve the problem? I doubt it very much." And he argued for a policy of regulated segregation as the most practical alternative.[52]

Many police chiefs also argued that a policy of segregation facilitated their law enforcement duties. James Doyle, superintendent of the Minneapolis police, argued in favor of "confining the disorderly elements into a compact and easily patrolled district." Prostitutes were widely used as police informants and it was believed that criminals tended to congregate in the vice districts and, therefore, were more easily apprehended. The author of a major national survey of the prostitution question pointed out that "the old type of policeman is generally in favor of segregation, because it enabled him to keep track of prostitutes in a rapid and convenient manner." There were also important practical arguments against suppression from a law enforcement perspective. As reformers in Chicago and other cities discovered to their dismay, the closing of the vice district only served to spread the practice of prostitution throughout the city to areas where it had not existed before. Chief Haver of the Memphis police told the IACP delegates that "the efficient way is to aggregate that which you cannot deny or destroy."[53]

As the antiprostitution movement gained momentum in the first decade of the century, police chiefs were caught up in the midst of a major social policy question. The debates at the IACP conventions were not only vigorous but were also conducted on an extremely sophisticated level. In an address to the 1907 IACP convention, Fred Kohler outlined the different options available. Essentially there were three alternatives: "First, official toleration; second, attempted supression by crusade; and, third, police repression." Kohler rejected the first alternative because it "could not be followed by a police administration seeking the end of civic decency." He also rejected the idea of an organized moral crusade, arguing that it had been tried and proven to be a failure: "The results are rather to scatter the social poison throughout the whole body of the city, and to cause it to hide itself from police knowledge and interference in neighborhoods and communities theretofore unpolluted."[54]

The most effective policy, Kohler argued, was something he called police repression and which he had implemented in Cleveland in 1905. He did not defend it as "a general principle of government," but simply as "the only practical method of genuine enforcement." There was a certain amount of wisdom in Kohler's attempt to develop a reasonable compromise between extremes, but in practice his police repression was highly arbitrary and involved questionable practices. Kohler directed his patrolmen to station themselves at the entrances to known houses of prostitution "to secure the names of visitors [and] their businesses." The object, of course, was to intimidate patrons with potential embarrassment. The possibility of outright blackmail was also not lost on potential customers. The police also undertook a selective enforcement of various city ordinances. Kohler pointed out that "We invariably refuse all permits to saloons in the tenderloin district [and] to saloons kept by or catering to disreputable characters, granting all others unless an objection is made by the police or some person residing in the vicinity." Meanwhile, "owners of low dives have been ordered to close up their places of business, and where the order was not complied with, a uniformed detail was established in front of such places." He also placed "under strict police surveillance" those cafes "frequented by females."[55]

Clearly, Kohler's approach to the prostitution question involved the same kind of arbitrary decisions as did the golden rule policy and the sunrise court. The definition of a "disreputable" saloon was vague to say the least. Nor was there evidence that Kohler enforced city ordinances in an impartial manner throughout the city. The stationing of police officers outside cafes frequented by women was also an unwarranted form of police harrassment. In the end, Kohler's police repression approach was little more than an attempt to limit prostitution by means of harrassment. Kohler boasted in his 1905 annual report that his campaign had succeeded and that prostitution and gambling "have been so far suppressed or regulated that to the general public they are a nonexistent question." This was an exaggeration, of course, and the prostitution question remained a major issue in Cleveland for more than another ten years.

Mayor Tom Johnson stepped up his antiprostitution effort in 1910 and in 1915, two years after Kohler had been removed as police chief, attempted to close down the vice district altogether.[56]

The intensified campaign in Cleveland was part of an antivice crusade that began in 1907 and reached its peak around 1913. A survey by the American Social Hygiene Association revealed that between 1893 and 1917 at least seventy-eight cities had adopted a policy of repression; that included fifteen cities in 1912 and twenty-four cities in 1913. The *National Municipal Review* in 1916 reported that the segregated districts had been closed in Baltimore, St. Louis, Cleveland, and Lexington, Kentucky. The work of a Morals Efficiency Commission in Pittsburgh, meanwhile, reduced the number of open houses from 247 to 65, and the number of professional prostitutes from 1,000 to 342. Patronage, meanwhile, was down an estimated 80 percent. While for the most part the campaign against prostitution originated with non-law enforcement professionals (social workers, doctors, women's groups, etc.), a significant number of police chiefs also took up the cause. In an important respect, the policy of repression was consistent with emerging notions of professionalism. For some, the idea of professionalism, of being dedicated to high ideals, dictated a policy of full enforcement of the laws. The practice of toleration, whatever its practical advantages, was tainted by its close identification with traditional patterns of police corruption. J. L. Beavers, chief of the Atlanta police, summed up this point of view when he told the 1913 IACP convention that "none of us are wholly free from guilt who permit this open shame [of prostitution] . . . we become parties to it and we, in a degree, are as guilty as they are." He concluded by asking "how can any decent man say that he is in favor of public prostitution, or a public indecency, for a public indecency it is."[57]

Antiprostitution reformers discovered to their dismay that the problem was not easily eliminated. Investigators in New York and Chicago discovered once again how intimate was the relationship between the police and organized vice. The report of the Chicago Vice Commission was particularly revealing about law enforcement practices at the level of the beat patrolman. The typical cases described in the report included many of the following: "Investigator was solicited by Minnie to go upstairs. Saw two officers Nos. (X578) and (X579) drinking beer in this place"; "November 20th . . . Wabash Avenue . . . prostitutes solicit in the rear room. On this date, officer in uniform (X599), came in and asked for beer and cigars, for which he did not pay." Consequently, many reformers proposed taking responsibility for enforcement of the prostitution laws out of the hands of the police altogether. The report of the New York Citizens Commission recommended the "separation of the control of the vices from the constabulary forces of the police so that the regular police shall no longer be responsible for their control and shall be left to their original function of preserving peace and order." The Chicago Vice Commission recommended the establishment of a separate "Morals Commission of the City of Chicago," which presumably would be a social work agency clothed with police powers. Similar recommendations were made in Pittsburgh and Minneapolis and the idea was endorsed by Leonard Fuld in his 1909 text, *Police Administration*. The idea of a separate antivice agency was but another instance in which reformers, frustrated by their inability to control the municipal police, thought in terms of creation of an entirely new agency.[58]

World War I proved to be a major turning point in the crusade against prostitution. Bolstered by a sense of national emergency and an extraordinary accretion of power by the federal government, reformers were able to bring considerable new pressure to bear against organized prostitution. The ostensible justification for federal action was the protection of the health of soldiers. Significantly, reformers who had been active in municipal reform, and police reform in particular, directed the federal government's antiprostitution drive.

Secretary of War Newton D. Baker had previously been involved in closing down the vice district in Cleveland when he served as mayor there. He brought similar concerns to his new job in Washington. In 1916 he became alarmed over lurid reports of appalling conditions in military camps along the Mexican border. He then hired Raymond B. Fosdick to conduct an investigation of the situation. Fosdick represented the link between vice reform and police reform. His 1914 study, *European Police Systems*, had been suggested to him and ultimately funded by John D. Rockefeller, Jr., through the American Social Hygiene Association. Fosdick reported that "what I found in that five-week trip was recorded in my confidential report to the Secretary of War. It was an almost unrelieved story of army camps surrounded by growing batteries of saloons and houses of prostitution." In response to the report, Baker appointed Fosdick chairman of the Commission on Training Camp Activities. Under Sections 12 and 13 of the Military Conscription Act, which prohibited the sale of liquor to men in uniform and which gave the president the power to ban prostitution around military camps, Fosdick's Commission waged a strong antivice crusade. In this respect, the war effort marked the fulfillment of many aspects of the Progressive Era. Armed with unprecedented federal powers, reformers were able to attack prostitution, the liquor problem, housing conditions, and the lack of adequate recreational facilities. The war did not destroy the progressive movement, it helped to fulfill it.[59]

By the end of 1917 Fosdick was able to claim that "every red light district in the United States had been closed—a hundred and ten of them." One member of the commission argued that the military camps "are national universities—training schools to which the flower of American youth is being sent." The attack on prostitution and venereal disease was justified under the slogan "Fit to Fight" and the argument that "Men must live straight if they would shoot straight."

Certainly the most remarkable extension of federal power occurred in Philadelphia where, for all practical purposes, the military took control over the police department. In April 1918 the Commission on Training Camp Activities issued a report charging that "the police have been in collusion with wrongdoers" in the city and that organized prostitution was flourishing with official toleration. Secretary of the Navy Daniels distributed copies of the report to both the mayor and the governor of Pennsylvania in an effort to get some action taken. The next day Philadelphia Public Safety Director William H. Wilson ordered the police to clean up the city in forty-eight hours, although he denied that conditions were as bad as the commission's report had suggested. Individual officers who failed to enforce the law faced immediate dismissal from the police force.[60]

Unsatisfied with the progress made by the police department in the following three weeks, the navy effectively took control of the situation. Secretary Daniels dispatched Lieutenant Colonel Charles B. Hatch to Philadelphia to take charge. Meanwhile, Mayor Smith ordered Police Superintendent James B. Robinson to take a thirty-day vacation and appointed Captain William B. Mills acting superintendent. Mills and Hatch worked together closely. Hatch said, "I told Captain Mills that he is acting for the government and that I will back him in everything he does . . . . We intend to see, however, that young men in the service are protected and that evil resorts are wiped out." Meanwhile, the press headlined "Federal Control of the Police in Philadelphia" despite denials from the mayor and other city officials. Reportedly, hundreds of women left the city in the first day of the federally supported suppression drive. Hatch himself took a walking tour of the vice district twelve hours after taking command and found it "quiet as a tomb."

The suppression of prostitution in Philadelphia, in any event, was temporary. In 1923 General Smedley Butler of the U.S. Marines was brought in as public safety director largely to eradicate prostitution. The 1918 episode demonstrated the extent to which reformers were willing to overturn established precedents in order to achieve their objectives. The federal control of the Philadelphia police in 1918, however limited and brief, was a disturbing precedent.[61]

Cops as Social Workers: Critique from the Old Guard

Not all police officials in the Progressive Era believed either in the ideals of professionalism or the idea that the police should play a leading role in social reform. Attacks on reformers were frequently voiced in debates at the IACP conventions. The first issue of the *National Police Magazine* in 1912 offered the editorial comment that "One of the heaviest crosses that the policeman has to bear . . . is the interference of the so-called leagues of reformers—the short-haired woman and the long-haired man who want to tell the police just how to run their business, how to do police work, and how to conduct the city." The criticism of outside interference was particularly important in one respect. The ideology of professionalism could easily be used to argue that only the police could determine how police departments should be administered. This argument was increasingly used to justify the growing insularity of the police as the twentieth century progressed.[62]

Police officials also expressed considerable opposition to the idea of rehabilitation itself. Police chiefs such as Fred Kohler were clearly the exception rather than the rule. The views of Frank Cassada, chief of the Elmira, New York, police, were perhaps more typical. "There is no man more liberal than I am," he asserted, "but I want to tell you every chief of police ought to make every man take his hat off and respect the law. When we arrest a man we are too lenient." Cassada took particular exception to Kohler's golden rule and proposed the following alternative: "Put the 'iron rule' on them—not the 'golden rule.' Knock their blocks off."[63]

Other police officials expressed more sophisticated criticisms of rehabilitation programs. John Downey, chief of the Detroit police in 1906, asserted that "The indeterminate sentence and the parole system are both an aid to the criminal." Chief Dolan of the Wilmington, Delaware, police suggested that "Sentimentality will never prevent crime," and strongly defended the use of the whipping post which was still in effect in Delaware. Chief Price of the Vicksburg, Mississippi, police summed up the antireform point of view with the simple comment that "criminals do not reform." The overzealousness of the reformers was another point of attack. Captain John Ryan of the Chicago police complained that "one fault that at present exists among our paid and volunteer juvenile workers who just fall into the work, most of them women from private life, is overzealousness and a firm conviction in the infallibility and correctness of their own knowledge and judgment, coupled with a sneering contempt for the opinions of veteran police officers."[64]

Nowhere was the overzealousness of reformers and its implications for due process of law more sharply dramatized than in a curious debate over police policy in New York City in 1903. In a series of articles in the *North American Review*, a representative from Tammany Hall took up the defense of civil liberties. Justice William J. Gaynor, then of the New York State Supreme Court, criticized the reform activities of the New York City police which were then defended by Assistant District Attorney for New York County Howard S. Gans.[65]

According to Justice Gaynor, the New York police had engaged in blatant violations of the U.S. Constitution, particularly the Fourth Amendment guarantees against unreasonable searches and seizures. He described one incident in which the police raided a place "said to be a place of private gaming." Gaynor charged that "a large posse of policemen suddenly surrounded it and violently attacked it. They smashed in a window by means of some heavy weapon, and entered pell mell by the breach thus made, some of them flourishing revolvers and others armed with axes. After entering, the same course of lawless violence was continued. They had a search warrant from a magistrate but did not act under it in getting in."

Gaynor cited other examples of police abuse of citizens' rights. In the case of *People v. Hochstim*, for example, Mr. Hochstim was arrested for violating the voter registration laws. As it turned out, Hochstim was indeed a properly registered voter. Gaynor complained that "it is more than probable that, at the very next election, hundreds of similar lawless arrests will be made in the City of New York by officers at the polls . . ." While conceding that some illegal voting might be curbed, he charged that "for one illegal vote that might be prevented in that way, there would be scores of legal votes prevented."

Justice Gaynor did not attempt to defend Tammany Hall, with its notorious record of fraudulent voter registration and police corruption; in fact he did not even mention it. Rather, his attack on the "Lawlessness of the Police in New York" was couched in terms of a lengthy discussion of the rights of the individual as established by the English common law and the U.S. Constitution. "The experience of history shows that free government, once established, can be preserved only by keeping the individual standing upon his rights, or, more pointedly speaking, keeping government, i.e. the officers and agents of government, at arms length." In an argument worthy of a contemporary civil libertarian, Gaynor suggested that a free society was best preserved by severely circumscribing the powers of government officials.

The problem was not merely one of police practices, however. Gaynor extended the scope of his discussion to include a critique of the whole idea of social reform. "The notion that the morals of the community can be reformed and made better," he argued, "or that government can be purified and lifted up, instead of being debased and demoralized, by the policeman's club and axe, is so pernicious and dangerous in any government, let alone in a free government, that no one can harbor it. . . ." The real issue was not the prevalence of vice, but the rule of law: "Crimes and vices are evil to the community, but it behooves a free people never to forget that they have more to fear from the growth of the one vice of arbitrary power in government than from all the other vices and crimes combined."

District Attorney Gans defended the New York police and refuted some of Gaynor's specific allegations. His account of the raid on the gambling establishment was considerably less lurid than was Gaynor's. "We are confident," he suggested, "that a careful investigation of the subject will reveal that abuses of power on the part of the police, in the matter of unlawful arrests, are neither so frequent nor so flagrant as to warrant any serious concern that they are undermining our institutions." He also suggested that Gaynor's attacks "lulled the good citizen into security by distracting attention from the true lawlessness of the police—their systematic corruption and blackmail, their alliance with the keepers of brothels and of gambling houses, their partnership with criminals and their acceptance of the proceeds of thefts and burglaries"—in short, the whole organized system of police corruption.

Gan's point was well taken. Police abuses under Tammany Hall had been enormous and Gaynor rather conveniently neglected to mention that problem at all. Nonetheless, the problem of police overzealousness was a real one and would continue to grow increasingly important as the twentieth century progressed. In particular during the post-World War II era the notion of national security would justify both an enormous expansion of police powers and systematic violations of constitutional rights. It is an irony of history that in 1903 the strongest defense of individual rights against police abuses—couched in terms that a contemporary civil libertarian could easily accept—came from a spokesman for the old and corrupt Tammany Hall. It serves as an important reminder that social reformers were often the victim of their own zealousness. Not only did they exaggerate the meliorative effects of their reforms but often their prescriptions called for an ominous extension of state intervention into the lives of private citizens.

Part III:
The Police and the Nation, 1919-1940

5

The Age of the Crime Commission, 1919–1931

For the American police the decade of the 1920s was the age of the crime commission. The period opened with the creation of the Chicago Crime Commission in 1919 and closed with the publication of the multivolume Wickersham Commission reports in 1931. The intervening years witnessed a multitude of similar commissions at the state and local level. The crime commission became the primary vehicle for police reform, for the most part emulating the style pioneered by the New York Bureau of Municipal Research. The 1931 Wickersham Commission report on the police, in fact, resembled the earlier reports in terms of the substance of its recommendations. This illustrated an important aspect of the professionalization movement. The agenda of reform remained unchanged even as the circumstances of the urban police underwent a dramatic change.[1]

The most important change in policing was the advent of the automobile. As the automobile became a dominant feature of American life it not only altered the physical structure of the city and the patterns of daily life, but also effected a profound revolution in the nature of police work. Simply to keep up with the expanding size of urban areas, police departments put their patrolmen in cars. This simple administrative change removed the patrolman from the streets. Also, the advent of the two-way radio and the spread of the telephone altered the manner in which the police intervened in citizens' lives. This revolution in police work went largely unnoticed. One finds no recognition of it in the many crime commission reports of the period. Not until the 1960s would its full impact be noticed and analyzed.

The most widely known law enforcement problem of the 1920s, national prohibition, had little long-term impact on policing. The problem of enforcing prohibition fell largely to federal officials. For the municipal police, national prohibition represented a strong continuity with earlier traditions of nonenforcement and corruption. In a history of organized crime in America, historian Humbert Nelli observes that "The network of contacts with police, politicians, and members of the legal profession developed during the decades of illegal gambling activities, prostitution, and labor racketeering, readily adapted to the new situation." Prohibition came and went leaving little effect on the urban police.[2]

The decade of the 1920s opened with two violent conflicts that foreshadowed the police problems of the 1960s. The year 1919 was marked by the climax of a bloody wave of racial violence in American cities. The Chicago race riot of that year was the worst instance of urban racial violence to that time. The fall of 1919 also witnessed the culmination of the first chapter in the history of police unionism. The public opinion backlash that followed the September 1919 Boston police strike ended police unionism for several decades. The two issues represented by these conflicts also went largely unnoticed in surveys of police administration in the 1920s. Yet, the question of the police and race relations and of the role of the rank and file police officer would ultimately prove to be among the most important issues in police administration.

The Rise and Sudden Fall of Police Unionism

The history of police unionism in the United States falls into three distinct periods. The first two of those three periods, 1917-1919 and 1943-1947, ended with the defeat of unionism. The third period, from 1966 to the present, witnessed the establishment of police unionism as a permanent feature of police administration.[3]

The sources of police union activity are not hard to discover. Attention has focused on the immediate and short-term rather than the long-term factors. The first two periods of police union activity were years of wartime inflation in which police salaries lagged far behind the rising cost of living. The immediate factors that spurred union growth in the 1960s were more complex, a mixture of economic considerations and strong feelings of social and political isolation. Preoccupation with these immediate factors has obscured the more fundamental sources of police unionism. To an important degree unionism was an inevitable consequence of professionalization. One of the first goals of police reformers was to establish police work as a full time career. The constant turnover of police personnel was recognized as one of the most obvious indicators of political interference in policing during the nineteenth century. Gradually, however, reformers succeeded in stabilizing the career patterns of police officers and introducing the first rudimentary sense of police work as a profession.

A number of developments signalled the emergence of careerism among the police. By the 1890s fraternal associations were to be found in most of the larger police departments across the country. A few of those groups began to engage in open political activity to promote their own interests. The New York City Patrolmen's Benevolent Association (PBA), for example, began lobbying around the turn of the century. Before long a number of national periodicals devoted exclusively to rank and file policemen appeared. The Chicago-based *National Police Magazine* (1912-1913), the New York-based *Policeman's Monthly* 1915-1918), *Policeman's News* (1919-1921), and the *National Police Journal* addressed themselves not to police reformers and administrators but to rank-and-file patrolmen. They were generally filled with gossipy news items about developments in local departments and full-scale feature stories about particular departments. The style was calculated to appeal to the growing sense of occupational identity.[4]

It is a striking commentary on the leaders of the police professionalization movement that they failed to reckon with one of the most important implications of their work. Reformers were firmly committed to the gospel of strong executive leadership. Leonard Fuld, Raymond Fosdick, and others emphasized the personal qualities and institutional needs of the dynamic administrator. Little attention was given to the needs and perceptions of the rank-and-file patrolman. Indeed, the patrolman was regarded as clay, to be molded by the police executive. The reformers, in fact, were almost unanimous in their criticism of arrangements that protected the interests of patrolmen. Fosdick and the others strongly attacked civil service procedures because they stayed the hand of the administrator.

The transformation of police work from casual labor to career (a process that occurred very slowly and at different rates in different cities) altered the manner in which rank-and-file patrolmen responded to job-related problems. The discontented officer who regarded the job only as a temporary one would be most likely to simply quit. After all, there was little that bound him to the job. But the officer who regarded the job as a career was more likely to seek some resolution within the confines of the job. And as more officers began to think in career terms the stage was set first for the emergence of fraternal associations, later for political activity, and eventually for unionism.

The precipitating factor of police unionism was the inflation wrought by the American involvement in World War I. This, in turn, was the culmination of a long inflationary cycle that overtook the American economy in the 1890s. The cost of living rose by 25 percent between 1900 and 1915, while the relative attractiveness of police salaries vis-à-vis blue collar jobs, declined significantly. The average annual earnings of manufacturing and construction workers increased by nearly 50 percent between 1900 and 1915. Police salaries, less responsive to economic fluctuations, remained relatively static. The leading spokesmen for professionalization, concentrating their attention on administrative changes and the development of formal training programs, said almost nothing about establishing professional level salaries. In some instances, it required a major scandal to raise salaries. A 1913 investigation by the New York City Board of Aldermen uncovered widespread economic hardships among police officers and the expose did result in substantial salary increases.[5]

The war years only aggravated the inflationary spiral; between 1915 and 1920 the cost of living doubled. Once again, blue collar workers were able to keep pace. Earnings for manufacturing workers doubled while construction workers enjoyed nearly comparable gains. In part these gains were the result of a dramatic expansion of the trade unionism in the private sector during the war. To maintain war production, the federal government actively encouraged accommodation between management and labor. As a result, unionism flourished; membership in the American Federation of Labor (AFL) nearly doubled during the war years.

The advances scored by workers in the private sector only heightened the alienation of police officers who saw their economic status declining rapidly.

The idea of police unionism, however, was constrained by a number of other factors. Even police officers themselves were ambivalent about the propriety of unionism. The individual rights of police officers had long been restricted. Most police departments, for example, forbade open political activity, although the ban was usually honored in the breach. There existed the widespread belief that public service jobs in general were a privilege and the job holder implicitly agreed to give up certain rights. This view received its most forceful statement in an 1897 opinion written by Justice Oliver Wendell Holmes, then of the Massachusetts Supreme Court. In the case of *McAuliffe v. Mayor of New Bedford*, Patrolman McAuliffe had been dismissed for engaging in political activity, a violation of police regulation 35. Justice Holmes, ruling against McAuliffe, stated that "The petitioner may have a constitutional right to talk politics, but he has no constitutional right to be a policeman." Then, enunciating a view that prevailed until the late 1960s, Holmes argued that "The servant cannot complain, as he takes the employment on the terms which are offered to him. On the same principle, the city may impose any reasonable condition upon holding offices within its control."[6]

The right of police officers to join labor unions, to say nothing of the right to strike, was hardly an accepted idea in the early years of the twentieth century. Organized labor itself remained wary of police unionism, although it never confronted the issue directly prior to the World War I years. In 1897 the AFL executive council refused to issue a charter to a group of private police officers from Cleveland. The council argued that private police generally served management and were "too often controlled by forces inimical to the labor movement." At no point did the AFL explicitly rule out the possibility of organizing municipal police officers, although at the same time it never initiated an organizing effort. Beginning in 1917, pressure from nascent police unions forced Samuel Gompers, president of the AFL, to rethink his position on the police union issue. Particularly strong pressure came from New York City unions where police militancy was rising rapidly. In 1918 the New York PBA demanded a $300 a year raise and succeeded in gaining half of that.[7]

Finally, at its June 1919 convention the AFL pronounced itself in favor of police unions. Meeting in Atlantic City, the convention passed resolution No. 162, which stated ". . . that this convention go on record as favoring the organization of the city policemen and the officers of the Federation be instructed to issue charter to same when application is properly made." By then, the union idea had already spread across the country. In the next two months sixty-five local organizations applied for AFL charters and thirty-three of those were quickly granted.[8] The AFL action occurred in the midst of a developing crisis in Boston and the question of affiliation with the AFL became the central issue in that confrontation. The Boston police strike, however, should be viewed in light of the peaceful police strike in Cincinnati the year before. The Cincinnati affair, which received little publicity at the time and which has been virtually neglected by historians, suggested that the fate of police unionism could well have been very different.

From all appearances the three-day Cincinnati police strike was a spontaneous walkout. For several months prior to September 13 police officers had been agitating for an increase in their maximum salaries from $1260 to $1500 a year. There had been no attempt to organize a union per se, however, or to affiliate with any other labor organization. On the morning of September 13, 1918, patrolmen held a secret meeting which caught city officials off guard. Detectives were barred from the meeting on the suspicion that they were spies for the city. At three o'clock in the afternoon most of the patrolmen on the second shift refused to report for duty. For the next four hours there were only forty-eight officers on duty to protect the entire city. At seven o'clock in the evening the city mobilized the Home Guard, a 600 member volunteer force organized because of the war, and assigned it to police patrol duty.[9]

The second day of the strike offered considerable opportunities for violence and disorder. A previously scheduled selective service parade brought 25,000 registrants parading through downtown Cincinnati in a display of patriotism. Considering the rising tide of antialien and antiradical passions across the country during the war, the possibility of violence was extremely high, particularly in Cincinnati with its large German-American population. Surprisingly, however, the event passed with no disorder. The few nonstriking policemen and the Home Guard were joined by a cadre of Boy Scouts mobilized for police duty.

The mayor of Cincinnati offered to compromise on the wage demands of the patrolmen but remained firm on the question of disciplinary action against the leaders of the strike. The leaders would have to stand trial for conduct unbecoming an officer and for insubordination, but no penalties would be levied against the bulk of the patrolmen if they would return to their jobs immediately. It was not clear exactly how many men would be held liable for disciplinary action. Finally, at three o'clock in the afternoon of the third day, September 16, the strike ended as quickly and quietly as it had begun. Despite having received no firm promises from the city regarding their salaries, the entire second shift returned to work that afternoon. The strike passed without violence or disorder. Several weeks later the city did grant the patrolmen their demand by raising salaries to a maximum of $1500 a year.

The Boston police strike occurred in a very different context. Although the salary demands were similar, the heart of the conflict involved the question of the right of the Boston policeman to affiliate with a national labor organization. Boston officials conceded the right of the policemen to join their own local union but held firm on the issue of AFL affiliation. The issue of formal union ties had not arisen in the Cincinnati dispute.

Perhaps even more important, the national mood changed significantly between 1918 and 1919. Hysteria over real and imagined radicalism, which had been growing since the start of the war, reached its peak in the spring and summer of 1919. The Red Scare unleashed wholesale repression of suspected radicals by law enforcement officials and private vigilante groups. Antiradical hysteria soon spilled over into an attack on organized labor. The same economic pressures that stimulated police unionism also led to widespread union activity in other areas. Furthermore, the large numbers of recent immigrants in some of the major industries allowed many Americans to equate the labor movement with alien radicalism. These fears were further inflamed by such events as the Seattle General Strike in the spring of 1919, an event that also seemed to portend the importation of "foreign" labor tactics. Finally, the summer of 1919 marked the climax of a mounting wave of racial violence, with major riots in Chicago, Omaha, Louisville, and Washington, D.C.[10]

In short, the national mood had turned extremely grim in the twelve months between the Cincinnati and Boston police strikes. By September 1919, in the minds of a broad segment of middle-class America, a cloud of suspicion hung over organized labor. Fears of foreign radicalism whipped up by the Red Scare further encouraged a law and order mentality that had no tolerance for strikes by police officers. At the same time, the mood of police officers in Boston and other cities was angrier than ever. Inflation had continued unabated while salaries remained static. The police themselves were in no mood to compromise.

The Boston police strike was preceded by nearly two years of agitation by patrolmen for better wages and working conditions. In late 1917 representatives of the Boston Social Club, the police fraternal association, met with Police Commissioner Stephen O'Meara, to discuss the need for salary increases. By early 1918 the patrolmen had formulated a specific demand for a $200 a year raise; they also raised complaints about the deplorable physical conditions in many of the city's nineteen police station houses. A Boston patrolman at that time could earn a maximum salary of $1400 a year, a figure that had not changed since 1898. The 79 percent increase in the cost of living in the intervening years had seriously eroded their financial status. Entry to the police force, meanwhile, imposed severe financial hardships. An officer joined as a "probationer" with a salary of only $730 a year. The next year his salary rose to $821.25 and he could soon look forward to earning the official starting salary of $1000 a year. Much of the officers' discontent focused on the fact that they were required to purchase their own uniforms out of these meagre starting salaries. Wartime inflation had doubled the cost of clothing and by 1919 Boston police uniforms cost nearly $200.[11]

In the winter of 1918-1919 two fateful events set the stage for the eventual confrontation. The popular and respected Police Commissioner O'Meara died in December and was replaced by Edwin U. Curtis. The inflexible position taken by Curtis was a major cause of the final impasse. Two months after O'Meara's death the Boston Social Club voted to seek affiliation with the AFL. The question of the Boston Social Club's relationship with a national organization proved to be the central issue in the strike. Rule 35, Section 19 of the Boston police department's regulations stated that

No member of the force shall belong to any organization, club or body composed of present or present and past members of the force which is affiliated with or part of any organization, club or body outside the department, except that a post of the Grand Army of the Republic, the United Spanish War Veterans may be formed within the department.[12]

Through the late winter and spring of 1919 the Boston patrolmen continued to agitate for a salary increase with little success. After the AFL sanctioned police unionism at its June convention, the Boston Social Club voted overwhelmingly to apply for a charter. The press reported that on August 1 940 of the 1343 patrolmen voted in favor of this step. According to the *Boston Globe*, meanwhile, 891 officers had signed union cards. A week later the club telegrammed the AFL concerning its charter and the following day, August 8, the charter arrived. Boston was the thirteenth city to be issued a police union charter.

Commissioner Curtis, meanwhile, reaffirmed his opposition to union affiliation. On July 29 he issued a general order stating that "I am firmly of the opinion that a police officer cannot consistently belong to a union and perform his sworn duty." Two weeks later, on August 11, he reiterated his position in General Order 110, declaring that "It is or should be apparent to any thinking person that the police department of this or any other city cannot fulfill its duty to the entire public if its members are subject to the direction of an organization existing outside the department." Curtis then moved against the union itself and its leaders. After the union elected its officers on August 15 the commissioner "questioned [them] as to their connection with the organization, and charges of having violated the rule [35] were then brought against them." Eight officers stood trial on August 26 and eleven additional policemen were brought to trial before the commissioner three days later.[13]

As the conflict between the Boston Social Club and the commissioner worsened, the mayor sought a compromise. The mayor asked James J. Storrow, a wealthy Boston banker, to chair a special Citizens Committee to investigate conditions in the Boston police department and make recommendations for a settlement. The committee held its first meeting on August 29, just as the second group of departmental disciplinary trials were taking place. In a preliminary statement, the committee declared "its admiration of the Boston Police Force as a body of men which has won the respect and confidence of the whole community through years of firm, courteous, impartial and faithful service." The committee also stated that it was "not opposed to any organization by the members of the Boston Police Force within its own body." Affiliation with the AFL, however, was another matter. The committee opposed it "for the reason that such affiliation tends to divide allegiance of a body of men which in the very nature of its duties can have but one allegiance, and that to the whole community." The committee maintained this position throughout the crisis.

By the time the Citizens Committee met, however, events had seemingly passed the point of no return. The Boston Social Club had committed itself to affiliation with the AFL while the commissioner remained adamantly opposed. Neither side seemed ready to compromise, particularly after the initial disciplinary trials. The Citizens Committee issued its report and recommendations after a week of investigation. The September 6 report reiterated the basic position outlined in the initial statement: acceptance of a local union but opposition to affiliation with any outside group. Recommendation 5 was crucial to any hope for compromise. The committee recommended "That no member of the Boston Policemen's Union be discriminated against because of any previous affiliation with the American Federation of Labor." Mayor Peters, in a letter to Commissioner Curtis, strongly endorsed the committee's report, suggesting that "it affords a speedy, and, it seems to me, satisfactory settlement to the whole question."[14]

Commissioner Curtis, however, remained adamantly opposed to any compromise and suspended all nineteen policemen. In reply to the mayor, he stated that he could "discover nothing [in the report] which appears to him to be either consistent with his prescribed legal duties or calculated to aid him in their performance." That statement, issued by the commissioner on Monday, September 8, set the stage for the strike the following day. The patrolmen, left with no apparent room for compromise, voted to stand behind both their union and the disciplined officers. A total of 1,134 men voted to strike, against only two negative votes. Late in the afternoon of Tuesday, September 9, 1919, 1,117 Boston patrolmen went out on strike, while 427 police officers remained on duty.

The response of the city of Boston to the police walkout was complex and contradictory. No historian has attempted to examine the patterns of disorder in depth. Instead, stereotypes of "anarchy" and "lawlessness" have prevailed. The actual violence and disorder was far less than the legend of the strike would suggest. Moreover, it is difficult to discern a consistent pattern of disorder. Different members of the Boston community saw the strike in quite different terms. Some saw the absence of police protection as an opportunity for looting and property destruction. Stores were looted, false alarms turned in, and pedestrians accosted on the streets. Much of the violence, however, was directed at the striking police officers themselves, particularly as they were seen leaving their station houses to go on strike. We can only guess at the sources of this hostility. Certainly some people equated the strike with disloyalty and un-Americanism. Others may well have had an old grudge against the police, possibly for a previous arrest. The strike was simply an opportunity to settle the old scores.[15]

Still other violence was directed at those policemen who remained on duty. It was clear that the strike had considerable support among Boston's working class. The Boston Central Labor Union, the institutional voice of organized labor, came out solidly in support of the strike. On Wednesday, September 10, a general strike of all organized labor seemed a distinct possibility. At an evening meeting of representatives of 125 Boston unions, more than 80 percent of the delegates expressed support for a sympathy strike in an informal poll. The leaders of the Central Labor Union, fearful of the possible consequences of a general strike, refused to announce the results of the poll. Instead, they issued a statement stating that they would continue "to work in conjunction with the Police Union, to the end that justice be given the members of the Police Union." The Central Labor Union, of course, had a direct interest in the basic issue of union recognition.

Much of the subsequent controversy over the strike concerns the role of the supplementary forces that were mobilized to compensate for the absence of police protection. Weeks before the strike, Commissioner Curtis ordered the training of civilian volunteers. Members of Boston's social elite, including a number of students and faculty from Harvard University, enrolled in the volunteer corps. Yet, the 500 volunteers were not mobilized until 8:00 A.M. on Wednesday, a full fourteen hours after the initial walkout. Many have argued that earlier deployment of the volunteers might have preserved order Tuesday night. Even greater controversy surrounds the use of the nonstriking police officers. It was charged that they were deliberately kept off the streets and that this also encouraged the Tuesday night violence. The greatest controversy, of course, involves the mobilization of the state militia and the role of Governor Calvin Coolidge in particular. Only after much confusion and delay was the militia mobilized. Arriving gradually on Wednesday afternoon, the militia established control of the city by Thursday morning. Governor Coolidge built a national political career on his famous statement, "There is no right to strike against the public safety by anybody, anywhere, at any time." The statement, however, came after the fact and his direct role in the conflict had, if anything, served to delay the use of the militia.

Newspaper accounts across the country painted a picture of anarchy in Boston. The image did not fit the facts, however. The final cost of the strike in terms of life and property has been estimated at eight persons dead, at least twenty-one seriously injured, and property damage in the neighborhood of $300,000. Even by comparison with the racial violence in other cities that summer it was a relatively small affair. Nonetheless, in the inflamed political atmosphere of 1919 the image of anarchy stuck. The equation of police unions with strikes and anarchy dealt a death blow to the vigorous young police union movement.

In Boston the heaviest losers were the striking policemen. Commissioner Curtis announced that "the places in the police force formerly held by the men who deserted their posts of duty have by this action been rendered vacant." Curtis's use of the word desertion, was carefully chosen to hang the label of disloyalty on the strikers. All of the strikers were, in effect, suspended, and the Boston police department began to recruit virtually an entire new force. It is a commentary on the economic conditions of the period that there was no shortage of applicants. There were also important incentives for new recruits. Commissioner Curtis announced that starting salaries would be $1400 and that, for the first time, the city would provide uniforms free. The new Boston policemen, in other words, enjoyed real earnings that far exceeded even the demands of the dismissed strikers.

Events in Boston, Cincinnati, and elsewhere clearly demonstrated that city governments could afford higher police salaries. The New York City police had won a $150 a year raise in 1918. In Los Angeles the city raised police salaries twice in the year 1919 alone, evidently in response to the Boston strike. The maximum salaries of Los Angeles patrolmen were raised from $1224 to $1440 and then again to $1800.[16]

While the Boston conflict headed for its showdown in August and early September, a similar situation began to develop in the nation's capital. The rise in union sentiment among the Washington, D.C., police attracted the immediate attention of the federal government and Samuel Gompers, head of the AFL, was soon called before congressional committees to explain and defend police unionism. Initially, the board of commissioners of the Washington police attempted to forbid membership in any labor union. General Order 56, issued on August 22, 1919, required all members of the force to answer in writing the question "Are you a member of any organization of policemen which is affiliated directly or indirectly with any other labor organization?" Any officer who remained a member of such an organization after September 7 would be "deemed guilty of willful noncompliance with the rules and regulations" of the department and subject to dismissal. Gompers appeared before the police commissioners on September 4 to argue against this policy. Gompers emphasized the no strike clause of the incipient Washington police union and argued that the AFL itself had never initiated a strike.[17]

The Washington Board of Police Commissioners indicated that they were willing to accept in principle both police unionism and collective bargaining. But, as was the case in Boston, they refused to allow affiliation with any other labor organization. Developments in Washington were soon overtaken by the crisis in Boston. The strike and the image of anarchy cast a pall over police unionism. President Woodrow Wilson called police strikes "a crime against civilization" and in a September 19 telegram to the police commissioners declared his opposition to police organizations and any group "whose object is to bring pressure upon the public or the community." The District of Columbia police union then faded away as did most of the other unions across the country. The AFL tried to maintain a brave face. In 1920 it announced that it would form an International Police Union as soon as membership in local groups totalled 6,000. Nothing came of it, however, for by then police unionism had collapsed and disappeared.[18]

Events in England, which at first closely paralleled developments in the United States, provide an interesting comparative perspective on police unionism. Union sentiment among the London police had flickered on and off since early in the century. In 1907, in fact, Ramsay MacDonald argued their case before Parliament. Many Socialist MPs apparently supported the idea of police unionism. As was the case in most American cities, the London Metropolitan Police commissioners banned union membership. By 1918 inflation spurred union sentiment to new heights. Then, in late August a police officer was dismissed for his union activity. This precipitated a police strike on Friday, August 30, 1918. Londoners turned out to see more than 6,000 members of the Metropolitan Police parading, in columns of four, through the streets. Sensing that the public supported the police, the prime minister granted a substantial pay increase and promised to reinstate the dismissed officer.[19]

The question of union recognition, however, was not settled and this set the stage for another confrontation the next year. The nascent police union requested formal recognition in the spring of 1919 but was turned down by the home secretary. The government, meanwhile, appointed a high-level committee to investigate working conditions on the police force. A police bill establishing a government-sponsored police association was then introduced into the House of Commons. While the bill was pending members of the London police decided to strike over the issue of union recognition. Although union sentiment was strong, the possibility of government action divided the rank and file. More than a thousand London police officers went out on strike, but within twenty-four hours it was evident that the strike would fail. It quickly collapsed and all of the strikers were dismissed from the force.

The strike was followed by the passage of the Police Act which established the Police Federation. For all practical purposes the Police Federation was a government-sponsored company union. All police officers in England were required to join and the structure of the organization provided an orderly mechanism for dealing with the problems of the rank and file. It could be said that the Police Federation smothered the militant independence of the rank and file. But the rank and file did gain a vehicle for airing its grievances. The contrast between the post-1919 situation in England and the United States was significant. The American police rank and file retreated in defeat, finding themselves without any institutional voice. The fraternal associations that survived did so only by disavowing any interest in political action. The end result was the development of a police subculture, isolated from the public and without any formal means of making its voice heard. The defeat of police unionism in 1919 presents one of the great imponderables of American police history: how different the development of the police might have been had they gained rather than lost a formal voice in police administration.[20]

The Cops in the Ghetto: Racism and Riots

The year 1919 also marked the bloody climax of a mounting wave of racial violence in America. One historian has counted over twenty major race riots that year alone and there is evidence of countless smaller incidents. In addition to major riots in Washington, D.C., Knoxville, and Omaha, the summer of 1919 witnessed the worst urban race riot in American history to that time. In the Chicago riot at least thirty-eight persons died, over 500 were seriously injured, several hundred left homeless and property damage measured in the hundreds of thousands of dollars. The police played prominent and controversial roles in virtually all of the racial riots of the period. Despite apparent similarities to the riots of the 1960s, however, there were important differences, particularly in the official response to police misconduct. An examination of these differences provides an illuminating index of the state of American policing with reference to race relations by 1919.[21]

A one-day race riot in New York City on a hot August afternoon in 1900 provided an ominous portent of things to come over the next two decades. Relations between whites and blacks in New York had been steadily deteriorating, as they had across the entire country, particularly since the 1890s. On August 12, 1900, Arthur Harris, who was black, killed a New York City police officer. Three days later whites retaliated with what was described as a "general assault" on black New Yorkers. During a four-hour rampage blacks were chased through the streets, dragged from street cars, and assaulted with impunity. More than seventy blacks were injured. One observer described the affair as a "Nigger Chase."[22]

The conduct of the New York City police was reprehensible. According to the *New York Post*, "The police virtually led the hoodlums." In a typical incident "A Negro appealed to a policeman for help and received a smash over the head with a nightstick in reply." Blacks vented their anger by throwing objects at the police from windows and the police replied with gunfire. Not a single white person was arrested while many blacks were, and some of those complained of further police brutality in the station houses. A sudden rainstorm brought the violence to a halt, although there were reports of additional incidents over the next two days.

The official response to the riot was dominated by partisan political considerations. Black leaders organized a Citizens Protective League and published a list of seventy-eight specific acts of police brutality. A grand jury, however, dismissed all complaints by blacks on the grounds that they were unable to identify individual officers. The Board of Police Commissioners conducted its own investigation and absolved the police of all wrongdoing. Republican newspapers, always eager to embarrass the Democratic Tammany Hall, took up the cause of the black New Yorkers. The *New York Tribune* accused the police commissioners of a whitewash and the conduct of the city police in the riot became an issue in the 1901 municipal elections.

The New York City riot contained all the major forms of police misconduct that characterized most of the race riots of the 1900–1919 period. First, there was evidence of blatant discrimination in law enforcement. Along with discrimination in jobs and housing, this established the preconditions for violence. Second, the police were generally passive in the face of white lawlessness, refusing to arrest whites who attacked blacks. This only encouraged whites to assume that it was open season on blacks and led to additional violence. Blacks, meanwhile, concluded that their only hope lay in armed self-defense and their retaliatory violence served to escalate the general conflict. Finally, as was the case in New York City, the police were often active riot participants themselves, joining other whites in the assault on blacks.[23]

The pattern of racial violence found in the 1900 New York City riot was repeated elsewhere. In most cases the violence was white initiated and triggered by a rumor of black violence against a white person. The rumors were often false or grossly exaggerated and the alleged victim was usually a white woman. In northern cities racial tensions were aggravated by the influx of black migrants and the resulting competition for jobs, housing, and recreation areas. In a number of the southern racial incidents, white violence was touched off by independent economic action by blacks, such as the formation of cooperative cotton marketing plans. In both cases white violence was an attempt to keep blacks literally "in their place."

The 1917 East St. Louis riot was not only one of the larger riots of the period but also one of the most extensively documented. Because the riot disrupted rail transportation, it provoked a full-scale congressional investigation. The investigating committee concluded that economic factors precipitated the riot. In 1917 alone an estimated 10,000 to 12,000 blacks migrated to East St. Louis in response to promises of jobs at high wages. There was evidence that employers sought to use black workers as strike breakers and that the promises of high wages were deliberately exaggerated. The influx of blacks aggravated racial tensions which finally exploded on the night of July 1. An automobile driven by whites "went through a negro section of the city and fired promiscuously into their homes." The black community was apparently prepared for harassment. A church bell mobilized a large crowd of armed residents. When they encountered a police car containing several policemen, the mob opened fire. One police officer was killed immediately while another died later of gunshot wounds.[24]

Local newspapers the next day published inflammatory accounts of the incident, while the police placed the bullet-ridden police car outside police headquarters for all to see. The result was a massive retaliation by whites: "Men and boys, girls and women of the town began to attack every negro in sight. . . . The crowd soon grew to riotous proportions, and for hours the manhunt continued, stabbing, clubbing and shooting, not the guilty, but unoffending negroes." In some instances "The negroes were pursued into their homes, and the torch completed the work of destruction." In the end, a total of thirty-nine blacks and eight whites were reported dead, with an untold number injured.

The congressional investigators condemned the conduct of the East St. Louis police. Specifically, they accused the police of not acting quickly to stop the escalating violence: "When the lawlessness began to assume serious proportions on July 2, the police instantly could have quelled and dispersed the crowds, then made up of small groups; but they either fled into the safety of a cowardly seclusion or listlessly watched the depredations of the mob passively, in many instances sharing in its work." The report cited a number of specific instances of police misconduct: "After a number of rioters had been taken to jail by the soldiers under Col. Clayton, the police deliberately turned hundreds of them loose without bond. . . ." Police officers clubbed blacks who had committed no offense, "shot into a crowd of negroes who were huddled together, making no resistance," and attacked newspaper reporters who had taken pictures of the riot, smashing their cameras and destroying the negatives. Nor did the military units perform much better. The report stated that "The conduct of the soldiers who were sent to East St. Louis to protect life and property puts a blot on that part of the Illinois militia. . . . They seemed moved by the same spirit of indifference of cowardice that marked the conduct of the police force."

In several of the other riots, however, the conduct of military units stood in striking contrast to that of the local police. In the 1919 Omaha and Chicago riots the military units earned the praise of all sides. As would also be the case in the riots of the 1940s and 1960s, the military entered the riots with more effective leadership, a clearer chain of command, and more experience in coordinating large units, and a less immediate involvement in the specific local conflicts. The greater weaponry of the military also commanded far more respect from riot participants and potential rioters.[25]

The 1919 Chicago riot followed a pattern similar to that of the East St. Louis riot. A doubling of the black population of Chicago between 1917 and 1919 aggravated racial tensions over jobs, housing, and the use of recreational areas. The spark that ignited the riot resulted from an incident at one of the public beaches on July 27. A seventeen-year-old black youth crossed the imaginary line that separated the black and white sections of the water, was stoned by white youths, and drowned. Blacks demanded that the whites be arrested and, when the police refused, began to attack whites in retaliation. Soon the entire city was engulfed in a bloody race riot. In the next six days, thirty-eight people died, over 500 were injured, and more than 1,000 left homeless because of property destruction.[26]

The conduct of the Chicago police was a major factor in the continuing violence. At the height of the rioting, 2,800 of the 3,000 Chicago police were concentrated in the black ghetto. The rest of the city, especially the busy downtown Loop district, was left virtually without police protection. Many black workers, traveling to and from their jobs, were attacked and beaten by mobs of whites. Although much of the violence was white initiated (the riot was marked by organized attacks of white youth gangs on the ghetto), the police practiced discriminatory law enforcement. Of the 229 persons arrested in the course of the riot, 154 were black. Yet, 342 of the 520 people injured were black, a figure that indicated the discrepancy between white violence and arrests.

The 1917-1919 riots introduced another feature of twentieth-century American life: the postriot investigating commission. The East St. Louis riot was examined by a congressional committee, while the Chicago riot called forth a privately funded, biracial committee drawn largely from the social and economic elite of the city. The various riot commissions documented a wide range of problems. The final report of the Chicago Commission on Race Relations, *The Negro in Chicago: A Study of Race Relations and a Race Riot*, was a broad sociological study of changing race relations in the urban community. With respect to law enforcement, *The Negro in Chicago* recommended a number of specific riot control techniques. The police were asked to develop detailed plans for the control of racial disorders and for coordinating their efforts with military units. The report also recommended that the police be more even handed in the enforcement of the law, specifically "that all rioters, white and negro, be arrested without race discrimination," and that all charges of misconduct or discrimination be investigated and the offenders "promptly punished."

The recommendations of the Chicago riot commission fell on deaf ears. There is no evidence that the Chicago police, or the police of any other riot-torn communities, took positive steps to eliminate racism or improve race relations. The riots of the entire 1900-1919 period passed with almost no effect on the American police. At the annual conventions of the International Association of Chiefs of Police in 1919 and 1920, for example, the race problem was not even mentioned (nor did they mention the question of police unions, for that matter). Police administration experts were equally unconcerned about relations between the police and the black community. In his *American Police Systems* (1920), Raymond Fosdick mentioned blacks only with reference to their allegedly high rate of criminal behavior. Police conduct in race riots was not mentioned at all. A similar point of view—neglect of riots and emphasis on black criminality— characterized police administration texts through the early 1940s. August Vollmer's *The Police and Modern Society* (1936) and Bruce Smith's *Police Systems in the United States* (1940) were identical to Fosdick's work in this respect.[27]

The American police in 1919 were not yet ready for police-community relations. Police administrators shared the pervasive racism of the World War I era. The egalitarianism expressed by the Chicago riot commission report was far in advance of public opinion on the race issue. Few Americans were yet ready to affirm racial equality as a national goal and, consequently, few saw the need for affirmative race relations programs. With respect to the police, the idea of formal training itself had only recently won a tenuous foothold. Specialized race relations training was hardly a realistic prospect in an era when many cities still had no training programs at all.

The response to the 1943 riots was quite different. The riots of that year gave birth to the modern police-community relations movement, bringing together progressive-minded police administrators and race relations experts in allied fields. The difference was not simply a testimony to the changed national mood on race relations, but also an important index of police progress in the intervening twenty years. Training programs had become established features of most departments. Moreover, the police were more self-conscious of their own claim to professional status and, as a result, more willing to seek expert help from professionals in other fields.

One other factor must be taken into consideration when evaluating the police response to the racial conflicts of the 1900–1919 period. To some extent positive action was not forthcoming in the 1920s and 1930s because the urgency of the problem itself declined. After the bloody orgy of 1919, urban racial violence virtually disappeared for twenty years. This is not to say that racial conflict disappeared; American society in those years was still marked by a continuing pattern of racism and racial conflict. But that conflict did not take the form of large-scale urban riots. Scholars have been able to identify only two major racial disturbances between 1920 and 1940: the 1921 Tulsa race riot and the 1935 Harlem riot. The latter, in fact, was a relatively small-scale, one-day affair.[28]

Why did racial violence subside during this twenty-year period? A general theory of urban rioting in American society helps to explain this phenomenon. One can view mob violence as a response to the *initial* phase of a major social change. Thus, the urban riots of the 1830–1860 period were a response to the onset of massive immigration. Eventually, however, patterns of accommodation developed and ethnic group conflicts found other outlets. In his study of anti-abolitionist violence in the same period, Leo Richards finds that violence was more common in the early years (1830s–1840s) of the abolitionist movement rather than the later stages. The 1900–1919 racial violence, then, should be seen as a response to the Great Migration, the first massive movement of black Americans to northern cities. After an initial outburst of violence the races settled into an uneasy but peaceful truce. The creation of the modern black ghetto represented the major accommodation.[29]

Subsequent periods of urban racial violence also resulted from sudden changes in the racial status quo. In both the 1940s and the 1960s there occurred dramatic changes in the expectations of black Americans. Violent conflict, in

large part, was the result of an unwillingness to tolerate conditions that had previously been endured without protest. We return to this theme in due course. It
is important to recognize, however, that changes in police practices had little to
do with either the rise or disappearance of racial conflict. If anything, police
conduct may actually have improved somewhat between 1919 and the 1960s.
But the police were judged by ever-rising levels of public expectations.

The Police and the Crime Commissions

The World War I years also brought into being another feature of twentieth-
century criminal justice, the crime commission. In January 1919 business interests in Chicago established the Chicago Crime Commission to serve as a permanent watchdog over the municipal criminal justice system. The commission
was the result of a spectacular daylight payroll robbery in 1917 that greatly
aroused the business community. Meanwhile, in Cleveland events were setting
the stage for the creation of the Cleveland Survey of Criminal Justice, a quite
different crime commission from the one in Chicago. These two commissions
were the first of many similar agencies that appeared across the country during
the next decade. The 1920s might well be called the age of the crime commission; by 1931 there had appeared at least seven local, sixteen state, and two
national crime commissions. Publication in 1931 of the fourteen volumes of the
Wickersham Commission (officially the National Commission on Law Observance
and Enforcement) marked the high point of the movement.[30]

The significance of the crime commissions lies more with their style than
with the substance of their recommendations about the police. The crime commissions represented the fulfillment of the ideals of pre-World War I progressive
reform, particularly the belief that social problems required the ongoing attention of professional experts whose talents were mobilized through bureaucratic
agencies. What had been done haphazardly before World War I was done far
more systematically in the 1920s. The various crime commission reports introduced almost no new ideas in police administration. The important differences
were twofold. First, many of the crime commissions gave continuing attention
to police problems. Such was the case in Chicago, for example. Second, most of
the investigations viewed the police in the context of the entire criminal justice
system. This represented considerable progress in the level of sophistication in
thinking about the police. No longer were the police viewed merely as an extension of partisan politics; rather they were increasingly seen as an agency of social
control with a complex relationship to other formal agencies.

The Wickersham Commission marked another qualitative change in public
thinking about the police. Established in 1929 by President Herbert Hoover, it
was the first full-scale national investigation of the American criminal justice
system. Two of the fourteen volumes pertained to the police and one of those,

an expose of the third degree, attracted virtually all of the publicity. The fact that a president of the United States considered it important to appoint a national crime commission was evidence of growing national concern about crime and criminal justice. This development began slowly in the 1920s, reached an even higher plateau in the 1930s, ebbed somewhat in the 1940s and 1950s, and then experienced a dramatic resurgence in the 1960s. By the end of the 1960s the crime problem was one of the most important national political issues.

In some respects it is difficult to generalize about the crime comissions of the 1920s since they took many different forms and were designed to serve different purposes. While the Chicago Crime Commission became a permanent institution, most of the commissions were short-lived. The Cleveland Survey, for example, was designed as a temporary investigation that would produce one final report. And while the Cleveland, Missouri, and Illinois surveys embraced the entire criminal justice system, many of the others were created for the more limited purpose of revising the state criminal code. Crime commissions also represented different interest groups. The Kansas City Law Enforcement Association was blatantly partisan and represented the attack of one identifiable political faction upon its chief rival. The Chicago and Los Angeles Crime Commissions, meanwhile, were creations of and represented the interests of business groups. The Cleveland Survey represented a more sophisticated approach. Nominally it was a high-level academic study, involving some of the leading legal minds in the country. But it was created at the instigation of elite groups, notably the local bar, and funded by a private group, the Cleveland Foundation.[31]

Despite the variety of forms that crime commissions took, they all represented one common point of view: a growing dissatisfaction with the administration of criminal justice on the part of elite groups in society. Whereas investigations of different agencies, particularly the police, had been blatantly partisan in the nineteenth century, the twentieth-century approach was to camouflage partisan interests behind a facade of nonpartisanship. If the Lexow Investigation of the New York police represented the nineteenth-century approach to reform, the Cleveland Survey of Criminal Justice or the Wickersham Commission represented the modern style. The shift had important political consequences. It was possible for all sides to play the partisan game, and all did in the nineteenth century. But only elite groups—particularly business interests and the organized bar—commanded the resources and techniques of the modern crime commission.

The Cleveland Survey of Criminal Justice most clearly represented the new style of investigation. Its origins, however, were rooted in the familiar syndrome of scandal, expose, and demand for reform. In the spring of 1920, the chief judge of the municipal court was implicated in "a particularly sordid crime." In response, the bar association, the mayor, and a number of scholars at Western Reserve University called for a full-scale investigation of the entire Cleveland criminal justice system. The Cleveland Foundation, a private philanthropy which had previously sponsored studies of the local school system and municipal recreation, agreed to fund the project. With a budget of $50,000 and a staff of thirty-five the survey began in February 1921, and was completed in June. The sophistication of the final report, published in 1922, was largely the result of the influence of the codirectors: Felix Frankfurter and Roscoe Pound, two of the most eminent names in twentieth century American legal thought. To handle particular aspects of the survey, Pound and Frankfurter enlisted respected experts in different fields. The study of the Cleveland police department, for example, was conducted by Raymond Fosdick, author of the recently published *American Police Systems* and perhaps the leading expert on police administration.[32]

The Cleveland Survey was aggressively academic and nonpartisan in approach. According to Felix Frankfurter it "marked the introduction of the research method into the field of practical administration of our system of dealing with crime . . . a pioneer attempt to become objective in a field which lends itself with particular ease to the distortions of feeling and 'hunch.'" The directors disdained the partisan "good-man–bad-man explanation of political phenomena" and disavowed any intention of "head-hunting" for individual villains. Rather, they sought to identify the underlying social and economic conditions which had brought about what they termed "the practical breakdown of criminal machinery." To achieve this goal they employed "disinterested, scientific" researchers "whose professional interest is the scientific administration of justice adapted to modern industrial conditions."[33]

The stated pretentions toward scientific objectivity, however, masked an important set of assumptions. Unlike previous investigations, the Cleveland Survey viewed the police in terms of effective crime suppression. This represented the beginnings of a subtle but extremely important redefinition of the police role in society. Gradually in the 1920s and more openly in the 1930s, police experts emphasized the crime-fighting image of the police at the expense of the social service aspects. This development, which was fostered by a number of different factors, was only encouraged by crime commission investigations which inevitably viewed the police in terms of the entire system of crime control.

Raymond Fosdick's report on the Cleveland police department was no surprise to anyone familiar with his previous work. His report was even guardedly favorable, concluding that "A general picture of the police service in Cleveland gives the impression of a group of men, singularly free from scandal and vicious corruption, but working in a rut, without intelligence or constructive policy, on an unimaginitive, perfunctory routine." This statement reflected the changing standards by which the police would be measured. It was no longer sufficient that the police were not doing something blatantly wrong; they were now expected to take an imaginitive and innovative approach to crime control. Fosdick emphasized sins of omission rather than sins of commission.[34]

Fosdick's list of police problems in Cleveland reflected a concern for administrative efficiency. Continuing the work of police reformers of the two previous decades, he stressed the need for strong leadership from a police executive who enjoyed security of tenure and who was free from direct political influence. With respect to rank-and-file patrolmen, Fosdick praised the existing eight-week training course, but expressed great concern about the high rate of personnel turnover. More selective recruitment procedures, he believed, would produce a greater number of men committed to police work as a career. Fosdick was also greatly disturbed over the apparently lax disciplinary standards that prevailed within the department. Only four of the twenty-three officers cited for drunkenness on duty were in fact dismissed from service. All in all, however, the record of internal discipline was far higher than prevailing conditions in most police departments two decades earlier. This indicated that the first stages of professionalization were comfortably underway.

In the latter portions of his report, Fosdick turned his attention to a set of issues that would increasingly dominate police thinking for the next four decades: the rational and efficient deployment of patrolmen. To achieve this, Fosdick recommended greater use of automobile patrols, a reduction in foot patrol, the closing of many existing precinct station houses, and in general a greater centralization of administrative procedures.

Efficiency in the suppression of crime dominated crime commission reports on the police in the twenties. This point of view was particularly evident in the work of the Chicago Crime Commission. In an October 1919 issue of its regular *Bulletin* the commission declared that "The business of crime is being more expertly conducted. Modern crime, like modern business, is tending towards centralization, organization and commercialization. Ours is a business nation. Our criminals apply business methods. . . ." As Mark Haller has argued in a study of the Chicago Crime Commission, that organization represented one of two major thrusts in police reform in Chicago. Business interests, concerned about property crime, pushed for administrative efficiency as a means of improving crime control. A very different group of reformers emphasized political corruption and the connections between the police and organized vice. This division in Chicago reflected the general split in police reform thinking during the Progressive Era.[35]

Haller argues that the efficiency-minded reformers, working through the crime commission, were far more successful than were the moral reformers. While this was generally true—almost all departments to some degree adopted the techniques of modern management—it would be a mistake to overemphasize their success. The history of the Chicago police in the 1920s is a case study in the persistence of partisan political influence and the frequent reorganization of the department. The effects of one "reform" were often nullified a few years later. During his first two terms as mayor (1915–1923) William H. ("Big Bill") Thompson actively cooperated with the crime commission. The businessmen behind the commission had little interest in combating vice while the mayor had strong political reasons for allowing it to flourish. Thus, both found a common interest in emphasizing ordinary property crime. The election of William H. Dever as mayor in 1923, however, brought about a dramatic change. Elected on a reform platform, Dever ended the overt toleration of bootlegging and other illegal vice activities in the city. This also resulted in an end to formal cooperation between the Mayor's office and the crime commission. But in 1927 Big Bill Thompson pledged to return Chicago to a "wide-open status and was reelected to a third term.[36]

The return of Thompson to power was then followed by a major reorganization of the Chicago police department. To permit the flourishing of illegal activities, the department was radically decentralized. No fewer than nineteen subordinates reported directly to the chief of police. Given the growing emphasis on administrative efficiency, and particularly the new concept of limiting the chief administrator's *span of control* (the number of subordinates who reported directly to him), the Chicago reorganization was a scandal. It was not only attacked by police reformers in Chicago, but was repeatedly cited years later as a classic example of administrative inefficiency. But radical decentralization represented inefficiency with a purpose. It served the mayor's intention of allowing illegal activities to flourish free from police interference.

Thompson's reorganization of the police department overstepped the tolerance limits of the members of the Chicago Crime Commission with whom he had previously had a good working relationship. Violence associated with the bootlegging industry soon began making national headlines and, in the eyes of businessmen, severely tarnishing the image of the city. Thompson quickly began to backtrack and appointed a new police chief, William F. Russell. A new reform group, the Citizens' Police Committee, began working on a full-scale reorganization of the Chicago police department. That same year, 1929, also saw the publication of the massive *Illinois Crime Survey* which included a critical appraisal of the Chicago police by August Vollmer. The citizens' committee published its own criticism in 1931 and by 1932 its recommended reforms were in the process of being implemented. The subsequent housecleaning, however, merely eliminated the most obvious signs of administrative inefficiency. Along with a more centralized command structure came higher standards of recruitment and training. It would be difficult to maintain that Chicago achieved a modern or efficient police department by these reforms alone or that they ended the persistent connection between the police and corrupt politics.[37]

The frustration of police reform was also evident in August Vollmer's one-year experience in Los Angeles, 1923-1924. Vollmer was brought to the city by the Los Angeles Crime Commission, a businessman's group modeled closely after the Chicago Crime Commission. The Los Angeles police for nearly twenty years had experienced an endless cycle of reform, scandal, and reform. The leaders of the Los Angeles Crime Commission believed that by bringing in Vollmer the situation could be corrected once and for all. Vollmer took a leave of absence from his job as chief of the Berkeley police and accepted a similar post in Los Angeles.

By the mid-1920s Vollmer was unquestionably the recognized dean of police chiefs. Through innovations in Berkeley, his extensive writings on a variety of police topics, and his year as president of the IACP in 1922, he had won an enormous national reputation. He was particularly noted for his pioneering work in developing college-level police education programs, automobile patrol, and scientific crime detection aids. His year as president of the IACP was an instructive experience. The published convention proceedings consisted of an enormous two-volume document that dwarfed previous convention proceedings and could serve as a comprehensive textbook on a wide range of police administration issues. Vollmer's year in Los Angeles was only one of many instances in which he would be asked to serve as a consultant for police departments across the country during the twenties and thirties.

Vollmer's experience in Los Angeles, however, was not a happy one. He immediately set out to implement some of his Berkeley-style reforms by cultivating ties with the local educational establishment and launching an internal police academy. But he increasingly found that refashioning a large metropolitan police department was far more difficult than it was in the much smaller Berkeley department located in a small and relatively homogeneous community. The legend of Vollmer's skill as an administrator rested largely on the force of his personal charisma in a small department. But in Los Angeles he found himself frustrated by the same factors that stymied reformers in other large cities: first, the sheer size of the bureaucracy itself and, second, the continuing and powerful influence of political pressure from many sectors of the metropolitan community. On top of this, he became personally involved in a public scandal involving a woman who allegedly attempted suicide on his account. Thus, Vollmer gladly left Los Angeles and returned to the happier pastures of Berkeley. His final report, issued as his annual report for 1924, analyzed the problems of the Los Angeles police department and contained a familiar set of recommendations for reform. The recommendations were ignored and the department remained unreformed and scandal ridden for another twenty-five years.[38]

The failure in Los Angeles did little to diminish Vollmer's steadily growing national reputation. Perhaps the pinnacle of his success as the acknowledged authority on police administration came in 1931 with the publication of the Wickersham Commission reports. Vollmer was the principal author of Volume 14, the report on *The Police*.

The Wickersham Commission was not the first national crime commission. In 1925 a group of prominent business leaders, led by Elbert H. Gary, then head of U. S. Steel, organized the National Crime Commission. The commission was conceived in Gary's New York office and formally announced to the public in November. Membership on the executive committee included a number of noted public figures, such as Charles Evans Hughes, former chief justice of the United States Supreme Court, and Newton D. Baker, former secretary of war. Baker had been intimately involved in police reform during his years as civic activist and mayor of Cleveland, Ohio. Perhaps even more significant, in terms of future developments, was the presence of Franklin D. Roosevelt, former assistant secretary of the navy and future governor of New York and president of the United States. As we later see, the decade of the 1930s was dominated by a hard-line law-and-order mood. Roosevelt's New Deal, moreover, contributed to a significant expansion of the federal role in criminal justice and police reform. His membership with the National Crime Commission in the mid-1920s, then, was an early indication of Roosevelt's concern about the crime problem and his receptivity to expanded federal action.[39]

The National Crime Commission was a private organization, closely resembling the Chicago Crime Commission. It was dominated by business interests concerned primarily with property crimes and adopted for itself the role of arousing public opinion. As one critic pointed out, few members of the commission had any direct expertise in criminal justice. Members were chosen with an eye toward their reputation rather than technical expertise. The work of the commission included sponsorship of two national conferences, assistance in the creation of a number of local organizations, and publication of several reports. The first conference, on April 28, 1926, ended with a call for the establishment of cooperating organizations in each state. Many of these new agencies were represented at a second conference in early November, 1927. The recommendations emerging from that conference, along with other commission documents, clearly indicated influence of the business community. The first recommendation proposed "Uniform state legislation and possibly national legislation to eliminate the receiver of stolen goods." The commission also published two reports on the problem of motor vehicle thefts.[40]

Significantly, concern over property crimes stimulated interest in gun control legislation. Various proposals were regularly debated at IACP conventions through the 1920s. And in 1922 the prestigious American Bar Association went so far as to propose the outright abolition of handguns: "We recommend that the manufacture and sale of pistols and of cartridges designed to be used in them, shall be absolutely prohibited, save as such manufacture shall be necessary for governmental and official use under legal regulation of control." Although interest in gun control was surprisingly high, the net result in terms of legislation was meager. Most states simply tightened their laws concerning the carrying of concealed weapons and sought to prohibit certain categories of persons from owning guns (delegates to the IACP conventions, for example, wanted to prevent "aliens" from owning guns). A number of gun control bills were introduced in Congress with little result. In the end, the 1920s marked the high tide of the gun control movement. The 1930s witnessed a significant shift in the direction of gun fetishism.[41]

The growing national concern about the crime problem in the late 1920s set the stage for President Herbert Hoover's appointment of the Wickersham Commission. In his March 1929 inaugural address Hoover warned that "the most malign of all these dangers today is disregard and disobedience of law. Crime is increasing. Confidence in rigid and speedy justice is decreasing." Undoubtedly, the national experiment with prohibition had helped to arouse concern over lawlessness. Not only was there widespread law breaking by ordinary citizens who continued to drink, but the spectacular crimes associated with the boot-legging industry further dramatized the problem. In spite of this, one is struck by the relatively moderate mood of public opinion and the cautious approach of President Hoover in particular. Hoover recognized that the crime problem was complex and that there were no easy solutions. In appointing the National Com-mission on Law Observance and Enforcement, he promised no quick results. Rather, he asked the commission to undertake an exhaustive and patient study of the many different aspects of the problem. This approach stands in sharp contrast to the approach taken by the New Deal under Roosevelt which, in turn, was influenced by a dramatic increase in national paranoia over an alleged crime wave. The law-and-order mood of the 1930s is examined in depth in the following chapter.[42]

The Wickersham Commission reports were supplemented by a second com-mission established by President Hoover. The report of the President's Com-mission on Social Trends, published in 1933 as *Recent Social Trends*, was a comprehensive examination of virtually every facet of American society. The chapter on "Crime and Punishment," written by criminologists Edwin Suther-land and C. E. Gehlke (a prominent figure in the Cleveland Survey), was a com-plete survey of developments in criminal justice through the first three decades of the century. A sober and detailed account, it effectively debunked the growing myth of a national crime wave.[43]

Of the fourteen volumes published by the Wickersham Commission in 1931, two volumes dealt specifically with the American police. Other volumes con-sidered such issues as the enforcement of prohibition, the causes and cost of crime, the state of criminal statistics, and the operations of various criminal justice agencies. Unfortunately there has been no detailed examination of the work of the Wickersham Commission. The two volumes devoted to the police differed radically, both in content and public reception. Volume 14, *The Police*, contained the latest statement of August Vollmer's views on police reform. The basic ideas were by then familiar to most people in the field: the need for strong leadership, the importance of eliminating political influence, the necessity of upgrading recruitment and training standards, and so on. The report merely ratified what was by then the established consensus of opinion on police profes-sionalization and Vollmer's status as its leading spokesperson.

Vollmer's report was completely overshadowed by the other volume on the police, Report 11, *Lawlessness in Law Enforcement*. In fact, the revelations about police misconduct contained in this report eclipsed all the other volumes published by the Wickersham Commission. The official report was accompanied by the publication of a popular account, *Our Lawless Police*, and marked the culmination of growing national concern about police misconduct in general and the so-called third degree in particular. The significance of the third degree controversy was twofold. On the one hand it reflected the heightened public concern about the police. At the same time, however, it represented a dramatic shift in public expectations about the quality of law enforcement. Brutality and uncivil conduct had long been a part of the American police tradition. However, by the early 1930s the public was not only increasingly intolerant of the more flagrant abuses of power but also began to expect the police to conform to constitutional standards of due process. This revolution in public expectations reached a plateau in the early 1930s but would continue to rise, bursting into national controversy again in the 1960s as a result of a series of major Supreme Court decisions.[44]

Lawlessness in Law Enforcement found a widespread pattern of police abuse. While acknowledging that accurate information was difficult to obtain—the police could be expected to deny accusations and victims would be prone to exaggerate—the authors concluded unambiguously that "The third degree—the inflicting of pain, physical or mental, to extract confessions or statements—is widespread throughout the country." They reported that "physical brutality is extensively practiced. The methods are various. They range from beating to harsher forms of torture. The commoner forms are beating with the fists or with some implement, especially the rubber hose that inflicts pain but it not likely to leave permanent visible scars." Other abuses included protracted questioning, the use of threats (usually of physical harm), illegal detention, and the use of physical brutality in making arrests.[45]

Evidence of routine beatings was extensively documented in the report. The police in a number of cities had devised incredibly perverse methods for extracting confessions. Suspects were suspended by their ankles out of upper story windows until they confessed, while a number of murder suspects were made to stand for extended periods of time with their hands on the body of the victim. In Cleveland one suspect was stripped, made to lie naked on the floor, and repeatedly lifted up by his genitals. Detroit police occasionally took suspects "around the loop," transporting them from police station to police station to keep them isolated from friends, family, or legal counsel. Indigent suspects received the bulk of the abuse, and blacks were disproportionately represented in both north and south.

Only a few cities managed to keep misconduct under control. The authors cited Cincinnati as a notable example of professional standards: "There has been little third degree in Cincinnati during the past three years. The present policy of the department is sincerely opposed to it. The consensus of opinion is that, with the installation of the present city-manager system and the retirement of an administration which used the rubber hose and other accessories a change began." The Cincinnati police department did achieve a considerable reputation for professionalism in the 1920s and 1930s, taking its place alongside Milwaukee as the most advanced police department in the country. Reform, however, did not necessarily mean the elimination of the third degree, as the case of Buffalo suggests. The report commented that "It is noteworthy that third degree methods and illegal detentions in Buffalo are not the result of any lack of discipline, but are the practices of a department which has many modern traits and is under rigid control." The Buffalo commissioner of police proudly defended his policy of aggressive crime control: "If I have to violate the Constitution or my oath of office, I'll violate the Constitution . . . A policeman should be free as a fireman to protect his community . . . Nobody ever thinks of hedging a fireman about with a lot of laws that favor the fire . . . Shysters have turned the Constitution into a refuge for the criminal."[46]

The publicity arising from the Wickersham Commission revelations threw the police on the defensive. Public attention focused on the scandal of police misconduct and ignored the more mundane areas of recruitment, training, and records where considerable progress had been made. At the 1931 convention of the California Peace Officer's Association the Wickersham Commission report was attacked by police chiefs. (The California group, it should be noted, was then a first-rate professional association whose work and accomplishments far exceeded those of the IACP.) Chief C. H. Kelley of Pasadena complained that the American police had been judged unfairly. "It would seem fair to state," he argued, "that the Commission has charged, arraigned, tried and convicted many of the larger police departments in the United States on the charge of extreme cruelty and, in some instances brutality in the handling of criminals. . . ." Kelley complained that "This conclusion has been arrived at without the police officials being accorded the formality of appearing before a court of record. . . ." Kelley further charged that "Public opinion in the United States is against the police officer who is actually engaged in bringing criminals to justice. . . ." The Wickersham report only encouraged the public stereotype of the police officer as "a man with a thick neck, rather low mentality, but possessed of a remarkable degree of physical strength and animal courage. . . ."[47]

Complain as they might, police officials had to face the fact that the Wickersham report greatly influenced public thinking about the police. While the abuses surrounding police misconduct are not to be denied, the ensuing publicity obscured the progress the police had made in the previous two decades. Professionalization, at least in terms of internal efficiency, had moved steadily forward in the 1920s, fulfilling much of the promise of the pre–World War I movement.

The Police in the Twenties: Progress with Problems

In 1933, two years after publication of the Wickersham Commission reports, the *Journal of Criminal Law and Criminology* asked August Vollmer to survey "Police Progress in the Past Twenty-Five Years." As the recognized authority on police administration, Vollmer was the logical choice for the assignment. Contrary to the image conveyed by the Wickersham Commission, Vollmer boldly asserted that "In no other branch of government have such remarkable changes been made as those made in the field of police organization and administration during the last quarter of a century." In fact, he continued, "One can hardly believe that such great advances could be made is so short a time." This observation could, of course, be viewed as self-serving since the time period involved coincided exactly with Vollmer's career and progress was most evident in areas he had emphasized. But it was probably an accurate assessment, objectively considered, for there had in fact been genuine, even remarkable progress in police reform.[48]

What evidence of police progress did Vollmer cite? He identified ten specific areas, five concerned with internal administration and five dealing with scientific crime fighting. The latter represented an important shift in Vollmer's own thinking as well as the general definition of police professionalism. As recently as 1921 Vollmer had been one of the leading proponents of the social work aspects of policing. By the early 1930s, however, the tide had shifted dramatically. The idea of the police as social workers fell into almost total eclipse, replaced by the image of the cop as crime fighter. As we have already seen, the mid-1920s marked the ossification and gradual demise of the policewomen's movement. And, as we see in the following chapter, the crime fighting aspects became even more pronounced as the thirties progressed.

The areas of progress cited by Vollmer more accurately represented the bureaucratization of the police rather than professionalization. That is to say, police organizations became more complex, more elaborate, and more governed by impersonal rules of procedure. Changes in personnel procedures were perhaps the most notable area of progress. With the exception of Kansas City (a corruption-ridden exception to the rule) civil service was nearly universal. Police work was increasingly recognized as a permanent career and most departments had begun to offer a wide range of fringe benefits and ancillary services. A 1929 survey, for example, revealed that it was "a fairly general practice to allow sick-leave with pay," that fifty-seven of seventy-eight cities surveyed provided two-week vacations with pay, and that all but seven of seventy-eight cities maintained some form of pension plan. Employment in police work had stabilized significantly. Wholesale removals were largely a thing of the past (again with the exception of Kansas City and a few other cities). In 1928 the personnel turnover in the seventy-eight cities averaged 4.17 percent a year.[49]

Additional progress had also been made in the area of police education and training. The gospel according to August Vollmer was spreading. He cited New York, St. Louis, Louisville, and Milwaukee as police departments with particularly strong in-house training programs. In New York and California, meanwhile, the first steps had been taken to provide training for smaller police departments on a regular basis in regional or "zone" schools. Finally, another milestone was passed when San Jose State College, with Vollmer's assistance, created the first four-year college-level law enforcement program in 1931.[50]

The difference between the bureaucratization of the police and professionalization was more than a matter of semantics. Bureaucratization entailed the development of formal and elaborate internal procedures (civil service, training programs, etc.) that subjected the police officer to more direct control and supervision. The control of the rank and file was in fact regarded as the great accomplishment of police reform. But this was not the same as professionalization, if by that concept we mean enhancing the independent judgment of the practitioner. The police in the 1920s, however, were not evolving in the same direction as the recognized professions. Rather, police officers were regarded as objects to be controlled and directed by chief administrators. If anything, it was the police chiefs who were professionalizing, and doing so at the expense of the rank and file.[51]

The inherent problems of bureaucratic organizations went largely unnoticed as the police progressed in the 1920s. Observers such as Vollmer were too busy measuring the police against the standards of the past—and finding much to celebrate—to notice the emerging problems of the future. The progress noted by Vollmer also failed to take into account other sweeping changes that were overtaking the American police. Technology provided the mainspring of those changes and the automobile, the telephone, and the two-way radio slowly began to effect a revolution in the nature of police service.

The police patrol car, which had been largely a novelty prior to World War I, had become an inescapable necessity by the 1920s. Urban growth in the prosperous twenties expanded both the population and physical size of American cities. Police departments faced the problem of spreading their limited manpower throughout the city in such a way as to provide at least the appearance of full police protection. Gradually the patrol car replaced foot patrol. Most of the police surveys in the decade, beginning with the Cleveland Survey, recommended the greater use of auto patrol. August Vollmer made auto patrol one of his major points of emphasis and claimed credit for making Berkeley the first police department entirely mobilized by car. The patrol car was also an extremely visible manifestation of the police and, beginning in the 1920s, the police increasingly equated progress and professionalism with the latest in automobile equipment.[52]

The patrol car was eventually joined by another major technological innovation, the two-way radio. The radio began to come into widespread use in the early 1930s. The radio-dispatched patrol car effected a hidden but far-reaching revolution in the nature of police work. The impact was twofold. First, the two-way radio allowed supervisors to maintain a far closer supervision of patrolmen than ever before. This in effect greatly enhanced the general trend toward more centralized command and control procedures within police departments. Complete control, of course, was never fully achieved. For their part, patrolmen developed ingenious techniques for subverting the effect of the new communications system and preserving for themselves an important degree of autonomy.

The second major impact of the new technology was on relations between the police and the public. The growth of telephone service completed the new communications system. While the patrol car removed the patrolman from the street, thereby isolating him from the general public, the telphone, two-way radio, and patrol car made it possible for citizens to make heavier demands for police service. A telephone call to police headquarters could produce a patrol car. Proud of their new equipment and the possibilities it opened up, the police themselves encouraged this practice. The change, of course, was not immediate. The communications network developed gradually, more rapidly in some cities than others. And it took some time for the public to learn new habits of calling the police. The long-term result was a revolution in public expectations about both police service and the level of order that should prevail in urban society. Because it was now possible to call the police to complain about even the smallest disturbance, the public gradually began to regard even the smallest disturbance as intolerable. Technological innovation effected an unforeseen and largely unnoticed social revolution. The result, of course, was not simply an added burden for the police but an important qualitative redefinition of the police role.[53]

The decade of the twenties, then, was most important not because of the problems of enforcing prohibition, the most obvious law enforcement issue of the times. After all, the urban police had long before lerned how to deal with unenforceable laws that tried to regulate human behavior. Rather, the period was most important for the subtle but profound shift in public expectations about the police role. Police experts such as August Vollmer, proud of their accomplishments in dealing with past problems, failed to notice the sweeping changes that were developing as the world changed around them.

**The Law-and-Order Decade,
1932–1940**

The decade of the 1930s marked an important turning point in the history of police reform. The financial crisis brought on by the depression forced many reluctant police departments to initiate long-delayed changes. The emergency gave an important measure of authority to efficiency-minded experts, many of whom came from the developing profession of public administration. This second generation of police reformers undertook studies of policing that represented a considerable advance in sophistication over previous investigations. The first genuine empirical studies of police work began to appear in the 1930s. The advance of professionalization was also marked by the emergence of a second generation of reform-oriented police administrators. By the end of the decade O. W. Wilson, disciple of August Vollmer, emerged as the leading authority on police administration. It was significant that Wilson was himself a police chief rather than an interested party from another profession. Police work, in other words, was able to produce its own experts.[1]

The most portentous development of the decade was a redefinition of the police role and the ascendancy of the crime-fighter image. The primary impetus for this development came from a national scare about a crime wave that swept the country in the early 1930s. More than anyone else, J. Edgar Hoover skillfully manipulated this public mood both to enlarge the role of the FBI and to emphasize the law enforcement aspects of policing at the expense of the more typical social service duties. By the end of the decade the public image of the police was far different from what it had been only ten years before. This change was also accompanied by a significant expansion of the role of the federal government in criminal matters that had traditionally been the exclusive domain of local governments. The FBI was the primary vehicle for that new role and the bureau played a major role in reorienting thinking about police professionalism.

The Police Occupation in Hard Times

The economic collapse of the 1930s had the curious effect of improving the relative economic status of police work. As the economy spiraled downward and as unemployment figures steadily rose, jobs on police forces became highly prized. Job security, of course, had always been one of the major attractions of police work and this had been enhanced in recent decades by the spread of civil service protection, pension programs, and a full range of fringe benefits. Massive unemployment in the private sector simply effected a quantum leap in the attractiveness of police jobs.

Even in terms of salaries—unemployment aside—the police made significant gains relative to the blue-collar jobs that most police officers considered as realistic alternatives. This continued a trend that had developed in the 1920s when local governments, flushed with prosperity and growth, found it possible to grant significant wage increases to their police. The crime commissions of the twenties, meanwhile, continually reiterated the necessity of providing decent police salaries. By 1928 the maximum salaries for patrolmen in New York City, Chicago, San Francisco, and Los Angeles equalled or approached $2500 a year. Workers in the manufacturing sector could expect average annual earnings of $1534 that year, while those in construction could expect $1719.[2]

In the depression years the police increased their relative advantage over other blue collar occupations. Between 1928 and 1938 the average annual earnings of manufacturing workers dropped from $1534 to $1296, while construction workers suffered an even greater loss, falling from $1719 to $1193. Police patrolmen, on the other hand, managed to hold their own and in some cases even register gains. The maximum salaries for patrolmen in New York City, for example, rose from $2500 to $3049 between 1928 and 1938. The New Orleans patrolmen, traditionally among the lowest paid among big cities, raised their maximum from $1500 to $2004 a year. And in a period when municipal governments were hard pressed simply to remain solvent, it was little short of miraculous that salaries remained stable in such cities as Cincinnati and Chicago. Stable salaries, moreover, represented a de facto increase as the cost of living fell by nearly 10 percent between 1925 and 1938.[3]

Police departments were not completely immune from the effects of the depression by any means. Budgets in many cases were reduced and some departments found it necessary to discharge officers. There was no consistent pattern across the country. A 1933 survey of 104 cities with 50,000 or more people found that three-quarters had reduced minimum salaries by an average of about 10 percent. Twenty-six departments had made no changes while three had actually increased salaries. The year 1933, however, was the worst year of the entire depression. As economic conditions improved slightly over the next few years, many police departments restored cuts that had been made earlier.[4]

The case of the Milwaukee police illustrates how salaries could fluctuate from year to year as the economic picture changed. Starting salaries had reached a high of $2040 a year in 1930. Two years later they were reduced to $1836. In 1935 salaries were raised to $1938 and the next year restored to the original high of $2040. Another downturn in the economy soon followed, however, and salaries were reduced to $1800 in 1938. This represented the same salary that Milwaukee police officers had earned in 1925; the drop in the cost of living over the intervening thirteen years resulted in a substantial de facto raise. Some police departments laid off officers, either as an alternative or in addition to cutting salaries. The Department of Justice reported that between 1930 and 1937 fourteen of the twenty-six largest cities in the country had reduced the size of their forces. In the same period, however, the other twelve departments had increased in size.[5]

The depression also gave an important boost to many police reforms. A number of police administrators welcomed the financial crisis as an opportunity to eliminate inefficient practices that had grown up over the years and were difficult to eliminate. Hard times generated a heightened interest in administrative efficiency in several important areas. The 1930s witnessed the first efforts to analyze the actual work of patrol officers and to develop a scientific basis for their assignment. There was also considerable interest in consolidating police departments in metropolitan regions. Short of consolidation, which remained more a dream than a reality, some progress was made in the direction of establishing formal cooperation between neighboring law enforcement agencies.[6]

The drive for efficiency was led, in large part, by experts from the developing field of municipal administration. Whereas in the Progressive Era many police reformers emerged from the social work profession, in the 1930s there were no prominent police experts from that field. Bruce Smith of the National Institute of Public Administration was more typical of the cost-conscious efficiency experts of the period. In the mid-1930s police reform found a new institutional locus with the International City Management Association. In 1934 the association began publishing an annual *Municipal Yearbook* with a chapter devoted to developments in "Police Administration." August Vollmer surveyed the field in the first edition, but for the following nine years (1935-1943) the assignment went to his chief disciple, O. W. Wilson. As police chief of Wichita, Kansas, Wilson established a reputation for expertise on automobile patrol. Wilson succeeded his mentor, Vollmer, as the recognized "dean" of police administrators, and maintained that status until the early 1960s.[7]

In early 1934, *Public Management*, a municipal administration journal, asked Bruce Smith to survey "What the Depression Has Done to Police Service." Smith's observations were rather optimistic. He commented on "the favorable effects of an occasional disruption of established procedures" and argued that the depression "encouraged police administrators to review with a critical eye the facilities placed at their disposal and encouraged adoption of new devices and procedures." In particular, he found an excellent opportunity to eliminate unnecessary indoor assignments for uniformed officers, to close down district police stations, and to make greater use of police radios and automobile patrol. The depression, in short, provided an excuse to institute reforms that various crime commissions had been advocating through the 1920s.[8]

Two other public administration experts, also writing in *Public Management*, saw in the depression an opportunity to institute cost-saving reforms. Clarence Ridley and Ernest Nolting argued in favor of consolidating agencies in metropolitan areas, greater cooperation between the police and other social agencies, and more scientific methods for both selecting and assigning police officers. In general, the 1930s witnessed a considerable expansion in the use of social science concepts and techniques in police administration. Much of that impetus came from the growing contacts between police and universities, as well as trained professionals in the field of public administration. It was in the last area mentioned by Ridley and Nolting, the scientific distribution of patrolmen, that the most notable advances were made.[9]

The attempt to scientifically measure police work, and thus to plan work loads accordingly, received a strong impetus from the federal government. Police departments found themselves eligible for federal relief funds along with other public agencies. The WPA sponsored a limited number of police projects, but they included a few extremely important ones. The *Cincinnati Police Beat Survey*, one of the two pioneering documents in this area, for example, was funded in part by the WPA. The agency also sponsored an analysis of arrest patterns by the Buffalo police and supplied the personnel who modernized the Patterson, New Jersey, police department records system. By 1938 the WPA had funded a total of 101 police-related projects costing a total of $1,275,000. The figure, of course, seems ridiculously small by the standards of LEAA grantsmanship in the 1970s. But for its time it represented an important precedent in federal support for police research.[10]

The *Cincinnati Police Beat Survey* was jointly sponsored by the Cincinnati police and the Cincinnati Regional Crime Commission, which also took a leadership role in the area of law enforcement consolidation. The idea behind the survey was quite simple; in fact, one is struck by the fact that no agency had undertaken such a study earlier. The experts focused on the Basin district of Cincinnati, a four-square-mile area consisting of the heart of the business district and some suburban areas. Through the use of "the cold fact of statistics" for the year 1934 the researchers sought to gain an accurate picture of the actual work police officers performed. Official departmental statistics were used and the resulting report did not take into account differences that reflected discretionary decisions not to intervene on the part of individual officers. Methodological problems aside, the authors of the final report were confident that they had taken a giant step forward. Not surprisngly, they found that police beats had not changed for many years and, as a result "there is no uniformity whatsoever in the amount of activity required to police them." The report then recommended an equalization of beat assignments based on work-load factors.[11]

The Cincinnati project was soon followed by a similar research effort undertaken by Chief O. W. Wilson of Wichita, Kansas. By the late 1930s Wilson was well on his way toward supplanting his mentor, August Vollmer, as the foremost authority on police administration. That recognition was based largely on his concern for automobile patrol, which was increasingly the main preoccupation of efficiency-minded police administrators. Wilson's intellectual debt to Vollmer was a direct one. Vollmer had steadily abandoned his own concern with the social work aspects of policing in the 1920s and early 1930s and increasingly emphasized technological developments such as the crime lab, the radio, and the patrol car.

Wilson was even more confident than the authors of the Cincinnati survey that he had established the basis for scientific police administration. He concluded his study with the claim that the "application of more scientific methods in the chronological and geographical distribution of personnel may be the first step toward developing the objective criteria by which the size of force necessary for effective police service can be determined." Wilson's report was published in 1941 by the Chicago-based Public Administration Service. In a foreword, Eliot Ness, then public safety director of Cleveland, announced that "For the first time police officials have a reliable standard with which to measure the effectiveness of the distribution of their respective forces."[12]

The question of what constituted a "reliable standard," however, remained an open one. Unfortunately, attempts to measure police work were distorted in the 1930s by another important innovation: the Uniform Crime Reports (UCR). The UCR system, launched in 1930 after decades of agitation for a national crime statistics system, was filled with innumerable flaws. The figures themselves remained unaudited, reflected official police activities not actual crime rates, and were subject to all sorts of manipulation. Even more serious was the fact that the UCR focused attention exclusively on the law enforcement activities of the police. Thus, the UCR and the drive for measurement techniques contributed significantly to the reorientation of the police role and the emphasis on the cop as crime fighter. Not for another thirty years would researchers rediscover the fact that the bulk of police time is devoted to service activities and begin to press for a more accurate definition of the police role.[13]

The analysis of actual police work which began to develop in the late 1930s was short-circuited by World War II. The war effort diverted energies away from empirical research projects on the police. One of the potentially most significant studies was undertaken in 1940 by the Baltimore Crime Commission. The commission examined various aspects of police work on a "typical day," April 11, 1940. The Commission sought to answer the question "Does Baltimore Need More Policemen?" and reflected the cost-conscious concerns of the 1930s. The commission did conclude that the city needed an additional 124 police officers, but, more importantly, other aspects of the investigation were rich with potential insights. The researchers undertook an hour-by-hour analysis of the number of officers actually on patrol duty and found that the percentage fluctuated wildly. Only 28 percent of the assigned force was actually on patrol between 8 and 9 A.M.; the figure rose to 69 percent between 10 and 11 A.M., but dropped to 20 percent between noon and 1:00 P.M. Had this particular avenue of research been pursued to its logical conclusion—perhaps by researchers in other cities—the result would have been a far more realistic picture of routine police work than was emerging from the O. W. Wilson-style investigations based largely on arrest statistics.[14]

The Baltimore Crime Commission report also reached two other significant conclusions. The size of the police department as a whole grew by 80 percent between 1912 and 1939, increasing from 1073 to 1919 sworn officers. Yet, the relative percentage of patrolmen had dropped from 75 percent to 72 percent. This development reflected the growing bureaucratization of the police department. As it became larger and subdivided into specialized units (traffic, vice, juvenile, etc.), a higher proportion of supervisory personnel was required. To the cost-conscious members of the crime commission this decline in the number of patrolmen on the street was a disturbing development. It seemed to run counter to the goal of greater efficiency in law enforcement. Nonetheless, it was an almost inevitable part of the professionalization process which resulted in an ever more complex police bureaucracy.

In an even more significant line of inquiry, the Baltimore report raised disturbing questions about the efficacy of automobile patrol. It reported that "Law enforcement officials have discovered that radio cars can never replace the peculiar type of service rendered by patrolmen." The traditional foot patrolman, inefficient as he might appear from one perspective, performed important functions that could not be accomplished from the patrol car, particularly in terms of direct contact with citizens on the street. This conclusion, however, was an isolated and lonely dissent from the growing consensus on the use of automobile patrol. Not until the 1960s, in the midst of a serious police–community relations crisis, would police administrators again think seriously about the value of foot patrol. In the end, the Baltimore Crime Commission study was an important lost opportunity. It raised a number of significant questions about police administration which deserved far more consideration than the neglect they did receive.[15]

O. W. Wilson's main influence beginning in the late 1930s involved not the question of automobile patrol per se, but whether to staff them with one or two patrolmen. Wilson emerged as the leading exponent of the one-man patrol car. The source of his growing influence was no mystery. The idea of the one-man patrol car had enormous appeal to those city officials and police administrators attempting to spread thin resources as broadly as possible. The depression gave a direct boost to this kind of cost consciousness, but the same concerns continued through the 1940s and 1950s. First the war and then urban growth through the prosperous late 1940s and 1950s put strains upon the manpower reserves of big city police departments.

Wilson advanced a number of different arguments in favor of the one-man patrol car. There was the obvious reason that it allowed the department to put up to twice as many patrol cars into service. Wilson argued that this reduced risk of victimization to citizens by half. At the same time, Wilson maintained that the patrol officer working alone was more efficient than when accompanied by a partner. "When together," he argued, "two officers spend part of their time visiting, swapping stories, and neglecting their regular routine duties." He also concluded that the individual officer was much safer when working alone. His statistics from Wichita indicated that in the nine years prior to 1928 a total of nine police officers had been killed on duty, while in the twelve years between 1928 and 1940 only one had died. Wilson suggested that this was due to the shift to one-man patrol cars, although he carefully avoided considering alternative explanations.[16]

The safety of the police officer was the main argument raised in defense of the two-man patrol car. Spokesmen for this position argued that serious crimes required two police officers, with one to serve as backup for the other. Also, it was suggested that patrol duty was safer with one officer driving and the other observing the district. And, finally, traffic accidents required one officer to handle the accident and another to direct traffic. The advocates of the two-man patrol car, however, waged a losing battle. In the long run, cost considerations outweighed other factors. By 1948 the *Police Journal* could report that 535 out of 840 cities (10,000 or more people) used at least some one-man cars and that 150 cities used them exclusively.[17]

The quest for efficiency in the 1930s gave impetus to another reform proposal, the consolidation of law enforcement agencies in metropolitan areas. Most of the leadership came from public administration experts who had an ingrained bias against the fragmentation of government agencies in urban regions and the consequent duplication of effort. Police experts contributed two concerns of their own. First, they sought additional ways of reducing expenses and, second, they increasingly argued that fragmentation of agencies hindered crime control efforts. Since the advent of the automobile, police officials had increasingly argued that the mobility of criminals allowed them to elude apprehension. This was but one more manifestation of the growing emphasis on the law enforcement aspects of policing at the expense of noncriminal service duties.

The fragmentation of governmental units in large metropolitan areas was documented in two major studies published during the 1930s. Charles Merriam of the University of Chicago pointed out that there were 1642 separate governmental units in the Chicago region, including not only cities, counties, and townships, but also various school, park, and sanitation districts. Within the area there were 350 law enforcement agencies, supplemented by another 350 private police organizations. The Cincinnati Regional Crime Commission hired police expert Bruce Smith to survey the situation in that area. Smith discovered a total of 147 law enforcement agencies spread out over two states and six counties.[18]

Bruce Smith's report, *A Regional Police Plan for Cincinnati and its Environs*, published in 1932 by the Institute for Public Administration, represented the single most important statement of the metropolitan coordination ideal. Luther Gulick, in his foreword to the report, hailed it as "a pioneer work . . . the first specific study of policing as both a local and regional problem." Smith found that of the 147 different law enforcement agencies, only the Cincinnati police department offered any meaningful training for its officers or made any serious attempt to provide systematic patrol service. The Cincinnati police at that time, it should be noted, was rapidly earning a reputation as one of the most advanced and professional of large city departments. Smith, however, acknowledged the political obstacles to the consolidation of police agencies. "The plan presented here," he wrote, "frankly accepts the highly decentralized scheme which characterizes police service throughout the United States." Instead, Smith recommended increased cooperation between agencies. In particular he called for coordination of communications systems, the sharing of criminal records, and the development of a crime lab available to all units in the area. It should be noted that all these recommendations pertained to crime fighting efforts.[19]

Some additional cooperation did develop in the wake of Smith's report (although frankly there had been considerable cooperation beforehand). A Cincinnati Regional Police Association representing seventy-eight law enforcement agencies began a regular series of bimonthly meetings and from this emerged a monthly crime reporting system and a plan to maintain a single fingerprint file. Also, the Cincinnati police began providing free radio service to twenty-nine other agencies.

In the long run, however, police consolidation and cooperation remained more a dream than an accomplishment. The alleged inefficiency of small governmental units and the problems of cooperation remained a standard item on the agenda of mnay policy reformers through the 1970s. Both the 1967 President's Crime Commission and the 1973 report of the National Advisory Commission on Criminal Justice Standards and Goals called for the consolidation of small units. The latter report, for example, recommended the consolidation of all law enforcement agencies with fewer than ten officers. Yet, none of the many reports of this sort over the years effectively addressed themselves realistically to the political obstacles to consolidation.[20]

In the end, then, the economic impact of the depression on police service was surprisingly benign. Police department budgets did not suffer much and the relative economic standing of police officers actually improved to a great degree. Experts such as Bruce Smith were probably right in that the financial crisis stimulated efforts to cut costs and helped to eliminate many old and inefficient practices. Unfortunately, however, it also led to an even more uncritical faith in the efficacy of automobile patrol.

The Police and the Labor Movement

An important consequence of the depression and the New Deal was the upsurge of the American labor movement, particularly the expansion of the CIO into industries previously unorganized. The resulting social conflicts, which in many localities constituted a virtual civil war, inevitably embroiled the police in controversy. The role of the police in the industrial conflicts of the 1930s, however, cannot be explained in terms of a simple formula. The situation differed from city to city and was influenced by economic, political, and administrative factors.

There is no question but that in most cities the police were major antagonists of the burgeoning labor movement. The entire decade of the thirties was punctuated by instances of police violence. The most notorious single episode was the Memorial Day Massacre in Chicago on May 30, 1937. Striking steelworkers and their families had gathered for a massive rally and picnic near the Republic Steel works in south Chicago. When the strikers began to move toward the steelworks to set up a picket line, the Chicago police went on a rampage, shooting indiscriminantly into the crowd and attacking with their billy clubs. When the rampage was over, four people were dead and more than eighty hospitalized with injuries. More than twenty of those hospitalized were policemen, injured when the enraged steelworkers fought back.[21]

Charges of police brutality were raised in many other cities as a result of police actions. Labor organizers in San Francisco charged that there has been a "police riot" (perhaps the first use of that term) on May 30, 1934. During the protracted Minneapolis Teamsters' strike the same year there was evidence of open collusion between the police, business interests, and private vigilante groups. Skirmishes between the police and strikers took on all the characteristics of full-scale military actions, with the strikers utilizing organized and coordinated movements to neutralize the police. And in Jersey City, Mayor Frank Hague used a full range of municipal powers—denial of speaking permits, harassment arrests, and outright brutality—to suppress a CIO organizing campaign.[22]

The sources of police antagonism to the labor movement were many. It would be an oversimplification to maintain it was solely the result of direct control by industrialists. A variety of social, economic, and political factors came into play. In some cities the police sought to play a scrupulously nonpartisan role. In others the police department assumed the role of labor mediator, actively seeking to resolve disputes.

A good deal of the antagonism of the police to the labor movement can be attributed to their relatively secure and improving economic situation. Conscious of their own good fortune, rank-and-file officers easily fell into a conservative mood and, like businessmen, viewed the labor upsurge as a threat to the status quo. Contributing to this was an important element of ethnic group consciousness. In Chicago, for example, it was estimated that more than three-quarters of the members of the police department were Irish-Americans. The labor movement, and the new CIO industrial unions in particular, were heavily dominated by Americans of southern and eastern European extraction—Poles, Italians, Hungarians, etc. Thus, the Memorial Day Massacre, for example, represented a confrontation between an older and more established ethnic group on the one hand, and the rising aspirations of more recent immigrant groups on the other.[23]

Police hostility to the labor movement also represented, in some cases, the cynical calculations of elected public officials. The most notorious case was Jersey City, where Mayor Frank ("Boss") Hague attempted to completely suppress the CIO. Ultimately, Hague's campaign became a national *cause celebre* and the American Civil Liberties Union joined with the CIO in a major legal struggle that eventually went to the U.S. Supreme Court. The court's decision in *Hague v. CIO* was a landmark case in the annals of free speech. The CIO and the ACLU documented a systematic pattern of harassment in which the police played a prominent role. Vagrancy arrests for example, were a common technique for harassing union organizers, along with many other blatant violations of constitutional rights.[24]

Hague's interest in keeping the CIO out of Jersey City arose from the burden of maintaining his bloated and corrupt political machine. During his tenure as mayor, between 1917 and 1940, the per capita cost of city government in Jersey City rose fivefold, from $14 to $78 a year. The police department was one of the most expensive items in the budget. By 1940 Jersey City had the largest and most expensive police department of any city in its population class. One observer called the 968 person force a "Mexican army" because it was so top-heavy with officials who performed little if any real police work. The $3,552,624 annual budget far exceeded the $1.2 million and $1.4 million budgets of Rochester and Seattle, cities of comparable size.

Not surprisingly, Jersey City also had the highest tax rates of any city its size in the United States. And it was concern for tax revenues that led Hague to end his former sympathy with organized labor and launch a full-scale attack on the CIO. To support the machine Hague realized that he needed a solid tax base. The antiunion campaign, then, was designed to make Jersey City attractive to business investment. The institutional needs of the machine, then, accounted for the policy of the Jersey City police toward the labor movement.

In other cities, conscious policy decisions by elected officials resulted in very different approaches. The dramatic upheaval of labor organizing placed enormous burdens on even the most fair-minded official. In Milwaukee, for example, there were 107 strikes in 1934 alone and the 868 policemen registered a total of 99,627 hours of overtime. In Cleveland, the police spent 84,928 hours on strike duty during 1938, responding to a total of ninety-eight different strikes. Cleveland Public Safety Director Eliot Ness created a special Labor Relations Bureau in the police department. "The major activity of the Bureau," he explained, "has been to promote peaceful settlements of strikes. . . . It seeks to effect compromises and the granting of concessions in the interests of avoiding violence. It also seeks to bring the parties together in conference if this procedure seems advisable." Cleveland was not the only city that adopted this practice. Similar labor mediation efforts emerged in Toledo, St. Louis, and Louisville, with the active participation of police officials.[25]

Although the Kansas City police department was almost as notoriously corrupt as Jersey City's, it took a strictly impartial position in labor disputes. Chief Otto P. Higgins (who later went to prison along with several other members of the Pendergast machine), created a special thirty-eight-man unit to handle strikes. "Right in the beginning," he argued, "we place ourselves in the position of umpires—umpires in a game that is to be played strictly according to the rules." In contrast to the situation in Jersey City, the Kansas City police recognized that the rules of the game included freedom of speech. We permit strikers to hold all the meetings they want and, in fact, encourage them to the extent of permitting them to use the city auditorium . . . free of charge."[26]

In New York officials went even further in their efforts to ensure police neutrality. Lewis J. Valentine, commissioner of the New York City police stressed the provisions of Article #33 of the departmental Manual of Procedure which stated that "It is to be assumed, unless advice to the contrary is had from the courts or other competent authority, that the purposes of a peaceful, orderly strike are legal." Valentine also indicated that it was his policy to "act swiftly and vigorously" against professional strikebreakers who fomented violence. In 1937, the Police Conference of New York State, which represented most departments in the state, adopted a policy statement of neutrality during strikes.[27]

Still other police departments, while not going to the extremes found in Jersey City, did institute formal antilabor policies, usually in the guise of special units to investigate alleged subversive activity. The mid-1930s, in fact, witnessed a subtle but profoundly important change in the prevailing definition of the chief threat to law and order. At the beginning of the decade the so-called crime wave was seen in terms of a few isolated bandits—the highly publicized John Dillingers and Pretty Boy Floyds. By 1937 and 1938 law enforcement officials increasingly emphasized alleged subversives, which included labor organizers and other radicals, as the chief law and order problem. J. Edgar Hoover and the enormous publicity operations of the FBI contributed greatly to the creation of the radical bogey. The late 1930s introduced into American police thinking an explicit antiradical political perspective. Previously, this outlook had been weak and unfocused at best. By the 1960s this antiradicalism would play a major role in the police response to the civil rights movement and other political developments. It gave the police a more formal identification with the status quo and an increased readiness to view all political protest activities as subversive.[28]

The activities of the antisubversive Red Squad of the Los Angeles Police Department were extensively documented by the investigations of the U.S. Senate Committee on Education and Labor—the famous Lafollette Committee. Beginning in the early 1920s the Los Angeles police kept a close surveillance of alleged radicals. Most of the attention focused on labor unions. The intelligence bureau infiltrated unions, kept files of active or potential members, and in numerous instances broke up planned union meetings. Throughout California concern about radicalism rose significantly in the late 1930s. The subject became a major theme in the annual debates of the California Peace Officers Association. And in 1938 the International Association of Chiefs of Police devoted a special session at their annual convention to the question of "Techniques For Handling Public Disorders."[29]

In one important respect, however, the depression years helped to eliminate some of the worst abuses of police power relating to organized labor. The LaFollette Committee hearings exposed a wide range of antilabor abuses on the part of private businesses. One of the worst of those practices had been the use of quasi-public private police. The system was most extensive in Pennsylvania where it could be traced back to the Civil War Era. Under the Coal and Iron Police Act, Pennsylvania permitted private corporations in rural areas to have their own security personnel deputized by the county sheriff and, thereby, clothed with police powers.

In the 1920s an attack on the private police system was mounted both by Governor Gifford Pinchot (first term: 1923-1927) and by the American Civil Liberties Union. After widespread violations of civil rights in the 1922 coal strike, Pinchot revoked the commissions of 3,670 of the 6,639 Coal and Iron Police. The abuses continued, but by the 1930s public opinion was more sympathetic to the plight of workingmen. At the start of his second term as governor (1931-1935), Pinchot simply revoked the commissions of all Coal and Iron Police. He also directed the state Department of Labor and Industry to undertake a full-scale investigation of the matter. The 1934 "Report to Governor Gifford Pinchot by the Commission on Special Policing in Industry" was a searing indictment of the special police system. The investigators charged that in some of the rural mining communities there existed "a curious feudal state"; the coal operators not only supplied most of the jobs, but also provided the company store and a company doctor, and controlled, directly or indirectly, law enforcement. The investigators also found that eliminating law enforcement abuses was more difficult than the governor had realized. When the Coal and Iron Police commissions were revoked in 1931, many of the large companies secured deputy sheriff appointments for the same men "so that the old Coal and Iron Police system continued, frequently with the same personnel, but under a new name."[30]

On the whole, however, the New Deal years created a political climate unfavorable to private police abuses in the labor area. Governor Pinchot's investigations were paralleled by the LaFollette Committee exposes on the national level. The new political power of organized labor itself also helped to put new constraints on official law enforcement agencies.

With respect to the poor and the destitute, the depression also brought about a revival of the police-sponsored social welfare activities that had largely disappeared since the nineteenth century. The Milwaukee police, for example, took in large numbers of station house lodgers. The annual numbers rose from

2,987 in 1930 to a high of 4,677 in 1932; by 1934 the number had fallen to 1,714 lodgers for the year. In New York City the police dispensed coffee and food. "During the extreme cold weather in the early part of 1935" the police distributed coffee and food "to all applicants" between the hours of noon and 2:00 P.M. and again between 5:00 and 7:00 P.M. A total of 307,557 people availed themselves of this sustenance, provided to the police by the Salvation Army.[31]

The New Deal, the FBI and the "War on Crime"

The decade of the 1930s witnessed a virtual revolution in the political dimensions of the crime problem, a development that had profound and lasting implications for the American police. Early in the decade there emerged a widespread feeling of a national crime wave. This represented a degree of national concern about the crime problem unlike anything before in American history. The political response to this mood was immediate and sweeping in impact. The role of the federal government in criminal justice matters, formerly the exclusive domain of state and local governments, expanded greatly. The Federal Bureau of Investigation suddenly emerged as a major factor in policing. Accompanying this institutional change was an even more profound intellectual reorientation: the 1930s marked the flowering of the crime-fighting role-image of the police. Concern about the crime problem was also felt in terms of a more conservative approach to a wide range of criminal justice policy issues.

The expansion of the federal government role, and of the FBI in particular, was intimately related to the New Deal itself. The Roosevelt administration effected a sweeping expansion of government intervention in all aspects of American life. The economic collapse brought about this expansion in economic and social affairs and, in the process, facilitated a similar development in the criminal justice sphere. The latter, however, had a justification of its own similar to, but largely independent of the economic crisis. Publicity over the alleged crime wave played an important catalytic role.

As historian William Leuchtenburg argues in a study of the New Deal, major expansions of the federal government role have been justified in terms of a national emergency. Those emergencies have usually been major wars, or social crises defined as the equivalent of war. The metaphor of foreign war was used as a definition of the economic collapse of the 1930s. In his inaugural address, Franklin D. Roosevelt declared that he would "ask the Congress for the one remaining instrument to meet the crisis—broad executive power to wage a war against the emergency, as great as the power that would be given to me if we were in fact invaded by a foreign foe." The new president also indicated that he would ask the people themselves to mobilize the energies "as a trained and loyal army willing to sacrifice for the common good of a common discipline."[32]

The sense of national emergency with respect to crime derived largely from a few spectacular and well-publicized crimes in the early 1930s. The stage had been set in the 1920s with the problem of prohibition and the highly publicized gangland killings in Chicago. But the mood of the 1920s, as reflected in the national media and by national political leaders, was remarkably restrained. As we have already noted, the primary political response to the crime problem in the 1920s was the spread of crime commissions. These, for the most part, were rather sober and often scholarly ventures. The decade of the 1930s proved to be very different.

Perhaps the major turning point was the Lindberg kidnapping in 1932. In March, the year-and-a-half-old son of Charles and Anne Lindberg was kidnapped from their New Jersey home. Because of Lindberg's national fame, the case became one of the most highly publicized events of the year. Congress wasted little time rushing through the so-called Lindberg Law making kidnapping a federal offense. The sequence of events in the Lindberg case foreshadowed developments in the next few years: highly publicized crimes, increased public fears of a crime wave, and an expanded role for the federal government.[33]

The kidnapping and the passage of the Lindberg Law preceded the election of 1932 and the coming to power of the Roosevelt administration. Nonetheless, J. Edgar Hoover, director of the Bureau of Investigation, sensed the opportunities dramatized by the Lindberg case. Since becoming director in 1924, in the wake of massive scandals, Hoover had presided over a small and unobtrusive agency (in some of his early reports, in fact, Hoover proudly announced that he had managed to reduce its size). In 1930 the bureau scored a major coup when it was designated the national clearing house for the new Uniform Crime Reports (UCR) system. But nothing prior to 1933 suggested the dramatic transformation of the bureau in the years that followed.[34]

Between 1934 and 1936 the public relations department of the bureau, under Hoover's guidance, mounted a publicity blitz that emphasized both the threat of a crime wave and the role of the bureau as a bulwark of law and order. The publicity surrounded a few criminals, inflated to heroic proportions by the bureau's press releases, who were to become the main figures in the new mythology of the bureau. In the summer of 1934 bureau agents gunned down John Dillinger and, in the next few years, killed or apprehended Pretty Boy Floyd, Baby Face Nelson, Ma Barker, and Alvin "Creepy" Karpis.[35]

Students of both American crime and the FBI generally acknowledge that the publicity surrounding these particular criminals was inflated out of all proportion to reality. In fact, professional criminologists doubted that there was anything approaching a national crime wave. In their contribution to the 1933 *Recent Social Trends*, criminologists Edwin H. Sutherland and C. E. Gehlke asserted that "No support is found for the belief that an immense crime wave has engulfed the United States." Their figures suggested that "the number of arrests and of court cases per 100,000 population increased moderately from

1900 to 1930, with a tendency to rise more rapidly after 1920 than before. A large part, however, of the increase in the last decade is explained by traffic cases, which increased at approximately the same rate as automobile registrations." Another writer debunked the notion that kidnapping was becoming a massive national crime problem. Analysis of figures from specific cities indicated that kidnapping, in 1932, was a relatively rare event, usually conducted by amateurs who only infrequently transported their victims across state lines.[36]

Sober analyses of crime statistics, however, had little impact on public opinion which was more susceptible to the FBI's press releases. The mass media played an important role in shaping public thinking. The development of the motion picture industry and then radio in the 1920s greatly altered the context of media influence. Not only did news travel faster than ever before, but the media had the power to create national heroes. Law enforcement officials were acutely conscious of the potential for glamorizing crime and criminals. J. Edgar Hoover made little secret of the fact that he set out to create a law enforcement hero. The IACP, meanwhile, created a special committee to lobby in Hollywood for more positive images of law enforcement and "less glorification of the criminal."[37]

One of the most disturbing aspects of rising concern about crime in the early 1930s was the particularly vicious quality of the rhetoric that public officials now used. J. Edgar Hoover was possibly the worst offender and may well have been responsible for the new style. At the 1934 Attorney General's Conference on Crime he referred to criminals as "vermin of the worst type." Lewis J. Valentine, commissioner of the New York City police, at the same conference, labeled criminals "mad dogs" and "human vultures" and called the crime problem "an infamous, vicious, cancerous growth," a "national menace," that required "a definite and aggressive program." Hoover, meanwhile, preferred to call a certain criminal as "Public Rat Number One."[38]

Congress responded to the alleged menace of a crime wave with a series of new laws rushed through to passage in the heat of the early New Deal. One of the first of these new laws was an extension of the 1932 Lindberg Law. On May 18, 1934, Congress enacted legislation making it a federal crime to either transport or aid in the transportation of a kidnap victim across state lines. Furthermore, it constituted a criminal conspiracy for two or more persons to enter into an agreement to carry out a kidnapping that would involve interstate commerce. On the same day, Congress enacted the Fugitive Felon Act making it a federal offense to cross state lines to avoid prosecution or to avoid testifying in a criminal case that involved a felony. Four days later, on May 22, 1934, Congress passed the Interstate Theft Act which made it a federal crime to transport across state lines stolen goods valued at more than $5000. This legislation was essentially an expansion of the 1919 Motor Vehicle Theft Act, one of the earliest intrusions of the federal government into state and local criminal activities. Finally, on June 26, 1934, Congress enacted the National

Firearms Act. The new law was heavily compromised, however, as public opinion, especially among police chiefs and in the legal profession, had swung against gun control. The new law provided for a tax on machine guns and other types of weapons, the licensing of gun dealers and some limitation on gun imports. Additional crime legislation followed in the next two years. Like much of the early New Deal legislation, the new crime laws sailed through Congress with remarkably little debate.[39]

In the midst of the economic crisis and the mounting hysteria over the "crime wave," few people raised objections to the expanding federal role. One dissenting voice was heard in *Harper's Magazine* where William Seagle issued a somewhat prophetic warning about the potential dangers of "The American National Police." Seagle pointed out that "The Seventy-Third Congress, in session last spring, added more to the provisions of the Federal criminal code than all previous Congresses." He challenged the basic justification for this new legislation: "The 'crime wave' has indeed been very much advertised since the early days of Prohibition but its existence has been very much doubted by the more sensible criminologists." Seagle cited statistics indicating that kidnapping, along with bank robbery the most publicized crime, was primarily a local offense. A 1932 survey showed that there were 285 reported kidnappings in 502 cities (which the author thought a rather low figure compared with 15,000 homicides nationally). And in only 16 percent of those cases had the victim been transported across state lines.[40]

Seagle raised other objections to the new federal thrust in law enforcement. The new federal law against using the mail to threaten a kidnapping imposed more severe punishments than did state laws against the act of kidnapping itself. He labeled this "a grotesque penological perversion." The severity of the new laws reflected the crime-control mood of Congress. Even more to the point, Seagle attacked the notion of efficiency in law enforcement itself. He argued that efficiency "can be bought at too high a price." "The unprecedented concentration of federal power," he argued, raised "a danger of widespread assault upon civil liberties." Concerning the role of the FBI, he warned that "a federal police force would not be responsive to local feeling." A centralized federal law enforcement agency, concerned primarily with "efficient" law enforcement, and fueled by a sense of national emergency over the crime problem presented enormous opportunities for abuse. The subsequent history of the FBI, the most sordid aspects of which did not come to light until the 1970s, proved that Seagle warnings were prophetic. Unfortunately, few listened in the overheated atmosphere of the early 1930s.

To dramatize its commitment to attacking the crime problem the Roosevelt Administration convened a national conference in late 1934. Roosevelt himself opened the Attorney General's Conference on Crime by directly linking the fight against crime with the struggle for economic recovery. "During the past two years," he declared, "there have been uppermost in our minds the problems of feeding and clothing the destitute, making secure the foundations of our agricultural, industrial and financial structures. As a component part of the large objective we include our constant struggle to safeguard ourselves against the attacks of the lawless and the criminal elements of our population." The president closed by mandating the conferees to "plan and construct with scientific care a constantly improving administrative structure—a structure which will tie together every crime preventing, law enforcing agency of every branch of Government—the Federal Government, the forty-eight state governments and all of the local governments, including counties, cities and towns." Roosevelt's personal interest in the crime problem could be traced back to the mid-1920s and his participation in the National Crime Commission. But as president he was mainly preoccupied with other problems and took little direct role in criminal justice matters.[41]

Attorney General Homer Cummings was the nominal leader of the Roosevelt administration's attack on the crime problem. Cummings was a prominent Connecticut attorney who owed his appointment to years of yeoman service in behalf of the Democratic Party. Most important, he had been a floor leader for Roosevelt at the 1932 Democratic convention. Cummings, however, was soon eclipsed by his nominal subordinate, J. Edgar Hoover. It would be more accurate to say that Hoover seized upon the opportunities raised by the crime-wave scare to carve out a new role for the bureau. The one specific proposal emerging from the Attorney General's Crime Conference serves as an illustration. The conferees endorsed the idea of some kind of national law enforcement educational or training center. Cummings proposed calling it the Institute of Criminology or the Federal School for Training in Law Administration. This new federal agency, in short, could have taken any number of different forms: a training academy, a scientific laboratory, or an academic law and social science institute. Under the FBI's leadership, however, it became the National Police Academy, a training institute that served as one of the major vehicles for the bureau's expanded influence over the whole sphere of law enforcement.[42]

The expansion of the FBI and its influence over local police consisted of several different elements. First, the bureau itself expanded in size and prominence; in this process Hoover managed to win for himself the image of the nation's "top cop." Second, the bureau assumed a number of new functions that gave it direct contact with local police departments. Those new activities included responsibility for the Uniform Crime Reports system in 1930, the National Police Academy in 1935, and its own crime lab established in 1932. The culmination of this process occurred at the end of the decade when, in 1940, Roosevelt gave the FBI formal responsibility for coordinating domestic security during war time.[43]

The Uniform Crime Reports system was the culmination of decades of thinking by police officials. At its first conventions in the 1890s the IACP began arguing the necessity of some national clearinghouse for crime statistics. And in

1897 the IACP itself began maintaining a rudimentary collection of criminal records. In the 1920s a number of states began maintaining their own crime statistics and by the end of the decade at least twenty-two states had some system in operation. Finally, in 1928 preliminary work began on a federal crime records system. Under the direction of Bruce Smith, the project involved a wide range of organizations and individuals. Prominent police administrators such as August Vollmer and William P. Rutledge, the respected commissioner of the Detroit police, were joined by J. Edgar Hoover and representatives from the International City Managers Association, the Bureau of Social Hygiene, the Census Bureau, and the National Institute of Public Administration. Funds from the Rockefeller Foundation and the Rockefeller-supported Bureau of Social Hygiene supported the project. In short, a broad consensus on the need for some sort of system had developed by the late 1920s. Only the lack of any precedents for federal involvement in local criminal justice activities delayed the new system.[44]

The impact of the UCR system was felt in many different areas. By virtue of becoming the clearinghouse and publisher of the national statistics, the FBI gained considerable prestige. It was ironic that in the 1930s the bureau eclipsed the IACP as the most important voice of law enforcement (the IACP did not fully reassert itself until the 1960s), for the IACP had led the fight for the UCR system. At the same time, the UCR system contributed to the reorientation of the police role. By providing a convenient statistical measure for evaluating police performance, it aided the growing emphasis on the law enforcement aspects of policing. The utility of the UCR statistics as a measure of police performance was questioned at the outset, significantly by an expert who had helped to create the system. Donald C. Stone, director of research for the International City Management Association, pointed out that the official figures were not accurate measures of actual crime and, even more important, it was inappropriate to hold the police alone responsible for changes in the crime rate since crime causation was an elusive and many-faceted phenomenon. Despite Stone's warnings, however, the UCR system became established, with all its obvious faults, as the measure of police effectiveness. Not until the 1970s did there begin a search for alternative and more realistic measures.[45]

The UCR system was only one of several developments in the 1930s that reflected a fascination with the science and technology of crime fighting. The crime lab, the lie detector, fingerprints, and various types of weapons also received an inordinate amount of attention. The direct application of scientific techniques to crime detection was one of August Vollmer's pet projects. In cooperation with Dr. Albert Schneider of the University of California, Vollmer established the first genuine crime lab in an American police department. Furthermore, in the 1920s Vollmer became fascinated with the newly developed lie detector and aggressively promoted it as a crime detection tool.[46]

Scientific crime fighting flowered in the 1930s. The first important developments occurred in Chicago. As a consequence of the famous 1929 St. Valentine's

Day Massacre, business, police, and academic leaders established the Scientific Crime Detection Laboratory. Located at Northwestern University, with the active cooperation of members of the law faculty, the lab was largely funded by donations from the business community. In conjunction with the lab there appeared a new journal, *American Journal of Police Science*, devoted to scientific crime detection. Two years later the FBI established its own crime lab. The influence of the bureau was enormous, far exceeding that of Vollmer's pioneering work. The crime lab lent an air of scientific precision to police activities that was far more effective as a public relations tool than the more mundane routine of patrol duty. The result, of course, was a further distortion of the role model and public image of the police.[47]

Even more publicity surrounded the expanded emphasis of fingerprints as a crime detection tool. The fingerprint system had been introduced in the early years of the twentieth century and quickly replaced the earlier and far more cumbersome Bertillion method of identification. Through the 1920s, however, fingerprint identification languished, receiving little in the way of emphasis. But in the 1930s, largely at the instigation of the FBI, there developed a genuine fingerprint fetish among law enforcement officials. When Hoover became director in 1924 the Bureau had 810,188 sets of fingerprints on file. Hoover set about reorganizing the files and, in the 1930s undertook a renewed effort to collect additional prints from every source imaginable. By 1974 the Bureau held an astronomical 159,000,000 sets of prints, with 3,000 new sets arriving every day. The bureau's policy of collecting prints indiscriminately contrasted sharply with European practices, especially that of Scotland Yard, which sought to limit the number of prints on file as much as possible. The Bureau's fingerprint fetish was consistent neither with civil liberties nor even efficient crime detection; public relations remained the primary purpose of fingerprints.[48]

Nothing better symbolized the more ominous aspects of the law and order mood of the 1930s than the abortive campaign for universal fingerprinting. Many American law enforcement experts had long admired European systems of requiring all citizens to either register with the police or carry some form of identification. Raymond Fosdick, for example, spoke highly of such systems in his 1914 study of the European police. Suddenly in 1935 and 1936 there developed an intense campaign to require all American citizens to submit their fingerprints to the FBI's Civil Identification Division. August Vollmer became a leading advocate of the idea and in 1932 the New York State Chiefs of Police Association proposed a similar idea, that all persons be required to carry a National Personal Identification Card. Two years later the same group recommended universal fingerprinting.[49]

In 1935 J. Edgar Hoover proposed "A Program for Voluntary Fingerprinting" and enlisted the support of a number of prominent individuals, including the president of the United States. In February 1935 John D. Rockefeller, Jr., along with 200 other business and financial leaders in New York, voluntarily submitted his fingerprints to the FBI. A picture of Rockefeller being printed appeared on the front page of the *New York Times*; two weeks later the *New York Post* published a picture of Jack Dempsey also being printed. Governor Lehman of New York recommended the fingerprinting of all misdemeanants, and the IACP in 1935 strongly endorsed universal fingerprinting. And in perhaps the most significant development, President Roosevelt himself submitted a copy of his fingerprints to the FBI. In promoting this campaign, Hoover contended that "There should be no stigma whatsoever attached to this method of identification." He argued that it would protect the law-abiding citizen against possible false arrest and aid greatly in identifying victims of disasters (which he suggested was a growing problem with the advent of commercial air travel).[50]

A few local communities embraced the universal fingerprinting idea wholeheartedly. Not surprisingly, Berkeley, California, was one of the most enthusiastic. Under the influence of Chief Vollmer, the project had begun in 1930 but managed to obtain only 2,000 sets of prints in the next five years. Then, with the impetus of national publicity, an intensive four-month campaign in 1935 resulted in over 52,000 sets of prints. This represented nearly half the population of the community. The campaign involved virtually every community organization. Convenient "fingerprint service stations" were established at fire stations, libraries, and in the schools. Robert G. Sproul, president of the University of California, posed for a photograph with Vollmer as he submitted his prints at a university-based service station. Some local businesses offered 5 percent discounts to customers who carried their fingerprint identification card. As many as fifty WPA workers aided in the collection of prints, while National Youth Authority employees connected with the university donated up to 500 hours of work. In addition, considerable time and effort was donated by such groups as the American Legion, the Boy and Girl Scouts, the local press and various churches. The total cost of the program in 1935 amounted to only $2,261.24. Police Chief John Greening hailed the effort a tremendous success. Organized labor in the area officially went on record as being opposed to universal fingerprinting, but did little to actively stop it. Local radicals, however, did distribute antifingerprint literature in opposition to the campaign.[51]

A few other cities across the country embraced the idea as well. In Detroit, a total of 75,000 prints were collected by 1941. Local officials seriously believed that the fingerprinting of students resulted in a decrease in juvenile delinquency. Officials in St. Paul, Minnesota, took a somewhat different approach. In 1936 they began to require that criminals who had been convicted of a felony in the previous ten years register with the police department. Failure to register could result in a ninety-day jail sentence or a $100 fine; each day that a person failed to register was regarded as a separate offense.[52]

The universal fingerprinting campaign faded almost as quickly as it had appeared. By 1936 the movement had lost its momentum and activity soon ceased, although the FBI did maintain its high interest in fingerprints generally. In retrospect, the universal fingerprinting idea stands as an eloquent testimony to the intensity of the law-and-order mood of the early 1930s and the threat to civil liberties that such a mood presented.

The FBI and the New Professionalism

In a subtle but important fashion, Hoover and the FBI in the 1930s succeeded in redefining the idea of police professionalism. This was not wholly the work of the bureau; events had been moving in the same direction for a number of years under the leadership of August Vollmer and others But the FBI did bring the movement to fulfillment and, simply by virtue of its enormous publicity apparatus, effect an important qualitative change in the whole notion of police professionalism.

The new image of police professionalism was that of a skilled, highly trained, and extremely efficient law enforcement agent. This particular definition of the police professional had always been latent in the reform movement. But a number of important developments in the 1930s—the UCR, the crime labs, fingerprints, and the interest in scientific measures of police activities—gave it a considerable boost. The social work aspects of policing receded into the background. No where was this shift more evident than in the fate of the police-women's movement. The movement had begun to stagnate in the mid-1920s, but by the 1930s women police officers were beginning to lose even their claim to head the separate juvenile or crime prevention units.[53]

J. Edgar Hoover proved to be the master bureaucrat, skillfully manipulating statistical data to justify his agency's existence. The 1932 annual report, for example, was a significantly larger and more impressive document than any of its predecessors. In this report Hoover also began to employ graphs showing a dramatic rise in both the number of fugitives apprehended (up from 923 in 1928 to 3690 in 1932) and the total number of years imposed in sentences on these individuals (up from 5547 in 1928 to 8003 in 1932). Hoover also began making the argument that over 90 percent of the suspects arrested by the bureau were subsequently convicted. To clinch his argument for bureau efficiency, Hoover pointed out that all this work had been accomplished with no increase in the number of special agents. In fact, the number had declined from 398 in 1925 to 362 in 1932.[54]

Efficient law enforcement, Hoover argued, was the result of high standards of recruitment and training. One of the more notable accomplishments in his first years as director of the bureau was to raise recruitment standards. Special agents with some legal training rose from 16.48 percent of the total in 1924 to 67.44 percent by 1938. Hoover also sought to distinguish special agents from local police officers with respect to the U.S. Constitution. In the wake of the Wickersham Commission revelations, he mounted an attack on the third degree. He argued that "a confession obtained by compulsion must be excluded as evidence in a trial. . . . The law enforcement officer is charged with the responsibility of enforcing the law without tearing down fundamental rights of the individual, while discharging these duties."[55]

Hoover's philosophy of law enforcement represented the "iron fist in the velvet glove." Vigorous pursuit of law breakers should be undertaken by the most "professional" means for two reasons. First, police abuse of citizens tarnished the image of law enforcement in the eyes of the public. Second, it ran the risk of having a conviction overturned, thus thwarting the ultimate goal. How much more effective, Hoover argued, to fight crime through "the application of scientific principles." This view underpinned his commitment to high recruitment standards, the crime lab, an extensive fingerprint system, and other advanced techniques. Professionalism, in short, was a means to efficient crime control.[56]

The National Police Academy became the means by which the FBI sought to extend training, and its own influence, to local police departments. The academy was a direct outgrowth of the 1934 attorney general's conference and the first session was held in late July 1935. The faculty for these brief sessions consisted of five full-time instructors and thirty special lecturers. Twenty-three local police officers attended this first twelve week course. In the following years two such sessions were held annually. Academy training was in turn supplemented by the FBI *Law Enforcement Bulletin* which also commenced publication in the early 1930s. At first a mimeographed circular, the *Bulletin* contained information on wanted fugitives, as well as technical articles on scientific crime fighting, particularly the details of fingerprint identification.[57]

One of the most pernicious influences of FBI training was the emphasis on firearms. In this area as in others, the bureau was not completely at fault; it simply gave enormous impetus to a movement that was already gaining ground. The law-and-order mood of the 1930s was characterized by a weapons fetish that rivalled the obsession with fingerprints. Publicity surrounding the FBI academy emphasized the firearms training. Perhaps the most extreme example was the training in the firing of machine guns from moving automobiles. According to one report, "The firearms course includes practice in 'running gunfire.' Experience with the Dillingers, Nelsons, Floyds, and Barkers has shown that such training may come in handy when the chase is on. To qualify in running gunfire an agent must be able to hit a moving target while firing from a rapidly moving automobile."[58]

The weapons craze of the 1930s then included not only expertise with service revolvers, but also an increased use of machine guns and alternative weapons such as tear gas. The *National Police Officer* magazine commented in 1937 that "never in the history of the United States have police departments been equipped as they are today." Emphasis on machine guns was largely in response to the Dillingers and Floyds, while tear gas was adopted for use in violent labor disputes. The increased armaments, of course, was a result of an aggressive sales campaign by the manufacturers themselves. Such magazines as the *National Police Officer* seemed to be little more than fronts for such companies as Federal Laboratories, a major producer of tear gas. Manufacturers were able to skillfully exploit the crime control mood of the country.[59]

The end result was that professionalism in law enforcement came to be identified in terms of firearms expertise. The link between guns and the police was a completely new phenomenon in the history of American law enforcement. The first police in the United States were generally not armed at all. And even around the turn of the century weaponry had been of little interest to police professionalizers. By 1935 an assistant chief of the Los Angeles police department could boast that revolver practice had helped to reduce robbery by 44 percent in two years and that burglary and auto theft were down 28 percent and 24 percent respectively. As he explained it, "bandits were being taken to the County Morgue instead of 'escaping in a hail of bullets.'" The city began paying bonuses for marksmanship and sponsoring competitive teams for national and international competition. An American Police Revolver League was organized in Chicago in 1938, joining such regional associations as the New England Police Revolver League in sponsoring organized competition. Meanwhile, the police participated actively in the annual competition sponsored by the National Rifle Association at Camp Perry, Ohio. The rising popularity of firearms put the police firmly in the antigun control camp. Calvin Goddard, writing in the *American Journal of Police Science*, complained that "for the past two decades, there has been a constantly increasing hue and cry against the 'menace of the pistol.'" As a result, "this erstwhile honorable weapon has become an outcast."[60]

The gun craze of the 1930s threatened to get completely out of hand. A few police departments attempted to impose some kind of control over the use of firearms. The Wichita *Duty Manual* prepared by Chief O. W. Wilson in 1935 directed: "In case anyone attempts to use a machine gun while driving a car it must be on 'single shot.'" Regulation 29 also specified that officers must report all firings of their weapons to the chief. The 1941 *Rules and Regulations* of the Boston Police Department declared that "the final warning which the Commissioner gives to all members of the Department is this: WHEN IN DOUBT, DO NOT FIRE." These efforts, however, were the exception. Most American police departments entered the 1960s with only limited procedures for limiting the use of weapons by their officers.[61]

The influence of the FBI, while extremely pernicious in its emphasis on weaponry and scientific crime fighting, was not wholly without positive benefit. Through the National Police Academy and the rhetoric and imagery of professionalism, the bureau did help to lead the way with new advances in the area of police education and training. The decade of the thirties, in fact, marked dramatic advances along three different lines in this area. First, college-level educational programs flourished as never before. Second, a number of states introduced regional training programs that, in many cases, brought formal training to smaller police departments. Finally, significant improvements were made in the area of police academy training programs.

College-level law enforcement programs, which had been the dream of August Vollmer since 1916, crossed a major watershed in the 1930s. Largely under Vollmer's influence, California led the way. A particularly notable advance occurred in 1930 with the development of a two-year law enforcement program at San Jose State College. Vollmer, of course, played a major role in developing that curriculum. At the same time, he was deeply involved in what proved to be an abortive law enforcement program at the University of Chicago. Vollmer had been in Chicago surveying the Chicago police department for the Illinois Crime Survey in 1928. Members of the faculty, impressed with his expertise, recruited him to teach at the university in 1929 and 1930. It was a measure of both Vollmer's personal prestige and of the growing national interest in law enforcement training that the University of Chicago would offer him such a post. Plans for a permanent program, however, did not materialize and Vollmer returned to California in 1931. There he joined the faculty of the University of California at Berkeley. The university began offering a major in criminology in 1933 and in 1951 Vollmer's work culminated in the creation of a School of Criminology offering graduate degrees.[62]

Many other universities, including some of the most pretigious in the nation, also began to develop law enforcement programs. Northwestern University, which cosponsored the Scientific Crime Detection Laboratory, initiated a traffic training program in 1932-1933. Following a 1932 conference of traffic officers from the midwestern region, the university established a permanent traffic institute in 1933. Insurance companies who had obvious interest in the problem, strongly supported the new program. The Kemper Insurance Co., for example, provided funds for twenty full-year fellowships. Between 1933 and 1938 more than 650 police officers were trained in the Northwestern program. In 1936 a grant from the Automobile Manufacturers Association, provided for fifteen fellowships for graduate-level study of traffic problems at Harvard University.[63]

In 1935 Michigan State College (later University) launched a five-year curriculum in police administration. The program called for three and one-half years of college work and a year and a half of in-service apprenticeship training. In Wichita, Kansas, Police Chief O. W. Wilson established a police cadet program in cooperation with the University of Kansas. Students who had completed two years of college work and who met the recruitment standards for the Wichita police department were eligible for the cadet program. Cadets worked half time with the Wichita police, for which they were paid $50 a month, and continued to carry twelve hours a semester of college course work.[64]

While Vollmer's ideal of the "college cop" continued to spread, it did not go unchallenged. Many law enforcement traditionalists questioned the practical value of college education for police officers. Duncan Matheson, secretary of the California Peace Officers Association in 1930, declared that some of the "scientific" policemen he had met were "stupidity personified." Furthermore, he maintained that "no person can point to anything that has been done to date by these so-called experts, to prevent crime. . . ." Even William Wiltberger, director of the San Jose State College Police School, confessed in 1939 that "one of the difficult problems of the pre-employment school is that the fundamentals and principles of police work must be discovered out of that great existing police knowledge and practices." The debate between the relative value of practical experience and higher education continued to dominate police education through the 1970s.[65]

A second important training development involved the emergence of the *zone school* or regional training center. New York and California led the way in this area. By 1923 New York had expanded its original state police training program to include twenty-three zone schools for officers in the smaller police departments. The State Conference of Mayors and the New York State Chiefs of Police Association joined with the State Police School in running the program. In 1929 the California legislature directed the Bureau of Criminal Identification "to arrange for and organize schools at convenient centers in the state for training police officers." Cooperation between the bureau, the State Department of Education and the California Peace Officers Association, resulted in a five-zone regional training system in 1935. The California approach, in fact, involved a comprehensive, multipronged police training program. Four distinct types of training schools existed: the in-house police academy, the zone school, technical training institutes during the summer, and preservice college programs.[66]

Other states followed suit with regional training. Pennsylvania established its Public Service Institute in 1938, while Virginia introduced a New York–style zone school system in 1932. The growing field of public administration also contributed significantly to the police training progress. By 1932 state leagues of municipalities helped to sponsor training programs in more than twenty states. O. W. Wilson's initial efforts in Kansas, for example, had been done in cooperation with the Kansas League of Municipalities.

The federal government gave a boost to police training with the passage of the George-Deen Act in 1936. A supplement to the 1917 Smith-Hughes Act, the new legislation greatly expanded federal aid to vocational education. In 1937 over $4,000,000 became available for police training. It was estimated that by 1939–1940 over 9,000 police officers were enrolled in training programs supported in part by George-Deen funds. As was the case with WPA-supported police projects, however, this pioneering effort in federal support was ended by the Second World War. In fact, many state programs and local police academies suspended operations during the war. California, for example, suspended its state training program between 1942 and 1946. As a result, much of the momentum toward police training that developed in the 1930s was dissipated in the early 1940s.[68]

An important consequence of police-training activities in California was the involvement of professional educators from the State Department of Education. With their prior experience in vocational education, they brought a new level of sophistication to police training. An effective training program, they pointed out, necessitated a detailed analysis of the job itself. Recognition of this elementary principle resulted in a pioneering effort to empirically study routine police work. In 1933 the State Department of Education published a *Job Analysis of Police Service*, based on "an analysis of duties performed in the various divisions of the Police Department of the City of Los Angeles . . . during the summer of 1932." This document was then followed by a 1934 *Instructional Analysis of Police Service* which attempted to present a training curriculum based on the evidence in the previous report.[69]

The California projects were soon followed by similar federal efforts. Responding to a 1936 request from the IACP, the Interior Department developed and published in 1938 a manual on *Training for Police Service*. The directors of the study acknowledged the "lack of substantive knowledge of law enforcement methods and also of experience with teaching methods." Although extremely rudimentary, the California and Interior Department manuals represented an enormous step forward: an effort to study police work empirically and develop relevant training programs and manuals.[70]

The third area of progress with respect to police training involved police academies. From a national perspective, the police training situation presented an ambiguous picture. A few departments offered extensive recruit training and clearly set new standards for the rest. But at the same time many departments still offered none whatsoever. The progress of professionalization was extremely uneven to say the least. A 1937 survey of eighty-one cities revealed that twenty-one offered some kind of formal training (three of those, however, offered less than a week of training). The most important factor perhaps was the simple fact that the idea of police training continued to gain ground. Bruce Smith, writing in 1940, commented on the progress made in the previous two decades. "Prior to 1920, formal training facilities for police were so rare that their influence upon the great mass of recruits was negligible," he argued. Nonetheless, "due allowance should be made for the veritible revolution in police attitudes which had to be effected before even a start at police training could be made." Smith concluded with the comment, "That revolution is now complete. . . ."[71]

If Kansas City and Jersey City held the distinction as the two most corrupt police departments by the 1930s—the two most unaffected by developments in professionalism since the turn of the century—the honor for the most thoroughly professional departments belonged to the Milwaukee and Cincinnati. In both cases, high standards in policing could be directly attributable to the quality of municipal government itself. Milwaukee's reputation for good government and professional police administration went as far back as the end of the nineteenth century. Standards in the Cincinnati police department slipped somewhat after reaching a peak in the early part of the century, but revived quickly with the advent of the city manager system in the early 1930s.

The reputation of these two police departments was based on their pursuit of the professional ideal as it had been defined early in the century. The major areas of progress, then, involved administrative centralization and stricter personnel standards. The Cincinnati police department, for example, centralized the registration and detention of arrested persons in the early thirties, abolishing the use of district police stations for this purpose. And with the assistance of the Cincinnati Regional Police Commisison, the department undertook one of the first beat patrol surveys, attempted to foster greater regional cooperation, and opened a scientific crime lab in 1934. It also maintained a two-month police training school, an impressive length of time by prevailing standards.[72]

The special strengths of the Milwaukee police department lay in the area of nonpartisan administration and personnel practices. What made Milwaukee famous was the long tenure it granted to police chiefs. Between 1888 and 1936 there were only two chiefs. John T. Janssen served for thirty-three years and his successor, Jacob G. Laubenheimer, served for fifteen. In the same period, Chicago had twenty-one police chiefs and Detroit sixteen. Laubenheimer's successor, Joseph T. Kluchesky, moreover, achieved a national reputation in the early 1940s as a leader in the new police–community relations movement. Report after report cited the Milwaukee case as the ideal in police administration.

Milwaukee also led the way by the 1930s in personnel practices. A police academy was introduced in 1923 with one and one-half hours of training per week for all members of the force. In 1922, meanwhile, the department began to publish a daily bulletin containing information about wanted persons and stolen property. In the early 1930s the training program was again expanded to include a total of 315 regular classes. Thirty-two of these were for officers with more than fifteen years service on the force. In an era when many departments had no recruit training at all, training for veteran officers was indeed remarkable. Complementing the training program was an elaborate personnel evaluation scheme. The department maintained a "3×5" card on each officer indicating special personal qualities, attendance record, arrest record (with an indication of the disposition of the case), the crime rate in the officer's district, citizen complaints, and, of course, his record on departmental examinations. A consultant for the New York State Conference on Mayors lauded the Milwaukee card file system: "This record quickly shows whether or not a patrolman is doing his duty. . . ."[73]

The 1930s, then, witnessed continued progress in the development of police professionalization. Writing in 1940, Bruce Smith was able to conclude that, despite certain enduring problems, "The past twenty years have witnessed some impressive advances in police personnel, material and management." This was similar to the judgment rendered by August Vollmer in 1933. Unfortunately, progress continued to be defined in terms of an agenda of professionalization that had been drawn up decades before. There was nothing wrong with that agenda—most departments had yet to begin to fulfill it. But it did not take into account a host of new police problems and in some respects was itself responsible for them. Technology was rapidly altering the nature of police service and relations between the police and the public. The legacy of the 1930s was extremely ambiguous, for just as the telephone, the radio, and the patrol car enhanced the service functions of the police, professionalism came to be defined almost exclusively in terms of crime fighting. A few isolated attempts were made to analyze the true nature of routine police work, but these insights were lost in the law-and-order mood that prevailed through the decade. Not until the late 1960s would a major crisis bring these new issues to the fore.[74]

Epilogue: The Legacy of Professionalization

The decade of the 1930s brought to an end the first phase in the history of police professionalization. From the 1940s through the early 1960s police reform continued along the lines that were already well established. Police professionalism was defined almost exclusively in terms of managerial efficiency, and administrators sought to refine techniques that would further strengthen their hand in commanding and controlling rank-and-file patrolmen. At the same time, the official mission of the police as a public service agency increasingly came to be seen in terms of the suppression of crime. There was a remarkable continuity in police reform from the 1940s through the early 1960s. No new important ideas appeared to challenge the conventional wisdom. The chief spokesperson for the dominant view was clearly O. W. Wilson, author of an influential textbook and superintendent of the Chicago police from 1960 to 1963.[1]

The legacy of professionalization was ambiguous. Much had been accomplished in elevating the level of police service. By the late 1930s policing had undergone a virtual revolution since the 1870s and 1880s. A man such as August Vollmer could take justifiable pride in the changes he had witnessed during the course of his own career—changes that he had done so much to bring about. Nonetheless, professionalization was not an unalloyed triumph. Despite the achievements, much remained to be done. Many of the old problems persisted, even into the 1970s. Even more serious, the professionalization process brought with it a number of unanticipated consequences. By the 1950s the police began to feel the pressure of problems that were at best only dimly understood by the leading administrators. These accumulating problems finally exploded in the turbulent decade of the 1960s. The racial crisis focused public attention on the police as never before and exposed the limitations of conventional police professionalization.[2]

The accomplishments of police reform by the end of the 1930s were considerable. Unfortunately, these very real gains are often lost sight of when the police are viewed in terms of the problems of the 1960s. Judged by the standards of the late nineteenth century, police reform had much to be proud of. A minimal definition of professionalism provides a convenient framework for identifying the most important changes. Police work by the late 1930s could legitimately claim to be a full-time occupation, with a commitment to abstract ideals of public service, the beginnings of an obligation to educate and train new practitioners and, finally, even the possibility of a body of scientific knowledge about policing. To be sure, the claim of professional status was more often an assertion of what ought to be done rather than a statement of actual achievement. But the mere fact that the idea of professionalism had gained ascendancy within police circles, that an agenda of reform had been defined, and that the first steps toward fulfilling it had been taken was itself a remarkable achievement.[3]

Careerism among police officers was the first minimal step towards professionalism. In the late nineteenth century, police work was essentially a form of casual labor. Political appointees filled police departments with little expectation that they would serve out the rest of their lives in that job. There were neither formal entrance requirements to screen out the unfit nor, with an occasional exception, was there any attempt to provide the recruit with any formal training for police work. How different the situation had become by the late 1930s. Civil service procedures had eliminated the more blatant forms of political patronage in almost all of the large police departments. Retirement plans and other fringe benefits, meanwhile, offered strong inducements for the police officer to remain in his job through the course of a full career. The economic collapse of the 1930s greatly enhanced the attractiveness of police service as a career but in doing so it only gave impetus to a trend that was already well under way.[4]

A virtual revolution had also occurred in the manner in which police departments handled both applicants and new recruits. In the late 1920s and early 1930s a few police departments sought to apply psychological tests to screen out the obviously unfit. Meanwhile, the more professionalized departments, such as Milwaukee, began to develop systematic forms of evaluating the performance of individual officers. In the nineteenth century, the training of police officers had been virtually nonexistent. Generally, officers were handed a copy of the department manual, which contained both department rules and municipal ordinances, and immediately placed on the street. By the 1930s most large police departments paid at least lip service to the idea of police academy training and the near-revolutionary idea of college educations for policemen was rapidly gaining ground. Whereas the police officer of the 1880s was required to meet only a political test, his counterpart in the 1930s was expected to meet at least some minimal job-related requirements.[5]

Accompanying the emergence of training programs was a redefinition of the meaning of police service. It is somewhat misleading, however, to suggest that it was a redefinition, since little thought was given in the nineteenth century to the meaning and purpose of police work. Although nominally committed to law enforcement, almost no thought was given to how those ends might be achieved. Around the turn of the century, reformers formulated lofty definitions of the police mission. Initially, this development took two forms. One school of thought emphasized efficient crime suppression through the use of scientific procedures: the emergence of the fingerprint process, elaborate criminal identification systems, scientific crime labs, and training in the natural sciences were all products of this thrust. Another school of thought viewed the police mission in terms of crime prevention. The police were to play a social work role, helping individuals in order to keep them out of the criminal process. In one of the more portentous developments of the 1920s and 1930s, the social work role model fell by the wayside and was almost completely replaced by the image of the police as a crime-fighting agency. Nonetheless, few could doubt that by the late 1930s there was a clear sense of mission for the police, a commitment to *public* service where one had not existed before.[6]

To achieve the new goals of police service, reformers effected a sweeping internal reorganization of police agencies. Following the precepts of scientific management, the reformers sought to achieve a rational and orderly process of administration. Most of all, rationality meant uniformity and that was to be achieved by centralizing command procedures. Reformers devoted much effort to closing district police stations and in many other ways breaking the traditional power of the captains in the precincts. The new communications technology in the 1930s greatly facilitated this movement and also helped to achieve a greater degree of direct control over patrol officers. Furthermore, consistent with the new goals of police service, police departments gradually evolved a wide range of specialized functions—homicide, vice, juvenile, records, training, etc.—all of which were integrated in a complex bureaucratic structure. Considerable reform effort was given to the creation and then the management of this complex bureaucracy.[7]

Finally, policing as an occupation began to develop its own sense of professional autonomy. Progress in this area was confined almost exclusively to police chiefs rather than rank-and-file patrolmen. The International Association of Chiefs of Police (IACP) established itself as the official voice of American law enforcement and an important forum for the dissemination of reform ideas. The IACP, however, fell short of realizing its full potential. As a professional association it was far outstripped by the work of at least one state group, the California Peace Officers Association. And in the 1930s, it was completely eclipsed by J. Edgar Hoover and the FBI. Rank-and-file police officers remained without any effective voice in police affairs. The network of local fraternal associations that survived the debacle of the Boston police strike carefully eschewed overt political activity and as a group remained largely isolated from each other. Throughout the history of police professionalization, the most articulate spokesmen and most creative thinking were to be found in nonpolice groups: the National Prison Association through the nineteenth century, the social work profession in the early years of the twentieth century, and the field of public administration in the 1920s and 1930s.[8]

Despite the major accomplishments of police reform, a wide range of problems remained. Professional status continued to be more an idea, a dream, and an ultimate goal, than an actuality. Many traditional police problems survived the reform process. The most highly publicized problem, police corruption, seemed to resist every effort to eliminate it. The history of the police down to the present continued to be punctuated by periodic scandals. A wave of particularly well-publicized scandals between 1959 and 1961, involving among others the Chicago and Denver police departments, did much to tarnish the national image of the police. To be sure, there were exceptions. The Los Angeles police, for example, gained a reputation for incorruptibility that even its severest critics acknowledged. But the reality of corruption persisted. In the early 1970s, a pattern of pervasive corruption in the New York City police department was fully documented by the Knapp Commission investigation and then immortalized in the book and the movie *Serpico*.[9]

Political influence over the police also resisted the long effort by reformers to establish independence and professional autonomy. The campagin to "get politics out of the police" was long the first item on the agenda of police reformers. Their efforts led to the demise of the police boards and, the vesting of full administrative authority in the office of police chief or public safety director. The case of Chicago only demonstrated the ease with which political influence could continue to pervade a major police department. In other cities, the situation became less blatant but, for that reason, all the more problematic. As William Westley argued in his study of the Gary, Indiana, police department, the police chief was a political appointee and was able to maintain informal influence over the department through a network of favorites. A complex bureaucracy created ample opportunities creating and maintaining an informal structure of power and influence.[10]

Furthermore, the rhetoric of professional autonomy could also be used to serve political ends. Cyril D. Robinson argues, in an impressive essay on the subject, that the nominal independence of the police disguised an informal pattern of influence and control. Thus, an elected official could disclaim responsibility for police problems, when expedient, and a police chief could resist reform proposals advanced by dissident groups. In the 1960s, for example, the police attacked many police–community relations proposals advanced by blacks (or their white liberal supporters) on the grounds of political pressure. Opposition to both civilian review boards and court decisions were infringements on their professional autonomy. Thus, the black community was placed on the defensive, advancing essentially political demands in an era when overt political influence was officially condemned. In this and many other areas, black activists found that the rhetoric and techniques of professionalism, expertise, and nonpartisanship were used to frustrate their legitimate claims.[11]

Police–community relations were another old police problem, but one that grew steadily more serious. The wave of urban racial disorders of the 1900-1919 period was repeated in 1943 as major violence erupted in Detroit, New York City, Los Angeles, and other communities. Once again, investigators found a widespread pattern of police misconduct: discrimination in law enforcement, a failure to stop white rioters, and in some cases active participation in antiblack activity. The 1943 riots, however, were followed by a major effort to improve police conduct and the relations between the police and the black community.

The birth of the modern police–community relations movement was an important index of the progress in police reform since 1919. There had emerged a group of experts willing to identify a major police problem and able to organize the resources to deal with it. The initial police–community relations efforts of the 1940s were an impressive first step but were woefully limited. The movement soon lost its initial momentum and the police–community relations problem reappeared with a vengance in the mid-1960s.[12]

The 1940s also witnessed the reappearance of police unionism. As had been the case during World War I, wartime pressures eroded the economic position of the police and engendered a union organizing drive. Although there was no single confrontation equal to the 1919 Boston police strike, the union movement encountered strong opposition. The police chiefs, far better organized than in the earlier period, issued a major statement opposing unionism, and the unions themselves suffered a series of devastating defeats in the courts. By 1947 the movement was again moribund. Like the police–community relations crisis, the issue of police unionism also experienced a dramatic resurgence in the mid-1960s.[13]

The issue of police unionism directs our attention to the host of new police problems that appeared as a consequence of professionalization. The emergence of careerism among police officers significantly altered their attitudes toward the job and toward the public they served. Committed to a permanent career in policing, police officers began to develop a distinct occupational outlook. William Westley was the first to explore the various dimensions of the police subculture in his pioneering study of the Gary, Indiana, police department. Whereas a professional subculture was an important mechanism for self-regulation with other occupations (law, medicine, teaching, etc.), the circumstances of police work made it problematic. Because the police had an often antagonistic relationship to their "clients," and low status vis-à-vis other professionals with whom they worked, they tended to develop an isolated and defensive perspective. Failing to win respect from the public, they came to feel that they could rely only on themselves for support and respect. Westley's conclusion, which proved to have an enormous influence on subsequent police research, was that the police subculture reinforced traditions of secrecy and violence.[14]

Many of the less attractive aspects of the police subculture were further reinforced by the organizational structure of police departments. Here the reformers failed to grasp the full consequences of their work. The hierarchical, semimilitary organizational form was one of the major fruits of professionalization. Prior to the turn of the century, police departments were largely decentralized, loosely controlled, and distinctly unmilitary. The military form and ethos were seized upon in an effort to assert some minimal degree of control over the rank and file. The tragedy of the militarization of the police lies in the fact that it addressed itself to very real problems and did in fact achieve many of the desired ends. It was no accident that in the early 1960s the Los Angeles police department was generally acknowledged to be the most efficient, the least corrupt, and the most militaristic department in the country. Unfortunately, the tradition of police reform developed blinders that prevented it from taking into account the consequences of the military model.

The hierarchical, military structure of police departments contravened the essence of true professionalism. The rank-and-file patrolman became an object to be controlled, a cog in the law enforcement machinery whose primary obligation it was to follow orders, to do it "by the book." While this did go a long way toward establishing some uniformity in police performance and eliminating some of the worst abuses, it also served to stifle talents and ambitions of many officers. The accumulated knowledge and insights of the rank and file had no effective outlet; the patrol officer was to follow orders, not make policy. By the 1960s, in the wake of the national crisis over the police in the city, a new generation of reformers began to explore various techniques tapping the talents and ambitions of patrol officers. Whether in the form of the much-discussed *team policing* concept, or in the use of policymaking task forces, or in strategies for career development, it was increasingly evident that the old model of police organization was not adequate to the present. In effect, the new generation of reformers sought to reorient the meaning of professionalism away from its exclusive emphasis upon managerial efficiency and toward encouraging a genuinely professional ethos among front-line practitioners.[15]

For their own part, the rank and file took the problem of alienation into their own hands. Provoked by the crisis of the mid-1960s, and the feeling that no one supported them in the face of criticism by blacks, intellectuals, radicals, and the courts, the police once again turned to unionism. A third upsurge of police union activity began in 1966 and by the 1970s unionism was an established and permanent feature of police administration. There was considerable irony in the fact that police unionism mimicked the militant spirit of their principal antagonists, the black power movement. "Blue power" was the response to "black power."[16]

Outside of the rank and file itself, police unionism found little support. Even those groups traditionally supportive of trade unionism expressed reservations about police unionism. It raised a host of disturbing questions about the degree of autonomy that could be allowed the police in a democratic society. One of the few hopeful views of police unionism was expressed by George Kelling and Robert B. Kliesmet—an academician and a police union official, respectively. They suggested that the union movement offered the possibility of an organizational infrastructure capable of mobilizing the necessary resources for the rank and file to promote their own professional development. Their suggestion was a long-shot idea but it was one of the few attempts to reconcile police unionism with the evident need to involve the rank and file in a fuller participation police policymaking.[17]

The police subculture was but one-half of the police–community relations issue. The racial crisis of the mid-1960s focused public attention on the problem of relations between the police and the public. In this area as well, professionalization bequeathed an ambiguous legacy. Both the 1967 report of the President's Crime Commission and the 1968 report of the Kerner Commission suggested that professionalism had often contributed to the problem of police–community relations. The patrol car, for example, had removed the police officer from the street and eliminated a great deal of routine contact between police and public. Although there was a tendency to romanticize the nineteenth-century foot patrolman (and ignore the long history of brutality and inefficiency), there was much to be said for the kind of direct contact that foot patrol yielded. Another problem involved law enforcement tactics. The impersonal style of professionalism, again exemplified by the Los Angeles police, often aggravated police–community relations. In particular, such tactics as aggressive preventive patrol, designed to suppress crime efficiently, exacerbated racial tensions.[18]

In response to the racial crisis, various proposals were made for improving the accountability of the police. Civilian review boards were frequently suggested but with little success. In fact, the mid-sixties marked the demise of the two most important civilian review boards in existence, those in Philadelphia and New York City. Radicals proposed direct community control of the police, through decentralization and neighborhood boards, but in its only major test, the idea was soundly defeated at the polls by the voters in Berkeley, California. Moderate reformers, meanwhile, searched for various strategies for decentralizing police departments or otherwise making them more open to the public. What James Q. Wilson referred to as "the bureaucracy problem" remained one of the most urgent police problems of the 1970s. Professionalization had led to the growth of complex bureaucratic structures; a new generation of reformers faced the problem of taming and humanizing the new animal.[19]

Finally, professionalization left an ambiguous legacy in terms of the official mission of the police. By the late 1930s the crime-fighter image was in the ascendancy, shaping both public expectations and the self-image of police officers. A wave of empirical research in the 1960s clearly demonstrated how useless this image was. The bulk of police activities were devoted to noncriminal, service duties. Studies even suggested that criminal investigation activities were vastly overrated in terms of effectiveness. The new agenda of police reform, then, emphasized reconciling image with reality. Considerable thought was given to developing reward structures and career incentives that recognized and valued the service aspects of policing.[20]

The idea that the police should function as a social service agency received renewed attention during the 1960s. Many reformers suggested that the police were uniquely situated to deal with a wide range of social problems, including race relations, chronic alcoholism, and family disputes. The much publicized Family Crisis Intervention Unit in the New York City police department was heralded as a model for innovative police service. (The fact that the grant-funded project was allowed to lapse once the grant expired was another problem.) The diversion of chronic alcoholics into detoxification programs also seemed a promising avenue. The idea of policing as social service, however, encountered two major obstacles. The first involved questions of civil liberties. As some of the experiments of the Progressive Era suggested, there were enormous dangers inherent in expanding the role of the police and utilizing their coercive powers in noncriminal matters. (Was a referral to a detoxification program an arrest or merely a suggestion? If it was an arrest, then standards of due process should apply; if it was only a suggestion, then the client should be free to reject it.) A second problem involved the difficulties of changing a complex, bureaucratic organization. Theorists talked glibly about reorienting police service and de-emphasizing the law enforcement role. The experience of attempts to change other large social service agencies (the public schools, for example) did not bode well for reform efforts.[21]

Whatever the prospects for changing the police in the last quarter of this century, it is clear that a new generation of reformers would have to confront the legacy of the first period of police professionalization. The new agenda of reform would have to consist not of completing the work of earlier generations but of transcending it. The tasks that lie ahead are not easy ones. Although there is widespread criticism of the hierarchical, semimilitary organizational form, alternative modes hold serious pitfalls. The enormous powers of the police to deprive citizens of their liberties demand both strict control and uniformity of procedures. Reconciling debureaucratization and the independent judgment of police officers with the requirement of equal protection of the laws presents reformers with no small dilemma.

In this regard, the history of police reform seems to suggest two lessons. First, reformers should take care to consider the full consequences of new techniques of police administration. The history of police reform illustrates the pitfalls of unanticipated consequences. But the second lesson suggests very real possibilities of change. The myth of the unchanging police, as well as a pervasive pessimism about "the bureaucracy problem," discourages creative thinking about change. The history of police reform suggests that significant, even radical changes are indeed possible. Both the opportunities and the perils of police reform confront a new generation of reformers.

Notes

Introduction

1. Samuel Walker, "The Urban Police in American History: A Review of the Literature," *Journal of Police Science and Administration* IV (September 1976): 252-260.

2. For the best summary of the literature, see W. E. Moore, *The Professions: Rules and Roles* (New York: Russell Sage, 1970).

3. Samuel Walker, "Police Professionalism: Another Look at the Issues," *Journal of Sociology and Social Welfare* III (July 1976): 701-710.

4. See Jerome Skolnick, *Justice Without Trial* (New York: John Wiley, 1966), pp. 230-245.

5. See Wallace S. Sayre and Herbert Kaufman, *Governing New York City: Politics in the Metropolis* (New York: Russell Sage, 1960).

6. For a suggestive discussion of the role of police unions, see George L. Kelling and Robert B. Kliesmet, "Resistance to the Professionalization of the Police," *The Law Officer* V (September 1972): 16-22.

7. Charles Reith, *The Blind Eye of History* (Montclair, New Jersey: Patterson Smith, 1975), pp. 13-21.

8. Allan Silver, "The Demand for Order in Civil Society: A Review of Some Themes in the History of Urban Crime, Police, and Riot." In *The Police: Six Sociological Essays* David J. Bordua, ed. (New York: John Wiley, 1967), pp. 1-24; Roger Lane, *Policing the City: Boston, 1822-1885* (Cambridge: Harvard University Press, 1967); James Richardson, *The New York Police: Colonial Times to 1901* (New York: Oxford University Press, 1970).

9. Sidney L. Harring and Lorraine M. McMullin, "The Buffalo Police 1872-1900: Labor Unrest, Political Power and the Creation of the Police Institution," *Crime and Social Justice* IV (Fall-Winter 1975): 5-14; *The Iron Fist and the Velvet Glove* (Berkeley: Center for Research on Criminal Justice, 1975).

10. This view builds upon the work of Samuel Hays, "The Politics of Municipal Reform in the Progressive Era," *Pacific Northwest Quarterly LV* (October 1965): 157-169; Robert Wiebe, *The Search for Order* (New York: Hill & Wang, 1967); and, Herbert G. Gutman, *Work, Culture, and Society in Industrializing America* (New York: Knopf, 1975).

11. Lawrence W. Sherman, "The Sociology and the Social Reform of the American Police: 1950-1973," *Journal of Police Science and Administration* II, no. 2 (1974): 255-262.

Chapter 1
The Police Unreformed

1. Mark H. Haller, "Historical Roots of Police Behavior: Chicago, 1890-1925," *Law and Society Review* 10 (Winter 1976): 303-324; Robert K. Merton, "The Latent Functions of the Machine," in *Social Theory and Social Structure,* Revised Edition (New York: The Free Press, 1957), pp. 71-81.

2. James Bryce, *The American Commonwealth,* vol. 2 (New York: Macmillan, 1889); Raymond B. Fosdick, *American Police Systems* (New York: The Century Co., 1920), pp. 3-4.

3. Gladys-Marie Fry, *Night Riders in Black Folk History* (Knoxville: University of Tennessee, 1975), pp. 82-109; Richard C. Wade, *Slavery in the Cities* (New York: Oxford University Press, 1967), pp. 80-82, 98-102.

4. Richard M. Brown, "Historical Patterns of Violence in America." H. D. Graham and T. R. Gurr, eds. *Violence in America: Historical and Comparative Perspectives* (New York: Bantam Books, 1969), pp. 45-84; Richard Hofstadter and Michael Wallace, eds., *American Violence: A Documentary History* (New York: Vintage Books, 1971).

5. Lincoln is cited in R. M. Brown, ed., *American Violence* (Englewood Cliffs: Prentice-Hall, 1970), p. 8; Jackson is cited by David Grimsted, "Rioting in its Jacksonian Setting," *American Historical Review* 77 (April 1972): 361-397.

6. John C. Schneider, "Riot and Reaction in St. Louis, 1854-1856," *Missouri Historical Review* LXVIII (January 1974): 171-185.

7. Brown, "Historical Patterns of American Violence;" Samuel Warner, *The Private City* (Philadelphia: University of Pennsylvania, 1971), chapter VII.

8. Albert J. Reiss, *The Police and the Public* (New Haven: Yale University Press, 1971).

9. Warner, *The Private City,* pp. 155-157.

10. Richardson, *The New York Police,* chapter 2.

11. Wilbur R. Miller, "Police Authority in London and New York City, 1830-1870," *Journal of Social History* VIII, no. 2 (1974-1975): 81-101.

12. Wilbur R. Miller, "Never On Sunday: Moralistic Reforms and the Police in London and New York City, 1830-1870," Paper, Conference on the Contextual Determinants of Police Behavior, Denver, February 1976.

13. Haller, "Historical Roots of Police Behavior."

14. Richardson, *New York City Police,* p. 193; Arthur Woods, *Policeman and Public* [1919] (New York: Arno Press, 1971), p. 27.

15. Augustine E. Costello, *Our Police Protectors* [1885] (Montclair: Patterson Smith, 1972).

16. A wealth of valuable information is contained in the 1880 Census reports. See U.S. Bureau of the Census, *Tenth Census of the United States,* Volumes 18 and 19, "Social Statistics of the Cities." Cincinnati, Police Department, *Annual Report,* 1886, pp. 181-186; Missouri Association for Criminal Justice, *The Missouri Crime Survey* (New York: Macmillan, 1926), pp. 19, 55.

17. John K. Maniha, "The Standardization of Elite Careers in Bureaucratizing Organizations," *Social Forces* 53 (December 1974): 282-288.

18. For survey data, see U.S. Bureau of the Census, *Tenth Census,* "Social Statistics of Cities"; Wood is cited by Richardson, *New York City Police,* p. 84.

19. Costello, *Our Police Protectors,* pp. 296-297; John J. Flinn, *History of the Chicago Police* (Chicago: Police Book Fund, 1887), pp. 151-206.

20. See, for example, the reports in Chicago, City Council, Committee on Crime, *Report,* March 22, 1915.

21. Cincinnati, Police Department, *Annual Report,* 1879, pp. 1022-3; for a systematic study, see Eugene J. Watts, "St. Louis Police Recruitment in the Twentieth Century," Paper, Conference on Historical Perspectives on American Criminal Justice, Omaha, Nebraska, April 22-23, 1976.

22. W. Marvin Dulaney, "Origins and Status of Black Policemen in the United States in Selected Northern Urban Cities and the South," Paper, Conference on Historical Perspectives on American Criminal Justice, Omaha, Nebraska, April 22-23, 1976.

23. Howard O. Sprogel, *The Philadelphia Police: Past and Present* [1887] (New York: AMS Press, 1974), pp. 172-173; Dubois cited in Dulaney, "Origins and Status of Black Policemen."

24. "Troubles of a Black Policeman," *Literary Digest* (January 27, 1912), pp. 177-179.

25. Lane, *Policing the City,* pp. 75-78; John K. Maniha, "Structural Supports for the Development of Professionalism Among Police Administrators," *Pacific Sociological Review* 16 (July 1973): 315-343; Samuel Walker, "Law and Order in Scranton," unpublished manuscript; Richardson, *New York City Police,* p. 70.

26. Fosdick, *American Police Systems,* p. 73.

27. James Robinson to International Association of Chiefs of Police, *Proceedings,* 1916 (Washington, D.C.; 1917), p. 81.

28. Edward H. Savage, *Police Records and Recollections* [1873] (Montclair: Patterson Smith, 1971), pp. 341-346; George M. Roe, ed., *Our Police: A History of the Cincinnati Police Force* (Cincinnati: n.p., 1890), pp. 132-135.

29. Costello, *Our Police Protectors,* p. 127; Sprogel, *The Philadelphia Police,* p. 103.

30. U.S. Bureau of the Census, *Tenth Census,* "Social Statistics of Cities."

31. Fuld, *Police Administration*, pp. 120–126; IACP, *Proceedings*, 1914, p. 28; New York City, Board of Aldermen, *Police in New York City: An Investigation* [1913] (New York: Arno Press, 1971), pp. 4497–4498.

32. Jonathan Rubinstein, *City Police* (New York: Ballantine, 1973), pp. 13–25.

33. Cincinnati, Police Department, *Annual Report,* 1887, p. 12; Fuld, *Police Administration,* p. 115; Herbert Asbury, *The Gangs of New York* (New York: Capricorn Books, 1970).

34. Miller, "Police Authority in London and New York," p. 85.

35. McKelvey to IACP, *Proceedings,* 1896, p. 28.

36. Lincoln Steffens, *Autobiography* (New York: Harcourt-Brace, 1931), pp. 206–207.

37. Haller, "Historical Roots of Police Behavior."

38. U.S. Bureau of the Census, *Tenth Census,* "Social Statistics of Cities." See chapter 6 for a discussion of the use of weapons in the twentieth century.

39. Richardson, *New York City Police,* pp. 157–158.

40. Gary T. Marx, "Civil Disorder and the Agents of Social Control," *Journal of Social Issues* 26, no. 1 (1970): 19–57.

41. Reiss, *Police and the Public,* p. 147.

42. Joel T. Headley, *The Great Riots of New York, 1712–1873* [1873] (Indianapolis: Bobbs-Merrill, 1970), pp. 305–306.

43. "The Politics of Municipal Reform in the Progressive Era," *Pacific Northwest Quarterly* LV (October 1964): 157–169; Walker, "Law and Order in Scranton."

44. Herbert G. Gutman, "The Tompkins Square 'Riot' in New York City on January 13, 1874: A Re-Examination of its Causes and its Aftermath," *Labor History* VI (Winter 1965): 44–70; Flinn, *History of the Chicago Police,* chapters 9–11; Robert V. Bruce, *1877: Year of Violence* (Chicago: Quadrangle, 1970), pp. 241–251.

45. Fuld, *Police Administration,* p. 148; Eugene Watts, comment, Conference, Historical Perspectives on American Criminal Justice.

46. U.S. Bureau of the Census, *Tenth Census,* "Social Statistics of Cities"; Sprogel, *The Philadelphia Police,* pp. 219–221.

47. U.S. Bureau of the Census, *Tenth Census,* vol. 19, p. 48. William McAdoo, *Guarding a Great City* [1906] (New York: Arno Press, 1971), pp. 134–137.

48. Jacob Riis, *How the Other Half Lives* (New York: Dover, 1971).

49. Haller, "Historical Roots of Police Behavior"; George L. Kelling, et al., *The Kansas City Preventive Patrol Experiment: A Summary Report* (Washington:

The Police Foundation, 1974); The Rand Corporation, *The Criminal Investigation Process,* 3 vol. (Santa Monica: The Rand Corporation, 1975).

50. Eugene F. Rider, "The Denver Police Department: An Administrative, Organizational, and Operational History, 1858-1905," Ph.D. dissertation, University of Denver, 1971, p. 42; Walker, "Law and Order in Scranton."

51. James W. Savage and John T. Bell, *History of the City of Omaha, Nebraska* (New York: Munsell, 1894), pp. 368-370.

52. Francis Russell, *A City in Terror–1919–The Boston Police Strike* (New York: The Viking Press, 1975), pp. 131-170; Sterling Spero, "The Rise, Fall and Revival of Police Unionism," in *Government as Employer* (Carbondale: Southern Illinois University Press, 1972), pp. 245-294. See chapter 5.

53. Richardson, *New York City Police,* p. 169; Flinn, *History of the Chicago Police,* p. 206; Fuld, *Police Administration,* p. 113.

54. U.S. Bureau of the Census, *Tenth Census,* "Social Statistics of Cities."

55. Fuld, *Police Administration,* p. 463; August Vollmer, "Police Progress in the Past Twenty-Five Years," *Journal of Criminal Law and Criminology* 24 (May 1933): 166.

56. Haller, "Historical Roots of Police Behavior"; the argument is central to Jerome Skolnick, *Justice Without Trial* (New York: John Wiley, 1967).

57. Richardson, *New York City Police,* pp. 209-210; Daniel Bell, "Crime as an American Way of Life: A Queer Ladder of Social Mobility," in *The End of Ideology,* rev. ed. (New York: Collier Books, 1961), pp. 127-150.

58. Allan Pinkerton, *Thirty Years as a Detective* [1884] (Montclair: Patterson Smith, 1975), pp. 177, et seq.

59. Flinn, *History of the Chicago Police;* Thomas Byrnes, *1886: Professional Criminals of America* (New York: Chelsea House, 1969).

60. Roger Lane, "Crime and the Industrial Revolution: British and American Views," *Journal of Social History* 7 (Spring 1974): 287-303.

61. Theodore N. Ferdinand, "The Criminal Patterns of Boston Since 1849," *American Journal of Sociology* 73 (July 1967): 84-99; Roger Lane, "Urbanization and Criminal Violence in the 19th Century: Massachusetts as a Test Case," *Journal of Social History* II (Winter 1968): 156-163; Warner, *The Private City.*

62. Theodore Roosevelt, "The Lawlessness of the Police," in *The Works of Theodore Roosevelt,* vol. XIV (New York: Charles Scribners, 1926), pp. 181-238.

63. Cincinnati, Police Department, *Annual Report,* 1882, p. 587.

64. Savage, *Police Records and Recollections,* pp. 254-260.

65. Wilbur Miller, "Never on Sunday: Moralistic Reforms and the Police in London and New York City, 1830-1870," Conference on Contextual Determinants of Police Behavior, Denver, March 1976.

66. Richardson, *New York City Police,* pp. 236-245; Charles H. Parkhurst, *Our Fight With Tammany* [1895] (New York: Arno Press, 1970); Senate Committee Appointed to Investigate the Police Department of the City of New York, *Report and Proceedings,* 5 vol. [1895] (New York: Arno Press, 1971).

67. Fosdick, *American Police Systems,* chapters II and III.

68. Ibid., pp. 112-3.

69. Ibid., p. 104.

70. Richardson, *New York City Police,* pp. 101-108; Fosdick, *American Police Systems,* p. 131; Savage & Bell, *History of the City of Omaha,* pp. 368-370.

71. Lane, "Crime and the Industrial Revolution"; J. J. Tobias, *Urban Crime in Victorian England* (New York: Schocken Books, 1972), pp. 244-255.

72. U.S. Bureau of the Census, *Tenth Census,* "Social Statistics of the Cities"; Cincinnati Police Department, *Annual Report,* 1882, p. 8.

73. J. P. Shalloo, *Private Police Systems in the United States* (New York: Arno Press, 1974).

74. Frank Morn, "Discipline and Disciplinarians: The Problem of Police Control in the Formative Years," Paper, American Historical Association, December 28-30, 1975.

75. Richard M. Brown, "The American Vigilante Tradition," in *Violence in America,* pp. 154-226.

76. Richard M. Brown, "Pivot of American Vigilantism: The San Francisco Vigilance Committee of 1856," in John A. Carroll, ed., *Reflections of Western Historians* (Tucson: University of Arizona, 1969), pp. 105-119.

Chapter 2
The Emergence of Professionalism

1. For a general introduction to the period, see Robert Wiebe, *The Search for Order* (New York: Hill & Wang, 1967).

2. John K. Maniha, "Structural Supports for the Development of Professionalism Among Police Administrators," *Pacific Sociological Review* 16 (July 1973): 315-343.

3. Richardson, *The New York Police,* pp. 216-217, 236-245; Haller, "Historial Roots of Police Behavior."

4. E. H. Savage, *Police Records and Recollections* [1873] (Montclair: Patterson Smith, 1971).

5. Costello, *Our Police Protectors*, pp. xix-xxi.

6. Flinn, *History of the Chicago Police;* Sprogel, *The Philadelphia Police;* Henry Mann, *Our Police: A History of the Pittsburgh Police Force, Under The Town and City* (Pittsburgh: The City, 1889); George M. Roe, *Our Police: A History of the Cincinnati Police* (Cincinnati: n.p., 1890); Thomas A. Knight, *History of the Cleveland Police Department* (Cleveland: n.p., 1898).

7. Costello, *Our Police Protectors,* pp. 465-466; Flinn, *History of the Chicago Police,* p. 203.

8. Sprogel, *The Philadelphia Police,* p. v. See also the pioneering investigations of police personnel practices by Maniha, "The Standardization of Elite Careers," and Watts, "St. Louis Police Recruitment in the Twentieth Century."

9. Costello, *Our Police Protectors,* pp. 466-467.

10. Savage, *Police Records and Recollections,* pp. 254-260; Lane, *Policing the City,* pp. 168-169.

11. Lane, *Policing the City,* p. 201.

12. For a convenient collection of the more important reports of the Standing Committee on Police, see National Prison Association, *Proceedings of the Annual Congress of the National Prison Association of the United States: Selected Articles* (New York: Arno Press, 1971).

13. National Prison Association, *Proceedings,* 1888, p. 215; ibid., 1890, p. 130.

14. Ibid., 1874, pp. 135-136; ibid., 1898, p. 304.

15. Ibid., 1888, p. 210.

16. Fuld, *Police Administration,* pp. 351-355.

17. Ibid., pp. 55-68, 342-351.

18. Cincinnati, Association of the Committee of One Hundred, *Proceedings,* February 11, 1886, March 26, 1886, October 5, 1886; Roe, *Our Police,* pp. 96-98.

19. Cincinnati Police Department, *Annual Report,* 1886, pp. 181-186; Roe, *Our Police,* pp. 178-185.

20. Ibid., pp. 158-162.

21. Cincinnati Police Department, *Annual Report,* 1886, p. 11; Roe, *Our Police,* pp. 161-162.

22. Ibid., pp. 132-135, 158-160.

23. Maniha, "The Standardization of Elite Careers in Bureaucratizing Organizations."

24. Cincinnati Police Department, *Annual Report,* 1900, pp. 485-486.

25. William H. Harbaugh, *Power and Responsibility: The Life & Times of Theodore Roosevelt* (New York: Farrar, Straus & Cudahy, 1961), pp. 3-64.

26. Richardson, *The New York Police*, pp. 236-245; Charles H. Parkhurst, *Our Fight With Tammany* (New York: Arno Press, 1970).

27. New York, Senate Committee Appointed to Investigate the Police Department of the City of New York, *Report and Proceedings*, 5 vol. (New York: Arno Press, 1971).

28. Richardson, *The New York Police*, pp. 246-267.

29. Theodore Roosevelt, "The Enforcement of Law," *Forum* (September 1895), pp. 1-10.

30. Richardson, *The New York Police*, p. 259.

31. Theodore Roosevelt, "The Roll of Honor of the New York Police," *The Century Magazine* LIV (October 1897), pp. 803-814.

32. Theodore Roosevelt, *The Works of Theodore Roosevelt: National Edition*, vol. XIV (New York: Charles Scribners & Sons, 1926), pp. 236-238.

33. Fosdick, *American Police Systems.*

34. National Police Convention, *Official Proceedings, 1871* (New York: Arno Press, 1971).

35. Omaha, *Municipal Reports*, 1892, pp. 350-351.

36. National Police Chiefs Union, *Proceedings*, 1895, p. 8.

37. On Richard Sylvester, see chapter 3.

38. *National Police Magazine* I (September 1912), p. 17; Eugene F. Rider, "The Denver Police Department: An Administrative, Organizational, and Operational History, 1858-1905," Ph.D. dissertation, University of Denver, 1971, pp. 338-339; Police Mutual Benevolent Association, *History of the New Orleans Police Department* (New Orleans: n.p., 1900), pp. 121-133.

39. Don Berney, "Law and Order Politics: A History and Role Analysis of Police Officer Organizations," Ph.D. dissertation, University of Washington, 1971; Rider, "The Denver Police Department," p. 257; Knight, *History of the Cleveland Police Department*, p. 125.

Chapter 3
Cleaning House: Professionalization as Administrative Reform

1. James Couzens, ed., *Story of the Detroit Police Department* (Detroit: The City, 1917), hereinafter cited as Detroit Police Department, *Annual Report*, 1917.

2. Raymond B. Fosdick, *Chronicle of a Generation* (New York: Harper and Bros., 1958); Fuld, *Police Administration*, p. 370.

3. President's Commission on Law Enforcement and the Administration of Justice, *The Challenge of Crime in a Free Society* (New York: Avon Books, 1968), pp. 258-259.

4. Wiebe, *The Search for Order;* Skolnick, *Justice Without Trial,* pp. 235-239.

5. Samuel P. Hays, *The Response to Industrialism* (Chicago: University of Chicago Press, 1957), p. 48.

6. John Russell Young, *The Metropolitan Police Department, Official Illustrated History* (Washington, D.C.: Lawrence Publishing Co., 1908), pp. 3, 16; Fuld, *Police Administration,* p. 181.

7. IACP, *Proceedings,* 1896, pp. 6, 11.

8. Ibid., 1901, pp. 44-46; ibid., 1911, p. 11.

9. Ibid., 1915, pp. 57, 71.

10. Ibid., 1911, p. 21; ibid., 1913, p. 70; ibid., 1914, pp. 32-37.

11. Jane Addams, *The Spirit of Youth and the City Streets* (New York: Macmillan, 1905), pp. 75-103; Robert Sklar, *Movie-Made America* (New York: Random House, 1975), pp. 122-140; Kathleen D. McCarthy, "Nickel Vice and Virtue: Movie Censorship in Chicago, 1907-1915," *Journal of Popular Film* V, no. 1 (1976): 37-55.

12. *National Police Magazine* I (July 1912), p. 63; IACP, *Proceedings,* 1909, p. 77; ibid., 1910, pp. 50, 58; *Journal of Criminal Law and Criminology* I (July 1910): 108-109.

13. IACP, *Proceedings,* 1895, pp. 10-11; *National Police Magazine* I (September 1912), p. 89; Pennsylvania Chiefs of Police Association, *Official Manual,* 1919, pp. 48-53, 68-69.

14. Bureau of Municipal Research, *Six Years of Municipal Research for New York City, 1906-1911* (New York: Bureau of Municipal Research, 1912); Jane S. Dahlberg, *The New York Bureau of Municipal Research* (New York: NYU Press, 1966), p. 22.

15. Dahlberg, *The New York Bureau of Municipal Research,* pp. 20-21.

16. Ibid., p. 47; Woods, *Policeman and Public,* p. 163, Detroit Police Department, *Annual Report,* 1917, p. 239.

17. Bureau of Municipal Research, *Report on a Survey of the City Government of Columbus, Ohio* (New York: Bureau of Municipal Research, 1916); Colorado Tax Payers League, *Report on a Survey of the Department of Safety* [of Denver] (New York: Bureau of Municipal Research, 1914); Bureau of Municipal Research, *A Report on a Preliminary Survey of Certain Departments of the City of Milwaukee* (New York: Bureau of Municipal Research, 1913); Chamber of Commerce of Reading, Pa., *Report on a Survey of the Department of Police* (New York: Bureau of Municipal Research, 1913); Bureau of Municipal

Research, *Government of the City of Rochester* (New York: Bureau of Municipal Research, 1915); San Francisco Real Estate Board, *Report on a Survey of the Government of the City and County of San Francisco* (New York: Bureau of Municipal Research, 1916).

18. Reading, Pa., Chamber of Commerce, *Report on a Survey of the Department of Police,* p. 111.

19. Ibid., pp. 113-114.

20. Lincoln Steffens, *The Shame of the Cities* (New York: Hill and Wang, 1957), pp. 134-161.

21. Robinson to IACP, *Proceedings,* 1914, pp. 26-28; Charles F. Jenkins, "The Blankenburg Administration in Philadelphia: A Symposium," *National Municipal Review* 5 (April 1916): 211-213.

22. Philadelphia, Department of Public Safety, *Annual Report,* 1913, pp. 49, 147-152; ibid., 1912, pp. 316-317.

23. Ibid., 1913, pp. 59, 147-152, 177.

24. Ibid., 1912, p. 311; IACP, *Proceedings,* 1914, pp. 26-28.

25. Philadelphia, Department of Public Safety, *Annual Report,* 1912, p. 307; ibid., 1913, pp. 172-174.

26. Ibid., 1913, p. 179.

27. Wallace S. Sayre and Herbert Kaufman, *Governing New York City: Politics in the Metropolis* (New York: Russell Sage Foundation, 1960), p. 286. Mark H. Haller, "Civic Reformers and Police Leadership: Chicago, 1905-1935," in Harlan Hahn, ed., *Police in Urban Society* (Beverly Hills: Sage Publications, 1971), pp. 39-56.

28. Austin F. MacDonald, "General Butler Cleans Up," *National Municipal Review* 13 (July 1924): 367-373.

29. Fosdick, *American Police Systems,* chapter IV, pp. 217-248.

30. Raymond B. Fosdick, *European Police Systems* (Montclair: Patterson Smith, 1969).

31. Nathan Douthit, "August Vollmer, Berkeley's First Chief of Police, and the Emergence of Police Professionalism," *California Historical Quarterly* LIV (Summer 1975): 100-124; Gene E. & Elaine H. Carte, *Police Reform in the United States: The Era of August Vollmer* (Berkeley: University of California Press, 1975).

32. Dayton David McKean, *The Boss: The Hague Machine in Action* (New York: Russell & Russell, 1940).

33. August Vollmer and Albert Schneider, "School for Police as Planned at Berkeley," *Journal of Criminal Law and Criminology* VII (1917): 877-898.

34. Woods, *Policeman and Public,* p. 27.

35. Cleveland Police Department, *Annual Report,* 1903, p. 15; ibid., 1906, p. 19; ibid., 1915, p. 1270.

36. Graham Taylor, "Police Work a Profession, Not a Job," *Journal of Criminal Law and Criminology* VII (1916-1917): 623.

37. New York City, Board of Aldermen, *Police In New York City: An Investigation* [1913] (New York: Arno Press, 1971).

38. Douthit, "August Vollmer"; Carte and Carte, *Police Reform.*

39. *National Police Magazine* I (September 1912), p. 17; *Policeman's Monthly* (March 1913), p. 3; IACP, *Proceedings,* 1904, pp. 91-97; ibid., 1915, p. 15.

40. Rand Corporation, *The Criminal Investigation Process,* 3 vol. (Santa Monica: The Rand Corporation, 1975).

41. U.S. Bureau of the Census, *General Statistics of Cities,* 1915, p. 24.

42. Ibid., p. 29.

43. Fosdick, *American Police Systems,* p. 271; Woods, *Policeman and Public,* pp. 96-97.

44. Bruce Smith, *Police Systems in the United States* (New York: Harper and Brothers, 1940), pp. 178-205.

45. J. P. Shalloo, *Private Police* [1933] (Montclair: Patterson Smith, 1974).

46. Smith, *Police Systems in the United States,* p. 205.

47. Pennsylvania State Federation of Labor, *The American Cossack* (New York: Arno Press, 1971); Katherine Mayo, *Justice to All: The Story of the Pennsylvania State Police* (New York: G. P. Putnam, 1917).

48. Max Lowenthal, *The Federal Bureau of Investigation* (New York: Harcourt, Brace & Jovanovich, 1950), pp. 3-79; Sanford J. Ungar, *FBI* (Boston: Little, Brown, 1976), pp. 37-63.

49. Lowenthal, *The Federal Bureau of Investigation,* p. 5.

50. See chapter 6.

Chapter 4
Reforming Society: Cops as Social Workers

1. Edwin H. Sutherland and C. E. Gehlke, "Crime and Punishment," in President's Research Committee on Social Trends, *Recent Social Trends in the United States* (New York: McGraw-Hill, 1933), pp. 1114-1167.

2. See chapter 6.

3. Francis A. Allen, "The Borderland of the Criminal Law: Problems of 'Socializing' Criminal Law," in *The Borderland of Criminal Justice* (Chicago:

University of Chicago Press, 1964), pp. 1-24. On the dilemmas of the police in a social work role, see Aaron Cicourel, *The Social Organization of Juvenile Justice* (New York: John Wiley, 1968).

4. George L. Kelling and Robert B. Kliesmet, "Resistance to the Professionalization of the Police," *The Law Officer* V (September 1972): 16-22.

5. Nathan Douthit, "August Vollmer, Berkeley's First Chief of Police, and the Emergence of Police Professionalism," *California Historical Quarterly* LIV (Summer 1975): 100-124 is far superior to the very disappointing Gene E. Carte and Elaine H. Carte, *Police Reform in the United States: The Era of August Vollmer* (Berkeley: University of California Press, 1975).

6. August Vollmer, *The Police and Modern Society* (Berkeley: University of California Press, 1936).

7. Arthur Woods, *Policeman and Public* [1919] (New York: Arno Press, 1971), p. 27; Joseph Quigley in IACP, *Proceedings,* 1912, p. 106; Graham Taylor, "Police Work a Profession, Not a Job," *Journal of Criminal Law, Criminology* VII (1916-1917): 622-624.

8. August Vollmer, "The Policeman as a Social Worker," IACP, *Proceedings,* 1919, pp. 32-38; Vollmer, "Predelinquency," ibid., 1921, pp. 77-80.

9. IACP, *Proceedings,* 1900, p. 24.

10. W. E. Moore, *The Professions: Rules and Roles* (Beverly Hills: Sage Publications, 1970).

11. Vollmer, "The Policeman as a Social Worker," p. 34.

12. Samuel Walker, "Police Professionalism: Another Look at the Issues," *Journal of Sociology and Social Welfare* III (July 1976): 701-710.

13. U.S. Bureau of the Census, *General Statistics of Cities, 1915;* Kathleen D. McCarthy, "Nickel Vice & Virtue: Movie Censorship in Chicago, 1907-1915," *Journal of Popular Film* V, no. 1 (1976): 37-55.

14. Fosdick, *American Police Systems,* pp. 211-212.

15. Los Angeles Police Department, *Annual Report,* 1915; *Toledo City Journal,* February 9, 1919, p. 76; Arthur Woods, *Crime Prevention* (Princeton: Princeton University Press, 1918), pp. 38-45.

16. *American City* III (August 1910): 151-152; ibid. IV (1911): 249; Fosdick, *American Police Systems,* p. 369.

17. The following discussion is drawn from Samuel Walker, "The Rise and Fall of the Policewomen's Movement," Paper presented to the Missouri Valley History Conference, Omaha, March 1976. The most valuable sources remain: Mary S. Allen, *The Pioneer Policewoman* (London: Chatto & Windus, 1925); Mary E. Hamilton, *The Policewoman* (New York: Frederick A. Stokes, 1924); and, Chloe Owings, *Woman Police* (New York: Frederick H. Hitchcock, 1925).

18. National Prison Association, *Proceedings*, 1886, pp. 301-306; Owings, *Women Police*, pp. 98-100.

19. Owings, *Women Police*, pp. 99-100, 166-167.

20. Ibid., pp. 101-103; Los Angeles Police Department, *Rules and Regulations, 1911*, p. 64; Los Angeles Police Department, *Annual Report*, 1915, pp. 34, 59; *Journal of Social Hygiene* I (1914-1915): 494-495.

21. Wells, IACP, *Proceedings*, 1914, pp. 129-130; National Conference of Charities and Corrections, *Proceedings*, 1915, pp. 411-418; ibid., 1916, pp. 547-552; Owings, *Women Police*, pp. 191-192.

22. Owings, *Women Police*, pp. 129-131.

23. Sabina Marshall, "Development of the Policewoman's Movement in Cleveland, Ohio," *Journal of Social Hygiene* XI (April 1925): 193-209.

24. Owings, *Women Police*, pp. 124-129.

25. Edna A. Beveridge, "Establishing Policewomen in Baltimore in 1912," National Conference of Charities and Corrections, *Proceedings*, 1915, pp. 418-421.

26. Hamilton, *The Policewoman*, p. 4; Louis Brownlow, *Policewoman's International Bulletin*, III (October 1927), p. 2.

27. Hamilton, *The Policewoman*, pp. 5, 33.

28. Wells to IACP, *Proceedings*, 1914, p. 129; Owings, *Women Police*, pp. 101-102.

29. Eleanor Hutzel and Madelin MacGregor, *The Policewoman's Handbook* (New York: Columbia University Press, 1933), p. 11; Hamilton, *The Policewoman*, p. 170.

30. *Policewoman's International Bulletin*, no 5 (1925), p. 13; U.S. Federal Security Agency, *Techniques of Law Enforcement in the Use of Policewomen*, 1945, pp. 5, 65.

31. Hamilton, *The Policewoman*, pp. 179-180.

32. Wells to IACP, *Proceedings*, 1914, pp. 129-130; Owings, *Women Police*, p. 197.

33. Owings, *Women Police*, pp. 270-275; Mina C. Van Winkle to National Conference of Charities and Corrections, *Proceedings*, 1924, p. 188; *Journal of Social Hygiene* X (1924): 108-109.

34. Women Police Officers Association of California, *Program*, 1937, p. 3; ibid., 1939, pp. 8-11.

35. U.S. Bureau of the Census, *General Statistics of Cities*, 1915, pp. 69-73.

36. Helen D. Pidgeon, "Policewomen in the United States," *Journal of Criminal Law, Criminology* XVIII (November 1927): 372-377; *Policewoman's International Bulletin*, 1925-1927.

37. Hamilton, *The Policewoman,* pp. 57-64; Henrietta Additon, "The Functions of Policewomen," *Journal of Social Hygiene* X (June 1924: 321-328; *Policeman's News* (March 1921), p. 21.

38. Owings, *Women Police,* pp. 123-124, 197.

39. *Policewoman's International Bulletin,* no. 18 (April 1926), pp. 8-10; Lois Higgins, "Historical Background of Policewomen's Service," *Journal of Criminal Law, Criminology, and Police Science* 41 (March-April 1951): 822-833.

40. Philadelphia, Bureau of Police, Crime Prevention Division, *The Philadelphia Policewoman,* April 1949 through December 1951.

41. O. W. Wilson, *Police Administration* (New York: McGraw-Hill, 1963), p. 334; International City Management Association, *Municipal Police Administration,* Seventh Edition (Washington: ICMA, 1971), p. 153.

42. Catherine Milton, *Women in Policing* (Washington: The Police Foundation, 1972).

43. "I, Fred Kohler," Scrapbook, Cleveland, Ohio, Public Library.

44. Kohler to IACP, *Proceedings,* 1908, pp. 30-43; ibid., 1909, pp. 28-35; Cleveland Police Department, *Annual Report,* 1909, p. 13.

45. Cleveland Police Department, *Annual Report,* 1905, p. 13; ibid., 1908, p. 16; Marshall, "Development of the Policewomen's Movement in Cleveland, Ohio," 197.

46. Detroit Police Department, *Annual Report,* 1917, pp. 58-59; *National Police Magazine* I (July 1912): pp. 11-17; Los Angeles Police Department, *Annual Report,* 1915, p. 7; IACP, *Proceedings,* 1908, p. 36.

47. Cleveland Police Department, *Annual Report,* 1908, p. 5.

48. William J. Norton, "Chief Kohler of Cleveland and His Golden Rule Policy," *The Outlook* 93 (November 6, 1909): 537-542.

49. Cleveland Police Department, *Annual Report,* 1908, p. 18; *National Police Magazine* I (July 1912): pp. 11-17.

50. Roy Lubove, "The Progressives and the Prostitute," *The Historian* 24 (May 1962): 308-330; Allen F. Davis, "Welfare Reform & World War I," *American Quarterly* XIX (Fall 1967): 516-533; Howard B. Woolston, *Prostitution in the United States* [1921] (Montclair: Patterson Smith, 1969); Chicago Vice Commission, *The Social Evil in Chicago* [1911] (New York: Arno Press, 1970).

51. Sylvester to IACP, *Proceedings,* 1913, p. 95; *National Municipal Review* 5 (October 1916): 698-702.

52. IACP, *Proceedings,* 1901, 19-20.

53. *Ibid.,* 1906, pp. 47, 66; Woolston, *Prostitution in the United States,* p. 129.

54. IACP, *Proceedings,* 1907, pp. 87-91.

55. Cleveland Police Department, *Annual Report,* 1905, p. 18; ibid., p. 6; ibid., 1912, p. 8.

56. *National Municipal Review* 5 (October 1916): 698-702.

57. Ibid.; IACP, *Proceedings,* 1913, pp. 20-21.

58. Chicago Vice Commission, *The Social Evil in Chicago,* pp. 154-156.

59. Davis, "Welfare Reform & World War I," pp. 528-531; Fosdick, *Chronicle of a Generation,* pp. 142-186.

60. *National Municipal Review* 7 (July 1918): 425; *New York Times,* April 1, 1918, April 2, 1918, April 21, 1918, April 22, 1918, April 23, 1918.

61. Austin F. MacDonald, "General Butler Cleans Up," *National Municipal Review* 13 (July 1924): 367-373.

62. *National Police Magazine* I (July 1912), p. 102.

63. IACP, *Proceedings,* 1908, p. 41.

64. Ibid., 1899, pp. 17-19; ibid., 1906, p. 54; *National Police Magazine* I (July 1912), p. 26.

65. William J. Gaynor, "Lawlessness of the Police in New York," *North American Review* CLXXVI (January 1903): 10-26; Howard S. Gans, "In the Matter of the Lawlessness of the Police—A Reply to Mr. Justice Gaynor," ibid., (February 1903): 287-296.

Chapter 5
The Age of the Crime Commission, 1919-1931

1. For developments in the period, see Nathan Douthit, "Police Professionalism and the War against Crime in the United States, 1920s-1930s," in George L. Mosse, ed., *Police Forces in History* (Beverly Hills: Sage Publications, 1975), pp. 317-333.

2. Humbert Nelli, *The Business of Crime* (New York: Oxford University Press, 1976), pp. 148-149.

3. On police unionism, see Sterling Spero, "The Rise, Fall and Revival of Police Unionism," in *Government as Employer* (Carbondale: Southern Illinois University Press, 1972), pp. 245-294; Don Berney, "Law and Order Politics: A History and Role Analysis of Police Officer Organizations," Ph.D. dissertation, University of Washington, 1971; Harvey A. Juris and Peter Feuille, *Police Unionism* (Lexington, Mass.: Lexington Books, 1973).

4. Berney, "Law and Order Politics," pp. 69-71. A nearly complete collection of police magazines is to be found in the New York Public Library.

5. United States, Department of Commerce, *Historical Statistics of the United States: Colonial Times to 1970* (Washington, 1975), vol. I, pp. 210-211; New York City, Board of Aldermen, *Police in New York City: An Investigation* (New York: Arno Press, 1971), pp. 4489-4498.

6. See Linda Alden Moody, "Extending the Shield of the First Amendment to the Outspoken Policeman," *Criminal Law Bulletin* VIII (April 1972): 171-205.

7. Spero, "Rise, Fall and Revival of Police Unionism," pp. 250-252.

8. Ibid.; U.S. Congress, House, *Congressional Record*, Sixty-sixth Congress, 1st Session, 1919, vol. 58, pp. 6844-6851.

9. *New York Times,* September 14, 1918, September 15, 1918, September 17, 1918.

10. For general background on the year 1919, see David Brody, *Labor in Crisis: The Steel Strike of 1919* (Philadelphia: J. B. Lippincott, 1965); Robert K. Murray, *Red Scare* (Minneapolis: University of Minnesota, 1955); Arthur Waskow, *From Race Riot to Sit-In: 1919 and the 1960's* (New York: Doubleday, 1967).

11. The following account of the Boston police strike is drawn from Spero, "The Rise and Fall and Revival of Police Unionism," pp. 252-284; Francis Russell, *A City in Terror—1919—The Boston Police Strike* (New York: Viking Press, 1975); Richard L. Lyons, "The Boston Police Strike of 1919," *New England Quarterly* 20 (June 1947): 147-168. Two important documents, "Fourteenth Annual Report of the Police Commissioner for the City of Boston" and "Report of Citizen's Committee Appointed By Mayor Peters to Consider the Police Situation," are available in *Boston Police Strike* (New York: Arno Press, 1971).

12. "Fourteenth Annual Report of the Police Commissioner," in *Boston Police Strike,* p. 11.

13. Ibid., p. 10.

14. "Report of the Citizen's Committee," in *Boston Police Strike,* appendix, pp. 11, 15-16, 18.

15. See the suggestive review of *A City in Terror* by Melvyn Dubofsky in *Labor History* 17 (Summer 1976): 437-440. Russell's account of the affair is wholly inadequate.

16. Spero, "The Rise, Fall and Revival of Police Unionism," pp. 251-252; Joseph G. Woods, "The Progressives and the Police: Urban Police Reform and the Professionalization of the Los Angeles Police," Ph.D dissertation, UCLA, 1973, pp. 147-149.

17. *New York Times,* October 13, 1919; U.S. Congress, House, *Congressional Record,* Sixty-sixth Congress, 1st Session, 1919, vol. 58, pp. 6844-6851.

18. *New York Times,* September 14, 1919, September 19, 1919, June 11, 1920.

19. T. A. Critchley, *A History of Police In England and Wales,* Second Edition, Revised (Montclair: Patterson Smith, 1973), pp. 182-189.

20. Ibid., pp. 190-198.

21. For general background, see Waskow, *From Race Riot to Sit-In* and Allen D. Grimshaw, ed., *Racial Violence in the United States* (Chicago: Aldine, 1969) which contains many articles, including Grimshaw's own important work on racial violence.

22. Seth Scheiner, *Negro Mecca* (New York: New York University Press, 1965), pp. 123-129.

23. This analysis is based on Waskow, *From Race Riot to Sit-In,* pp. 209-218.

24. Elliott M. Rudwick, *Race Riot at East St. Louis, July 2, 1917* (Carbondale: Southern Illinois University Press, 1964); U.S. Congress, House of Representatives, Thirty-fifth Congress, 2nd Session, Document No. 1231 (July 15, 1918), pp. 1-24.

25. Allen D. Grimshaw, "Actions of Police and the Military in American Race Riots," *Phylon* 24 (Fall 1963): 271-289.

26. Allan H. Spear, *Black Chicago* (Chicago: University of Chicago, 1967); William M. Tuttle, *Race Riot* (New York: Atheneum, 1970); The Chicago Commission on Race Relations, *The Negro in Chicago: A Study of Race Relations and a Race Riot* (Chicago: University of Chicago Press, 1922).

27. International Association of Chiefs of Police, *Proceedings,* 1919, 1920; Raymond B. Fosdick, *American Police Systems* (New York: The Century Co., 1920), pp. 22-23, 41; August Vollmer, *The Police and Modern Society* (Montclair: Patterson Smith, 1971), pp. 19-20. Bruce Smith, *Police Systems in the United States* (New York: Harper and Brothers, 1940).

28. Gary T. Marx, "Civil Disorder and the Agents of Social Control," *Journal of Social Issues* XXVI, no. 1 (1970): 19-57; see also the collection of documents and analysis by Anthony M. Platt, *The Politics of Riot Commissions, 1917-1970* (New York: Collier Books, 1971).

29. Leonard L. Richards, *Gentlemen of Property and Standing: Anti-Abolition Mobs in Jacksonian America* (New York: Oxford University Press, 1970); Richard M. Brown, "Historical Patterns of Violence in America," in H. D. Graham and T. R. Gurr, ed., *Violence in America: Historical and Comparative Perspectives* (New York: Bantam Books, 1969), pp. 45-84.

30. On the crime commissions of the period, see Virgil W. Peterson, *Crime Commissions in the United States* (Chicago: Chicago Crime Commission, 1945); Wayne L. Morse and Raymond L. Moley, "Crime Commissions as Aids in

the Legal-Social Field," *Annals of the American Academy of Political and Social Science* (September 1929): 68-73; an annotated bibliography is to be found in the *Journal of Criminal Law and Criminology* XXI (May 1930): 129-144.

31. The Cleveland Foundation, *Criminal Justice in Cleveland* (Montclair: Patterson Smith, 1968).

32. Raymond Moley, "The Cleveland Survey of Criminal Justice," National Conference of Charities and Corrections, *Proceedings,* 1922, 58-64.

33. Cleveland Foundation, *Criminal Justice in Cleveland,* pp. v-ix; Felix Frankfurter, "Surveys of Criminal Justice," National Conference of Charities and Corrections, *Proceedings,* 1930, pp. 63-69.

34. Cleveland Foundation, *Criminal Justice in Cleveland,* pp. 3-80.

35. Chicago Crime Commission, *Bulletin* 6 (October 1, 1919), p. 1; Mark H. Haller, "Civic Reformers and Police Leadership: Chicago, 1905-1935," in Harlan Hahn, ed., *Police in Urban Society* (Beverly Hills: Sage Publications, 1971), pp. 39-56.

36. Haller, "Civic Reformers and Police Leadership"; Illinois Association for Criminal Justice, *Illinois Crime Survey* (Montclair: Patterson Smith, 1968), pp. 357-372; The Citizens' Police Committee, *Chicago Police Problems* (Montclair: Patterson Smith, 1969).

37. Bruce Smith, *Police Systems in the United States* (New York: Harper and Bros., 1940), pp. 260-266.

38. Los Angeles Police Department, *Annual Report,* 1924 (reprinted as *Law Enforcement in Los Angeles* [New York: Arno Press, 1974]; Gene E. Carte and Elaine H. Carte, *Police Reform in the United States: The Era of August Vollmer* (Berkeley: University of California Press, 1975), pp. 58-62; Woods, "The Progressives and the Police."

39. John H. Wigmore, "The National Crime Commission: What Will It Achieve?," *Journal of Criminal Law and Criminology* XVI (November 1925): 314-315; Douthit, "Police Professionalism and the War Against Crime," pp. 323-324.

40. National Crime Commission, Committee on Motor Vehicle Thefts, *Reports,* 1930, 1931; National Crime Commission, *Outline of a Code of Criminal Procedure,* 1927.

41. Lee Kennett and James Laverne Anderson, *The Gun in America* (Westport: Greenwood Press, 1975), p. 192; IACP, *Proceedings,* 1924, pp. 31-32.

42. U.S. National Commission on Law Observance and Enforcement, *Reports,* 14 vol., 1931; George W. Wickersham, "Law Enforcement," National Conference of Charities and Corrections, *Proceedings,* 1930, pp. 20-33; Peterson, *Crime Commissions in the United States.*

43. President's Research Committee on Social Trends, *Recent Social Trends* (New York: McGraw-Hill, 1933).

44. U.S., National Commission on Law Observance and Enforcement, *Lawlessness in Law Enforcement,* vol. 11; Jerome Hopkins, *Our Lawless Police* (New York: Viking, 1931).

45. U.S. National Commission on Law Observance and Enforcement, *Lawlessness in Law Enforcement,* pp. 102-104; 152-155.

46. Ibid., p. 117.

47. California Peace Officers Association, *Proceedings,* 1931, pp. 86-95.

48. August Vollmer, "Police Progress in the Past Twenty-Five Years," *Journal of Criminal Law and Criminology* 24 (May 1933): 161-175.

49. William C. Beyer and Helen C. Toerring, "The Policeman's Hire," *Annals of the American Academy of Political and Social Sciences* CXLVI (November 1929): 135-146; *National Municipal Review* 17 (May 1928): 170-173; Missouri Association for Criminal Justice, *The Missouri Crime Survey* (New York: Macmillan, 1926), pp. 29-33.

50. University of Minnesota, *Survey of Police Training* (Minneapolis: University of Minnesota, 1937); American Municipal Association, *Municipal Training Schools for Police Officers* (Chicago: American Municipal Association, 1932); George H. Brereton, "Police Training in College and University," *American Journal of Police Science* III (January-February, 1932): 64-71.

51. Jerome Skolnick, *Justice Without Trial* (New York: John Wiley, 1966), pp. 235-239.

52. Cleveland Foundation, *Criminal Justice in Cleveland,* p. 63; Vollmer, *Police in Modern Society,* p. 164.

53. Albert Reiss, *The Police and the Public* (New Haven: Yale University Press, 1971).

Chapter 6
The Law and Order Decade, 1932-1940

1. On the 1930s, see Nathan Douthit, "Police Professionalism and the War Against Crime in the United States, 1920s-1930s," in George L. Mosse, ed., *Police Forces in History* (Beverly Hills: Sage Publications, 1975), pp. 317-333.

2. Samuel Walker, "The Changing Policeman's Lot: A Comparative Study of Police Salaries, 1870-1970" (unpublished manuscript); William C. Beyer and Helen C. Toerring, "The Policeman's Hire," in *Annals of the American Academy of Political and Social Sciences:* CXLVI (November 1929): 135-146; *National Municipal Review* 17 (May 1928): 270-273.

3. U.S. Department of Labor, *Bulletin* 685, "Salaries and Hours of Labor in Municipal Police Departments, July 1, 1938," (1941).

4. O. E. Carr, "Police and Fire Salaries, 1929–1933," *Public Management* XV (June 1933): 176-178.

5. Milwaukee, Police Department, *Annual Report,* 1938, pp. 2–10.

6. Clarence Ridley and Orin F. Nolting, "Economies in Police Administration," *Public Management* XV (January 1933): 15-17; Bruce Smith, "What the Depression Has Done to Police Service," ibid. XVI (March 1934): 67-70.

7. "Police Administration," in *The Municipal Yearbook* (Chicago: International City Management Association, 1934 to the present).

8. Smith, "What the Depression Has Done."

9. Ridley and Nolting, "Economies in Police Administration."

10. *Police Journal* (March 1937), p. 2; ibid., (August 1937), p. 14; ibid., (May 1938), pp. 11-15. *Police Chiefs' Newsletter* (December 1937), p. 3; *Public Management* XX (November 1938): 346.

11. Cincinnati, Division of Police, *The Cincinnati Police Beat Survey* (American Public Welfare Association, 1936).

12. O. W. Wilson, *The Distribution of Police Patrol Force* (Chicago: Public Administration Service, 1941).

13. International Association of Chiefs of Police, *Uniform Crime Reporting: A Complete Manual for Police* (New York: IACP, 1929); U.S. Department of Justice, Federal Bureau of Investigation, *Uniform Crime Reports,* vol. I, no. 1 (August 1930); U.S. Department of Justice, *Ten Years of Uniform Crime Reporting,* 1930-1939 (Washington, November 1939).

14. Baltimore Criminal Justice Commission, "Does Baltimore Need More Policemen?" (April 1940, mimeograph), pp. 5–13.

15. Albert Reiss, *The Police and the Public* (New Haven: Yale University Press, 1971).

16. O. W. Wilson, "One Man v. Two Men in Patrol Cars," *Public Management* XXII (April 1940): 111-112; *Police Journal* (September–October 1944), pp. 13, 20-21; IACP, *Police Yearbook, 1940,* pp. 52-56.

17. *Police Journal* (January-February 1948), p. 16.

18. Charles E. Merriam, et al., *The Government of the Metropolitan Region of Chicago* (Chicago: University of Chicago, 1933).

19. Bruce Smith, *A Regional Police Plan for Cincinnati and its Environs* (New York: Institute of Public Administration, 1932).

20. David L. Norrgard, *Regional Law Enforcement* (Chicago: Public Administration Service, 1969); President's Commission on Law Enforcement and Administration of Justice, *The Challenge of Crime in a Free Society* (New York:

Avon Books, 1968), pp. 301-309. Only recently has the conventional wisdom on consolidation been questioned, largely by Elinor Ostrom and her colleagues; see, for example, Elinor Ostrom and R. B. Parks, "Suburban Police Departments: Too Many and Too Small?," in L. Masotti, ed., *Urbanization of the Suburbs* (Beverly Hills: Sage Publications, 1973).

21. Irving Bernstein, *Turbulent Years* (Boston: Houghton Mifflin, 1971), pp. 485-490. For the police view of the conflict, see *American Police Review* (July-August 1937), p. 55.

22. Bernstein, *Turbulent Years,* passim. For a Marxist interpretation, see Sidney L. Harring, "Law and the Social Control of the Labor Force: The Suppression of Tramps in Buffalo During the Depression of the 1890's," paper, American Sociological Association, August 1976.

23. "Are Policemen Irish," *Police 13-13* (November 1929), p. 15.

24. Dayton David McKean, *The Boss: The Hague Machine in Action* (New York: Russell and Russell, 1940); Richard J. Connors, *A Cycle of Power: The Career of Jersey City Mayor Frank Hague* (Metuchen, N.J.: Scarecrow Press, 1971); National Committee for the Defense of Political Prisoners, *Report on the Denial of Labor and Civil Rights in Hudson County, New Jersey* (February 1937); American Civil Liberties Union, "Candid Views of Mayor Hague" (pamphlet, 1938).

25. Cleveland, Police Department, *Annual Report,* 1939, p. 86; Milwaukee, Police Department, *Annual Report,* 1934, p. 22; O. W. Wilson, "Police Administration," *Municipal Yearbook,* 1938, p. 97; IACP, *Police Yearbook,* 1937-1938, pp. 41-42.

26. Otto Higgins in IACP, *Police Yearbook,* 1938-1939, pp. 38-39, 80-82.

27. Lewis J. Valentine in ibid., pp. 38-39, 118-119.

28. California Police Officers Association, *Proceedings,* 1936, pp. 91-122.

29. Symposium, IACP, *Police Yearbook,* 1938-1939, pp. 77-119.

30. American Civil Liberties Union, *The Shame of Pennsylvania* (New York: ACLU, 1928); Pennsylvania, Department of Labor and Industry, *Special Bulletin* 38, "Report to Governor Gifford Pinchot by the Commission on Special Policing in Industry," (Harrisburg 1934).

31. Milwaukee, Police Department, *Annual Report,* 1938, table VI; New York City, Police Department, *Annual Report,* 1935, p. 65.

32. William E. Leuchtenburg, "The New Deal and the Analogue of War," in John Braeman, et al., eds., *Change and Continuity in Twentieth-Century America* (New York: Harper and Row, 1966), pp. 81-143.

33. Sanford J. Ungar, *FBI* (Boston: Little, Brown, 1976), pp. 72-73; Fred J. Cook, *The FBI Nobody Knows* (New York: Pyramid Books, 1965), pp. 150-151, 188-189.

34. Ungar, *FBI,* pp. 46-55. Hoover's image at first was such that even the ACLU supported his appointment in 1924; see Michael R. Belknap, "Reining in the Radical Hunters: An Historical Perspective on a Contemporary Controversy," paper, Conference on Historical Perspectives on American Criminal Justice, Omaha, April 1976.

35. U.S. Department of Justice, Bureau of Investigation, *A Booklet Concerning the Work of the United States Bureau of Investigation* (Washington, 1932); Federal Bureau of Investigation, *The Federal Bureau of Identification* (descriptive brochure, 1936, 1939, 1940, 1947).

36. Sutherland and Gehlke, "Crime and Punishment," in *Recent Social Trends;* William Seagle, "The American National Police," *Harper's Monthly Magazine* 169 (November 1934), pp. 751-761.

37. *Police Chiefs Newsletter* (March 1935), p. 3; *American Police Review* (May-June 1938), p. 9.

38. U.S. Attorney General's Conference on Crime, December 10-13, 1934, *Proceedings* (Washington 1934).

39. "Extending Federal Powers over Crime," *Law and Contemporary Problems* I (October 1934); Arthur Millspaugh, *Crime Control by the National Government* (Washington: The Brookings Institution, 1937).

40. Seagle, "The American National Police."

41. Roosevelt to Attorney General's Conference on Crime, *Proceedings,* pp. 17-20.

42. Ibid., pp. 1-7.

43. FBI *Law Enforcement Bulletin* IX (September 1940), p. 3; Ungar, *FBI,* p. 56.

44. IACP, *Uniform Crime Reporting: A Complete Manual for Police;* U.S. Department of Justice, *Ten Years of Uniform Crime Reporting.*

45. Extensive criticisms were voiced by Donald C. Stone, "Can Police Effectiveness Be Measured?," *Public Management* 12 (March 1930): 465-470; Thorsten Sellin, *Research Memorandum on Crime in the Depression* (New York: Social Science Research Council, 1937).

46. August Vollmer, "The Scientific Policeman," *American Journal of Police Science* I (January-February 1930): 8-12; Carte and Carte, *Police Reform in the United States,* pp. 49-50, 79-80.

47. Calvin Goddard in *American Journal of Police Science* I (January-February 1930): 13-37.

48. Cook, *The FBI Nobody Knows,* pp. 207-210.

49. Raymond B. Fosdick, *European Police Systems,* pp. 315-368; August Vollmer, "Police Administration," *Municipal Yearbook,* 1934, p. 77; New York Chiefs of Police Association, *Proceedings,* 1932, pp. 16, 34; *Police 13-13* (October 1930): 11-12.

50. *New York Times,* February 8, 1935; *New York Daily News,* February 22, 1935; *Police Chiefs Newsletter* (March 1935), p. 2, (July 1935), p. 2, (February 1936), p. 4; *Police Journal* (February 1937), p. 2.

51. Berkeley, City Manager, *Annual Report,* 1935, p. 21; IACP, *Police Yearbook,* 1936-1937, pp. 116-120; *Police Journal* (November 1936), pp. 3-4.

52. *Police Journal* (April 1936), p. 4; *National Sheriff* (February 1941), p. 7; *National Police Officer* (February 1936), p. 3.

53. For a suggestive analysis of the reorientation of the police image, see Peter K. Manning, "The Police: Mandate, Strategies, and Appearances," in Jack D. Douglas, ed., *Crime and Justice in American Society* (Indianapolis: Bobbs-Merrill, 1971), pp. 149-193.

54. FBI, *The Federal Bureau of Investigation* (1932, 1936, 1939).

55. J. Edgar Hoover, "The Confession and Third Degree Methods," *Law Enforcement Bulletin* V (January 1936), pp. 11-13.

56. J. Edgar Hoover, "Law Enforcement as a Profession," ibid VI (November 1937), pp. 3-4.

57. Federal Bureau of Investigation, *Training Schools: Selection of Personnel* (Washington 1936); FBI, *Standards in Police Training* (Washington 1939).

58. J. Edgar Hoover, "The Value of Marksmanship," ibid. (March 1941): 29; Alex Collier, *Training of Personnel* (Washington: The FBI, 1935), p. 6.

59. *National Police Officer* (January 1937), p. 6.

60. *American Police Review* (January-February 1939), p. 7; ibid., (September-October 1937), pp. 17-22; *New England Police Journal* (January 1935), p. 12.

61. Wichita Police Department, *Duty Manual,* 1935, pp. 9, 71; Boston Police Department, *Rules and Regulations,* 1941, pp. 317-320.

62. University of Minnesota, *Survey of Police Training* (Minneapolis: University of Minnesota, 1937); George H. Brereton, "Police Training in College and University," *American Journal of Police Science* III (January-February 1932): 64-71; Carte and Carte, *Police Reform in the United States,* pp. 68-71, 82.

63. *Pacific Coast International* VI (July 1939), p. 29; "Police Administration," *Municipal Yearbook,* 1937, p. 87.

64. League of Kansas Municipalities, Police Training School, "Outline of Instruction," June 1-6, 1931 (typescript).

65. California Peace Officers Association, *Proceedings,* 1930, *Police 13-13* (November 1930), pp. 11-12; *Pacific Coast International* IV (September 1939), pp. 11-12.

66. George H. Brereton, "The California Plan for Training Peace Officers," California Peace Officers Association, *Proceedings,* 1939, pp. 38-43; William A. Wiltberger,, "The Problems of Pre-Employment Police Training," ibid., 1938, 19-23.

67. University of Minnesota, *Survey of Police Training;* Smith, *Police Systems in the United States,* pp. 319-327.

68. O. W. Wilson, "Police Administration," *Municipal Yearbook,* 1938, p. 100; *Police Journal* (August 1936), p. 2; International City Management Association, *Municipal Police Administration* (Chicago, ICMA, 1943), p. 175.

69. California Department of Education, *Bulletin* 4, "Job Analysis of Police Service," February 15, 1933; California Department of Education, *Bulletin* 3, "Instructional Analysis of Police Service," February 1, 1934.

70. U.S. Department of Interior, Vocational Division, *Bulletin* 197, "Training for the Police Service," 1938.

71. Smith, *Police Systems in the United States,* pp. 319-327; Minnesota, *Survey of Police Training.*

72. Cincinnati City Manager, *Municipal Activities,* 1930-1937, passim.

73. Milwaukee Police Department, *Annual Report,* 1922-1941, passim.

74. Smith, *Police Systems in the United States,* p. xvii.

Epilogue: The Legacy of Professionalism

1. O. W. Wilson, *Police Administration,* 2nd ed. (McGraw-Hill, 1963); Donal E. J. MacNamara, "American Police Administration at Mid-Century," *Public Administration Review* X (Summer 1950): 181-189; Lawrence W. Sherman, "The Sociology and the Social Reform of the Police, 1950-1973," *Journal of Police Science and Administration* II (1974): 255-262.

2. The most perceptive assessment of the contemporary police in Herman Goldstein, *Policing a Free Society* (Cambridge: Ballinger, 1977).

3. W. E. Moore, *The Professions: Rules and Roles* (New York: Russell Sage Foundation, 1970); Samuel Walker, "Police Professionalism: Another Look at the Issues," *Journal of Sociology and Social Welfare* III (July 1976): 701-711.

4. On the stabilization of police careers, see John K. Maniha, "The Standardization of Elite Careers in Bureaucratizing Organizations," *Social Forces* 53 (December 1974): 282-288.

5. MacNamara, "American Police Administration at Mid-Century."

6. Peter K. Manning, "The Police: Mandate, Strategies, and Appearances," in Jack D. Douglas, ed., *Crime and Justice in American Society* (Indiana: Bobbs-Merrill, 1971), pp. 149-193.

7. For valuable insights into the efforts of reform on individual police departments, see James Q. Wilson, *Varieties of Police Behavior* (New York: Atheneum, 1973) and James Q. Wilson, "Police Morale, Reform, and Citizen

Respect: The Chicago Case," in David J. Bordua, ed., *The Police: Six Sociological Essays* (New York: John Wiley, 1967), pp. 137-162.

8. On the attempts by the Kennedy and Johnson administrations to elevate the IACP at the expense of the FBI, see Gerald Caplan, "Reflections on the Nationalization of Crime, 1964-1968," *Law and the Social Order* (1973): 583-635.

9. Ralph Lee Smith, *The Tarnished Badge* (New York: Thomas Y. Crowell, 1965); Paul Jacobs, *Prelude to Riot* (New York: Vintage Books, 1968), pp. 13-60; *The Knapp Commission Report on Police Corruption* (New York: George Braziller, 1973).

10. William A. Westley, *Violence and the Police* (Cambridge: MIT Press, 1970), pp. 22-30.

11. Cyril D. Robinson, "The Mayor and the Police—the Political Role of the Police in Society," in George L. Mosse, ed., *Police Forces in History* (Beverly Hills: Sage Publications, 1975), pp. 277-315.

12. Samuel Walker, "The Birth of the Police-Community Relations Movement: The Impact of World War II," unpublished manuscript.

13. Sterling D. Spero, "The Rise, Fall and Revival of Police Unionism," in *Government as Employer* (Carbondale: Southern Illinois University, 1972), pp. 245-294.

14. Westley, *Violence and the Police.*

15. Richard A. Myren, "A Crisis in Police Management," *Journal of Criminal Law, Criminology, and Police Science* 50 (March-April, 1960): 600-604 is perhaps the earliest statement of this theme. See also the important elaboration of the same idea by Jerome Skolnick, *Justice Without Trial: Law Enforcement in Democratic Society* (New York: John Wiley, 1967).

16. Hervey A. Juris and Peter Feuille, *Police Unionism* (Lexington, Mass.: Lexington Books, 1973).

17. George K. Kelling and Robert B. Kliesmet, "Resistance to the Professionalization of the Police," *The Law Officer* V (September 1972): 16-22.

18. The President's Commission on Law Enforcement and Administration of Justice, *The Challenge of Crime in a Free Society* (New York: Avon Books, 1967), pp. 258-259. *Report of the National Advisory Commission on Civil Disorders* (New York: Bantam Books, 1968), pp. 301-302.

19. "Securing Police Compliance With Constitutional Limitation: The Exclusionary Rule and Other Devices," in National Commission on the Causes and Prevention of Violence, *Law and Order Reconsidered* (New York: Bantam Books, 1970), pp. 411-415; Ronald Kahn, "Urban Reform and Police Accountability in New York City: 1950-1974," in Robert L. Lineberry and Louis H. Masotti, eds., *Urban Problems and Public Policy* (Lexington, Mass:

Lexington Books, 1975), pp. 107-127; Arthur Waskow, *Running Riot* (New York: Herder and Herder, 1970), pp. 35-50; Jerome Skolnick, "Neighborhood Police," *The Nation* (March 22, 1971), pp. 372-373. See the perceptive comments in Albert Reiss, *The Police and the Public* (New Haven: Yale University Press, 1971), pp. 207-212. Wilson, *Varieties of Police Behavior* explores the "bureaucracy problem."

20. Reiss, *The Police and the Public;* on the reorientation of the police role, see Goldstein, *Policing a Free Society.*

21. Goldstein, *Policing a Free Society*, chapter IV, "Developing Alternatives to the Criminal Justice System."

Index

Addams, Jane, 58
Additon, Henrietta, 92
American Civil Liberties Union, 78, 150
American Federation of Labor, 69, 111, 112, 113–119
American Female Reform Society, 85
American Journal of Police Science, 157, 161
American Police Systems, 27, 46, 67, 123
American Social Hygiene Association, 68, 87, 91, 102
Asbury, Herbert, 14
Atlanta, 56, 101
Attorney General's Conference on Crime (1934), 154–155
Automobile, impact on police, 109, 136, 153

Baker, Newton D., 102, 130
Baldwin, Lola, 85–86
Baltimore, 4, 5, 28, 35, 85, 88, 101; Crime Commission, 143–144
Bell, Daniel, 22
Berkeley, California, 68, 72, 80, 91, 130, 136, 158, 173
Bertillion System, 73, 157
Bingham, Theodore A., 66
Black police officers, 10–11
Blankenburg, Rudolph, 62–66
Bonaparte, Charles, 77–78
Boston, xi, 4, 5, 11, 12, 16, 20, 23, 35, 37–38, 85, 88, 91, 161; police strike (1919), 20, 49, 110, 113–118, 171
Boston Social Club, 114–116
Brockway, Zebulon R., 39
Brooklyn, N.Y., 15, 16, 39
Brown, Richard M., 30–31
Brownlow, Louis, 89
Bryce, James, 3
Brynes, Thomas, 8, 22, 23, 35
Buffalo, N.Y., 12, 83, 134, 142

Bureau of Municipal Research, 58–61, 79, 109
Burns, William J., 78
Butler, General Smedley D., 66–67, 71, 78, 103

California Department of Education, 164
California Peace Officers Association, 59, 73, 134, 150, 163, 169
Charleston, S.C., 4
Chicago, 10, 17–18, 20, 21, 23, 30, 35, 36, 37, 54, 60, 66, 71, 74, 79, 83, 85, 87, 92, 97, 98, 99, 101, 140, 147, 152, 156–157, 162, 167, 170; Commission on Race Relations, 123; race riot (1919), 109, 120, 122–123, 124
Chicago Crime Commission, 60, 109, 125, 126, 128–129
Chicago Vice Commission, 99, 101
Cincinnati, 5, 9, 10, 11, 12, 14, 20, 21, 25, 27, 29, 35, 40–43, 56, 70, 73, 84, 99, 133, 140, 164–165; police strike (1918), 112–113
Cincinnati Police Beat Survey, 142
Cincinnati Regional Crime Commission, 142, 145–146, 165
Civil liberties, 77–78, 90, 97–98, 104–106, 150, 174
Civil service, 7, 10, 39, 44, 70, 74–75, 168
Cleveland, 11, 49, 71, 87–88, 93, 93–98, 100–101, 102, 112, 133, 148
Cleveland Survey of Criminal Justice, 125–128, 136
Commission on Training Camp Activities, 102–103
Congress of Industrial Organizations (CIO), 70, 146, 147, 148
Congressional investigations, of police, 58, 121–122, 149

201

Consolidation, of police agencies, 141, 145–146
Coolidge, Calvin, 117
Costello, Augustine, 12, 35, 36, 37
Council Bluffs, Iowa, 84
Crime Commissions, 60, 109, 125–134, 143–144, 145–146, 155
Crime detection, 22–23, 39–40, 47, 72–73, 80, 168
Crime prevention, 7, 37–39, 54, 79–98, 168–169; role of women police, 84–94; *see also,* juveniles, rehabilitation
Crime statistics, 23–24, 38–39, 40, 64, 132, 143, 152–153, 155–156
Cummings, Homer, 155
Curtis, Edwin U., 114–117

Decriminalization, 95–96
Denver, 19, 49, 60, 170
Depression (1930's), impact on police, 139–146, 147, 154–155
Detroit, 53–54, 79, 89, 93, 97, 104, 133, 158, 170
Dietsch, Philip M., 41, 99
Dillinger, John, 149, 152, 160
Diversion, 95–96
DuBois, W.E.B., 11

East St. Louis, race riot (1919), 121–122
English police, xi, 7–8, 14–15, 28, 68, 119–120, 157
Ethnicity, xiii, 5, 6, 8, 11, 17, 18, 25, 30, 45, 113, 147
European Police Systems, 68, 102

Federal Bureau of Investigation (FBI), 40, 58, 59, 70, 75, 77–78, 139, 149, 151–161, 169; *Law Enforcement Bulletin,* 160
Federal government, and the police, 75, 77–78, 102–103, 106, 125–126, 130–134, 142, 146, 149–150, 151–166
Felton, Charles, 38, 39
Ferdinand, Theodore, 23

Fingerprints, 73, 157–159
Flinn, John J., 23, 35, 36, 37
Floyd, Pretty Boy, 149, 152, 160
Fosdick, Raymond B., 3, 27, 46, 54, 67–68, 74–75, 83–84, 102–103, 111, 123, 127–128, 157
Foundations, private, 68, 156
Frankfurter, Felix, 127
Fuld, Leonard, 14, 20, 21, 54, 56, 102, 111

Gangs of New York, The, 14
Gans, Howard S., 104–106
Gary, Elbert H., 130
Gary, Indiana, 170, 171
Gaynor, William J., 104–106
George-Deen Act., 163
German-Americans, 5, 11, 18, 25
Girard, Stephen, 6
Goddard, Calvin, 161
Golden Rule Policy, 94–98
Gompers, Samuel, 112, 118
Gulick, Luther, 145
Gun control, 131, 153–154

Hague, Frank, 69–70, 78, 147, 148
Haller, Mark, 8, 16, 19, 21, 24, 35, 128
Hamilton, Mary, 89, 90–93
Hays, Samuel, 7, 56
Headley, Joel T., 17
History of the Chicago Police, 35
Holmes, Oliver Wendell, 112
Hoover, Herbert, 125, 131–132
Hoover, J. Edgar, 59, 70, 73, 78, 80, 93, 139, 149, 152, 153, 155, 156, 157, 159–160, 169
Hutzel, Eleanor, 89–90

Illinois Crime Survey, 126, 129
Immigration, xii, xiii, 4, 11, 17
Indeterminate sentence, 79, 104
International Association of Chiefs of Police (IACP), 23, 38, 48, 56–59, 64, 73, 80, 81, 82, 86, 89, 91, 95, 97–101, 103, 130–131, 150, 153, 155, 164, 169

International Association of Police Matrons, 86
International Association of Police-women, 86, 91, 93
International City Management Association, 141, 156
Irish-Americans, 5, 6, 11, 12, 17, 18, 25, 30, 147

Jackson, Andrew, 4
Janssen, John T., 57, 165
Jersey City, N.J., 69–70, 147, 148, 149, 164
Johnson, Tom, 87
Journal of Criminal Law and Criminology, 134
"Junior Police," 84
Juveniles, 38, 47, 54, 58, 79, 81–82, 84, 85

Kansas City, 28, 54, 74, 126, 135, 149, 164
Kansas League of Municipalities, 163
Kelling, George, 172
Kerner Commission, 173
"Keystone Kops," 58
King, Rufus, 10
Kliesmet, Robert B., 172
Kluchesky, Joseph, 165
Knapp Commission, 170
Kohler, Fred, 71, 79, 95–98, 100–101, 104

Labor relations, and the police, xii, 4, 17–18, 20, 29–30, 36, 69, 76, 114, 146–151; *see also* police unions
LaFollette Committee, 149, 150
Lane, Roger, xi, 23–24
Laubenheimer, Jacob G., 165
Law Enforcement Assistance Administration (LEAA), 77, 142
Lawlessness in Law Enforcement, 133–134
Leuchtenburg, William, 151
Lexow Committee Investigation, 22, 24, 25, 35, 44–45, 59, 126

Lincoln, Abraham, 4
Lindberg, Charles, 152
Liquor, enforcement of laws, 24–25, 45, 65, 67; *see also* prohibition
London Metropolitan Police, 6, 7, 14–15, 28; police strike, 119–120
Los Angeles, 84, 86, 90, 97, 140, 149, 161, 170, 171–172, 173; crime commission, 126, 129
Lubove, Roy, 98

McAdoo, William G., 19
McAuliffe v. *Mayor of New Bedford*, 112
McDonough, James, 11, 34
McGinniskin, Barney, 11
McKelvey, William J., 15
Madison, Wisc., 21
Maniha, John K., 9, 34, 43
Marxism, interpretation of police history, xii, 17
Maryland, 27–28
Matheson, Duncan, 162–163
Matsell, George, 34–35
Merriam, Charles, 145
Michigan State College, 162
Militarization of the police, xv, 42, 45–46, 63, 66–67, 171–172
Miller, Wilbur, 7, 14, 16, 25
Milwaukee, 57, 60, 85, 135, 140, 148, 150, 164–165, 168
Minneapolis, 21, 99, 102, 147
Missouri, 28; *Missouri Crime Survey*, 126
"Modern" police, defined, 3–4, 5, 7, 19
Morn, Frank, 30
Motion pictures, image of the police, 57–58

National Advisory Commission on Criminal Justice Standards and Goals, 146
National Chiefs of Police Union, 48, 56
National Commission on Law Observance and Enforcement (see Wickersham Commission)

National Conference of Charities and Corrections, 86–87
National Crime Commission (1925), 130–131, 155
National Institute of Public Administration, 59, 141
National Police Academy, 155, 160, 161
National Police Convention (1871), 47–48
National Prison Association, 38–40, 47, 81
National Probation Association, 79
Native American Party, 6, 7
Negro in Chicago: A Study of Race Relations and a Race Riot, The, 123
Ness, Eliot, 143, 148
New Deal, The, 78, 146, 150, 151, 153
New Orleans, 9, 16, 49, 60, 140
New York City, xi, 4, 5, 6, 7, 8, 9, 11, 12, 13, 14, 15, 16, 17, 19, 20, 22, 23, 24, 25–26, 27, 28, 34, 35, 36, 43–47, 59, 66, 71–72, 74, 83, 84, 85, 89, 91, 92, 93, 101, 104–106, 111, 112, 118, 120–121, 124, 135, 140, 149, 151, 170, 173
New York State, Chiefs of Police Association, 157, 163; Conference of Mayors, 163, 165; Police Conference, 149
Night watch, 3, 35
Nolting, Ernest, 141–142
North American Review, 104
Northwestern University, 71, 157
Norton, William J., 97

Omaha, 20, 28, 48, 120, 122
O'Meara, Stephen, 114
Orange Riots, 17
Our Police Protectors, 35
Owen, Marie, 85
Owings, Chloe, 89

Parkhurst, Charles H., 26, 44, 45

Pennsylvania, 59; Coal and Iron Police, 29, 76, 150; Federation of Labor, 76; State Constabulary, 75–76
Peoples Party, Chicago, 10; San Francisco, 31
Philadelphia, 4, 5, 6, 10, 12, 13, 18, 23, 26, 35, 61–67, 71, 79, 83, 85, 92, 94
Philadelphia Negro, The, 11
Philadelphia Police: Past and Present, 35
Philadelphia Policewoman, 94
Pinchot, Gifford, 150
Pinkerton, Allan, 22, 29–30; Robert, 23; William, 23, 58
Pittsburgh, 18, 35, 101, 102
Police, brutality, 3, 15–16, 58, 120–122, 132–134; bureaucratization, x–xi, 55, 70, 74, 93, 135–136, 174; careers, 3, 34, 43, 139–141, 167–168; commissions, 26–28, 41–47, 67; corruption, 10, 22, 25, 26, 35, 44, 101, 105, 109, 129–130, 148, 164, 169–170; discretion, xiv, 8, 55, 71, 97; equipment, 12, 16, 71 (*see also* police weapons, technology); fraternal organizations, 20, 35, 49, 69, 110, 119 (*see also* police unions); history, xi–xiii, 35–37; law enforcement role, 19, 22–25, 37, 44–46, 64, 67, 83–84, 127–128, 131, 159, 173; lodgers, 18, 84, 150–151; magazines, 103, 110, 145, 161; matrons, 85, 86; organizations, structure, xv, 36, 56, 68, 129, 169, 171–172, 174; patrol, platoon systems, 13, 20–21, 42, 63–64; patrol, scientific study of, 142–144, 164, 173; patrol cars, 21, 136, 141, 142, 144–145; patrol wagons, 15; pensions, 35, 43, 135; personnel, 9–10, 11, 17, 20, 41–43, 45, 63–64, 69–70, 74, 165, 167–

168; police-community relations, 16, 123–124, 170–171, 173; professionalism, defined, ix–xi, 33–34, 159–166; salaries, 9–10, 92, 111–114, 118, 135, 140; service role, 6, 21, 150–151, 173–174; stations, 18–19, 169; strikes, 19–20, 49, 112–120, 169; subculture, xv, 49, 119–120, 171–173; supervision, 7, 10, 13, 21, 61, 67; training, 3, 11–12, 39, 42, 61, 63, 67, 70–73, 91, 124, 128, 130, 132, 135–136, 161–164; uniforms, 12–13; unions, xi, 110–120, 171–172; weapons, 16, 160–161
Police Federation, 119
Police Gazette, 35
Police and Modern Society, The, 80, 123
Police Records and Recollections, 35
Police Systems in the United States, 123
Policemen's benevolent associations, 35, 49, 110
Policewoman's International Bulletin, 89, 92, 93
Politics, influence on police, xii, 3, 6–7, 8–9, 10, 20, 24–25, 25–28, 30–31, 34, 39, 40–41, 44–47, 54, 60–61, 64–65, 66, 69–70, 148–149, 170
Porter, George D., 62–65
Portland, Oregon, 85–86
Pound, Roscoe, 127
President's Commission on Social Trends, 132
President's Crime Commission (1965–1967), 60, 146, 173
Private City, The, 23
Private police, 30–31, 150
Professional associations, police, 37–40, 47–49, 56–59, 73, 169; policewomen, 86, 93; public administration, 141–142, 156, 169
Professional Criminals of America, 23, 35

Progressive Era, 43, 61, 71, 79–80, 84, 94, 98, 102, 103, 174
Prohibition, 109, 129, 132, 154
Prostitution, 22, 24, 25, 37–38, 47, 69, 87–88, 98–103
Public attitudes toward police, 14, 21, 57–58, 116, 134, 137

Race relations, xiii, 4–6, 10, 16, 109–110, 120–125, 170–171, 173
Reading, Pa., 60–61
Recent Social Trends, 132, 152
Rehabilitation, 37–39, 54, 55, 79–80, 81, 94–98, 104
Richardson, James, xi, 16, 22, 45
Ridley, Clarence, 141–142
Riis, Jacob, 19, 44
Riots, 4–5, 6, 12, 16, 17–18, 109–110, 117, 120–125, 147, 170–171
Robinson, Cyril D., 170
Robinson, James, 12, 62–65, 103
Rockefeller, John D., Jr., 54, 68, 102, 157
Roosevelt, Franklin D., 131, 151, 154–155, 158
Roosevelt, Theodore, 24, 26, 28, 43–47, 67, 68, 77–78

St. Louis, 5, 9, 10, 11, 28, 34, 43, 47, 49, 73, 74, 85, 101, 135, 148
San Francisco, 9, 60, 140, 147; Vigilance Committee, 30–31
San Jose State College, 136, 162, 163
Savage, Edward H., 12, 25, 35, 37–38, 41, 81
Scientific Crime Detection Laboratory, 157, 162
Scranton, Pa., 11, 17, 19–20
Seagle, William, 154
Seavey, Webber S., 48
Serpico, 170
The Shame of the Cities, 62
Sherman, Lawrence W., xiv–xv
Silver, Allan, xi
Smith, Bruce, 123, 141, 146, 156, 164, 165
Social Control, role of police, xi–xii, 18, 28–31, 37

"Social evil" (*see* prostitution)
Social sciences, application to police, 59–60, 73–74, 81–82, 127
Sprogel, Howard O., 35, 36
State police, 75–77
Steffens, Lincoln, 15, 62
Stone, Donald C., 156
Sunrise Court, 94–98
Sylvester, Richard, 48, 56–57, 59, 68, 80, 99

Tammany Hall, 26, 44, 45, 54, 66, 104–106, 121
Taylor, Frederick W., 60
Taylor, Graham, 81
Technology, impact on police, ix–x, xiv, 9, 13, 21, 39–40, 80, 136–137, 166, 169
"Third Degree," 58, 125–126, 132–134, 159–160

Uniform Crime Reports (UCR), 40, 143, 152, 155–156, 159
University of California, 72–73, 81, 91, 156, 158
University of Chicago, 162
Urbanization, xi–xii, 23–24

Valentine, Lewis J., 149, 153
Van Winkle, Mina, 90
Vigilantism, 30–31
Vollmer, August, 21, 59, 68, 70–71, 72, 73, 79–83, 93, 123, 129–
130, 132, 134–136, 139, 141, 142, 156, 157, 158, 159, 162, 165

"War on Crime," 151–159
Warner, Sam Bass, 23–24
Washington, D.C., 4, 18, 48, 56, 68, 83, 90, 93, 99, 118, 120
Watts, Eugene, 10, 18
Wells, Alice Stebbins, 86, 89, 91
Westley, William, 170, 171
Wichita, Kan., 141, 142, 145, 161, 162
Wickersham Commission, 58, 60, 109, 125, 126, 130–134, 159
Wilmington, Del., 59, 104
Wilson, James Q., 173
Wilson, O. W., 73, 79–80, 93, 94, 139, 141, 142–143, 144, 145, 161, 162, 163, 167
Wilson, Woodrow, 67, 118
Wines, Frederick C., 38–39
Women police, 54, 84–94
Women's Christian Temperance Union (WCTU), 85, 86
Wood, Fernando, 9
Woods, Arthur, 8, 60, 66, 68, 71, 72, 75, 81, 84
World War I., 88, 98, 102–103, 111, 123, 125, 171
WPA, 142, 163

Zone Schools, 163

About the Author

Samuel Walker is assistant professor of criminal justice at the University of Nebraska at Omaha. He holds the Ph.D. in American History from Ohio State University (1973) and has a special interest in the history of social conflict in the urban community. He has contributed articles on the history of the police and the history of the American labor movement to several journals. As research director in the Department of Criminal Justice at the University of Nebraska at Omaha, he organized conferences on "Key Issues in Criminal Justice Doctoral Education" and "Historical Perspectives on American Criminal Justice." He is currently researching a history of criminal justice in the United States.